*Roland H. Worth, Jr.*

# The Seven Cities of the Apocalypse and Roman Culture

PAULIST PRESS
New York/Mahwah, N.J.

*Also by Roland H. Worth, Jr.*
*published by Paulist Press*

THE SEVEN CITIES OF THE APOCALYPSE AND GRECO-ASIAN CULTURE

Scripture excerpts are taken from the *New King James Version* as well as from the *New Revised Standard Version*.

*Cover design by Moe Berman*

Copyright © 1999 by Roland H. Worth, Jr.

ISBN 0-8091-3874-3

Published by Paulist Press
997 Macarthur Boulevard
Mahwah, New Jersey 07430

www.paulistpress.com

Printed and bound in the
United States of America

# Contents

iii

# Preface

Since my teenage years, I have always enjoyed the challenge of biblical study. Yet I have also been intrigued by what makes the world tick: its politics, its economic structures, its wars, its societal biases and preferences. Perhaps it is this desire to look at the *entire* picture that has fed my ongoing interest in those areas where the biblical and the then-surrounding world overlap. The Palestinian environment in which Jesus lived and in which the earliest church did its work represents an example of where such study can present an intellectually stimulating challenge. Yet my own interest has tended to the Roman world beyond Palestine—the Greek and Asian provinces that were the field of the labors of Paul and John.

In one sense this might be considered peripheral, but only if one considers the works of these two apostles to be peripheral to the New Testament! The more radical school of thought sees Christianity as the result of its expansion into these regions; the more conservative students of the matter (such as myself) see the *adaptation* of the doctrinal and moral demands of Christianity to the existing local situation. This was not a betrayal of existing beliefs any more than the adaptation to the Jewish-dominated culture of Palestine represented a renunciation of the inner essence of the movement. On the other hand, an understanding of those environments enables one to better understand the challenges to the new faith posed by the varying local cultures, politics, and religious structures.

No person could write a book such as this alone. A learned professor once stated that those who obtained their doctorates about the time he did in the 1950s were the last generation who could honestly claim to be masters of the entire literature of their field. Today, regardless of one's specialty, no one at any level of education can possess more than a working knowledge of a (hopefully) wide cross-section of the publications in his or her field and where to obtain access to the remainder on an as-needed basis.

This difficulty in attempting to be all-encompassing is even more pronounced in regard to a multidisciplinary study such as this, when the needed pieces of information are often found in isolation: a fact here, a fact there, perhaps a handful of data in yet a third place, and on those truly exciting days a single source that can be utilized repeatedly. By casting one's factual net often enough and broadly enough one can still hope to reap a sufficiently broad collection of data to form the foundation of a book-length analysis. One will not "catch" everything, but one will garner more than enough to do justice to one's topic.

Then comes the tedious job of piecing it all together. Indeed, courtesy of the wonders of the modern computer one may actually be piecing it together *while* continuing the research. In spite of the many annoying characteristics of the computer, it permits "instant" inclusion of new data and facilitates quick adaptation of the text as new information emerges. When one discovers that a blunder has been made, it is a simple task to revise the text to incorporate the correct information. This book would have taken a decade or two with a typewriter—if I had even considered making the effort with such a massive load of facts needing to be compiled. With a computer it was the product of a few years' labor—a few years of *intense* labor.

To *process* these facts was one man's endeavor. To *gain access* to these facts was the product of the numerous men and women who cooperate in the maintenance of the interlibrary loan system on the collegiate level. The interlibrary office of the University of Richmond's Boatwright Library was able to tap repeatedly into this resource to obtain for me scarce publications that added a depth of historical data that would have required wide travel and economic resources far above and beyond my own. Adequate words of appreciation are hard to find: I built the building, but they provided much of the brick and mortar! Nor should the value of their own in-house collection be minimized; it represented an additional resource that I abundantly utilized.

Also deserving the highest praise is the Union Theological Seminary of Richmond, Virginia. It possesses one of the largest religious and theological collections in the nation and provided an invaluable source of information not only on matters directly related to the exegesis of Revelation 2 and 3 but also on broader religious matters of the ancient world as well.

My family has seen me through three published works prior to this one. Their tolerance of this passion for historical and biblical research is deeply appreciated.

—ROLAND H. WORTH, JR.

# Introduction

To understand the immediate cultural and societal background of the cities to which John wrote in Revelation 1 and 2, we must first understand the broader background of Roman civilization and its impact upon the region of its Asian province. Both the great cities of Asia (such as Ephesus and Smyrna and Pergamon) as well as the less conspicuous ones (such as Laodicea and Thyatira) were influenced in their practices and aspirations by the attitudes and preferences encouraged by the Roman Empire, of which they were a small part. Hence to understand the *Asian* background of the book of Revelation, it is desirable to begin with the *Roman* background of the then-existing world and its impact upon that region. Indeed, there are issues and questions that do not readily fit into a discussion of the seven churches (and their surrounding cities) but which are useful in understanding the world in which they functioned.

This requires a consideration of a widely varying collection of questions. What were the life spans of that age? What was the tax structure? What were the regional customs that made Greek and Greek-influenced Asia different from the rest of the empire: in regard to women, religion, architecture, and other matters?

Then in regard to Asia proper we must deal with questions as diverse as the strange bequest of the area to the Roman Empire by its local ruler, and the role of the emperor cult in solidifying loyalty to the empire. Indeed, the cult of the emperor is significant not only important because of the role it played as a theological "glue" for diverse peoples, but also because participation in the cult later became the litmus test by which Christians could be brought to public attention and punishment.

This volume is complete in itself in that it paints the broad picture of the Roman world in general as well as emphasizing the regional peculiarities of the province of Asia. This was a background that John was fully familiar with when he wrote the book of Revelation, but alien to the modern reader. This study of the social and economic context of the world will be useful to those interested in the Roman Empire in general, to those interested in its regional peculiarities, and finally, to those interested in the unstated background that was a "given" in the New Testament writer's own age. To these readers this volume will provide the key information they seek.

Yet many other readers of these pages will approach them as only a prelude to their central area of concern, the seven specific cities to whose churches John wrote in the book of Revelation. For them the city-specific studies are the main subject—and these are examined in detail in the second volumn of this work, *The Seven Cities of the Apocalypse and Greco-Asian Culture.* Yet to understand that more specific topic, understanding of the broader background is also desirable, for it is within the context of that more universal scope that the peculiarities of each of those cities developed. Hence these two volumes supplement each other and can be profitably read either by themselves or together.

*1*

# Overview:
# First-Century Roman
# Government and Society

## General Background

In the first two centuries A.D. the population of the Roman Empire remained approximately stable,[1] at a figure perhaps as high as seventy million, though others prefer a significantly lower estimate.[2] Both Asia in particular and Asia Minor in general possessed substantial populations. Of the broader area of Asia Minor, the population estimate for the first century runs from a low of around eight[3] or nine million[4] to thirteen million or higher.[5] The vast bulk of this was located in urban centers.[6] For comparison, in 1935 Turkey's population—in approximately the same geographic area—was about 12,439,000 people.[7] As to the first-century population of Asia, that has been estimated at between four and five million.[8]

Typical life spans have been estimated as low as twenty or twenty-five years.[9] On the other hand, if the estimate is correct that over 50 percent of wives died due to childbirth-related problems by age forty,[10] half lived beyond that age, making a life span of forty years typical for married women—and in ancient society virtually all grown women would have enjoyed that status. Furthermore, a typical legionnaire in the Roman army entered service at age nineteen,[11] served twenty or more years,[12] and retired afterward to set down roots, marry, and raise a family.[13] This implies he entered his "fathering" years around forty and did not die till his children reached adulthood (otherwise marriage posed dangerous survival risk for both spouse and children). This indicates a theoretical life span going into at least the fifth decade. Hence, though many presumably died young at childbirth, due to childhood diseases, or as a result of harsh living conditions, a substantial life span could still be anticipated by large elements of the population.

Much of that adult population could read and write. But when we try to convert that broad generalization into a proportion or percentage, the evidence fails us. Perhaps the closest we can come is a *geographical* comparison: Based upon the number of epigraphic texts surviving from Asia it would appear that the region enjoyed literacy equivalent to that "of the more Romanized provinces of the west."[14]

The international language of the day was Greek. In Asia there were at least five distinct dialects of the language, some of which made purists cringe.[15] As in other pre-television societies, there were significant differences between urban and rural usage.[16] Hence this figure should be taken as a minimum.

## Social Structure

At the pinnacle of the socio-political hierarchy was the emperor himself. Below him were the senators, men who were required to possess a worth of at least one million sesterces in order to qualify for their high position. Their distinctive garb was the toga with a wide purple stripe. Only a few hundred families possessed the wealth and prestige to qualify. Since they desired to remain close to the position of top power—and since the emperor desired to avoid the danger of high-status opponents building up followings in distant parts of the empire—they had to obtain specific imperial permission whenever they wished to leave Italy. As a result, senators were more often found in Italy than anywhere else, with only a minority serving abroad in top government positions and on special assignments from the emperor.[17]

The next level, equestrians, had to be freeborn and to possess a more modest wealth of 400,000 sesterces. They did not bear the severe travel restrictions imposed upon their more prestigious superiors, the senators, and could therefore be found scattered throughout the empire in important government and military postings. They also were entitled to wear the toga, but their purple stripe had to be a narrow one. Only a few thousand individuals shared their position in society.[18]

Although those of equestrian status who resided in the provinces seem to have represented the elite of the provincial society in which they dwelled, this is most clearly the case in the second and third centuries.[19] Due to their larger numbers decurions also played an important role and, quite possibly, even the dominant one in the first century. These individuals had to have a minimum of 100,000 sesterces in their possession and were numerous in the role of civic officials (in the town) and as second-echelon administrators on the provincial level.[20] A freedman, no matter how successful, could not qualify for the post—but his son could.[21] In third-century Italy at least 25 percent of all having decurion status had fathers who once had been slaves.[22]

To become a senator, equestrian, or decurion required official action by the Roman senate.[23] Wealth was not the only prerequisite; one also had to convince the authorities that one *deserved* the honor. Hence one's attitude, friendships, obvious civic participation, and other intangibles played significant roles in being granted the honor.

Asians were freely admitted into responsible positions, beginning with Claudius and Nero.[24] Many educated Asians entered the Roman bureaucracy, not just in Asia itself but in other provinces as well.[25] Between A.D. 46 and 69 two different Asians served in the prestigious position of prefect of Egypt. One was a native of Ephesus; the other of Miletus.[26] Equestrian status began to come to Asians in substantial numbers,[27] nor did they stop at that level. A. N. Sherwin-White, a specialist on Roman citizenship issues, notes that "by the time of Trajan and Hadrian a remarkable proportion of new recruits to the senatorial order came from the cities of Asia, Bithynia, Galatia and Syria."[28] The empire was rewarding its faithful with its highest honor.

Internationally, the top official of the empire was the emperor, with the senate below him. The administrative organs and the Roman legions scattered throughout the

empire reported back to him. Policy evolved from the constant "interplay of five groups: the army, the plebeians, the
senate, the provinces and the 'intellectuals' (poets/writers
and philosophers). Each group had its own powerbase and its
own basic interest."[29] To the extent that each was united it
could, temporarily at least, play a significant role in modify-
ing or changing official policy. To the extent that such power
centers were in agreement, to that extent their attitudes were
likely to be reflected in government action. To the extent
there was intragroup disagreement—or unconcern—the
emperor had the maximum leeway to determine policy. In
turn, the very fact that the top authority figure had endorsed
and demanded a certain policy would normally cause the
other power centers to acquiesce—at least temporarily. A
"strong" emperor was one who might *consult* these alternative
authority elements but who, by brunt of argument, will
power, or plain brutality convinced or compelled their
acceptance. A "weak" emperor was one who felt compelled to
yield his preferred course because of uncertainty whether he
could enforce his program against substantial opposition.
The strength of the emperor was enhanced due to the fact
that these various groups had competing internal interests
(not to mention competing interests with other groups). The
astute emperor could take advantage of these divisions and
impose his own policy upon a divided opposition.

A different hierarchy was found on the provincial level. At
its height was the governor, with the various city and regional
assemblies reporting to him. Dominated by equestrians and
decurions, other individuals whose wealth, position, or reputation provided them respect and honor were also part of the
socio-political elite of any city and region. All of these high-status individuals were considered by themselves—and society at
large—as superior to the rank and file freeborn and freedmen.
The latter two groups, of course, ranked higher socially than
slaves.[30] Even here there could be ambiguity, because the slave
of an esteemed master might feel himself to be better than
most freedmen since most were poor and unrecognized while
he was the servant of an important and respected individual.
Furthermore, if he performed a significant function on behalf

of his master, he might easily exercise greater power than a freedman and even be publicly respected more than the individual already possessing his freedom.

When the Romans took over Asia, they did not oust the existing politico-economic power structure. Instead, they absorbed it into their own system, encouraging modification of the local structures rather than their abolishment. This permitted the development of a cooperative attitude between Rome and Asia rather than an antagonistic one.[31]

At the heart of the social system in any province was the patron-client relationship.[32] The higher-status individual gave benefits of some kind to the less-well-placed individual, and that person, in turn, owed loyalty, support, and whatever else would be of benefit to the patron and his interests. This could be either near-term or, more likely, at some indefinite point in the future. Instead of grounding the support in the needs of one's fellow man, on the basis of charity or love, the system rationalized (relative) charity for the poorer by the expectation of loyalty in the short term and repayment in some form if the recipient moved higher up the social scale. Perhaps because of the grave disparity between the societal levels of patron and client, the system could psychologically wear on the self-respect of the latter; the Romans minimized this danger by speaking of the system in terms of mutual "friendship."

The modern writer might describe this, crudely, as "you scratch my back and I'll scratch yours." The actual operation was far more subtle. Perhaps the best late-twentieth-century parallel would be a political IOU: Some fellow politician has gone above and beyond any personal need to provide special assistance for some project or legislation your district needs. Usually implicit in such generosity is the assumption that at some point when that politician is in equally urgent need of help you will act in a similar vein.

During Domitian's reign Plutarch wrote *Praecepta Gerendae Reipublicae* for the Asian Menemachus, who apparently hailed from Sardis.[33] Plutarch provides examples of a proper patron fulfilling his responsibility: introducing an individual to a rich citizen, passing on to a "friend" (client) a law case that will bring a good fee, intervening to help him gain a valuable contract. But when the client is successful, he must remember the implicit bargain to act in a reciprocal manner.

Pliny provides an example of when "pay-back time" arrives. Writing in an epistle to the Roman military legate Priscus, he says, "Your command of a large army gives you a plentiful source of benefits to confer, and...your tenure has been long enough for you to have provided for your own friends. Turn to mine—they are not many."[34] Pliny is specifically seeking "the highest office in your power" for a friend of his. Of course even here a justification—preferably beyond a mere rationalization—was desirable. So Pliny is careful to provide several significant evidences of the recommended man's reputation and civic commitment.[35]

## Economics and Business

Keith Hopkins estimates the *minimum* gross product of the Roman Empire as 8.24 billion sestercii annually.[36] "In reality," he observes, "the gross product of the Roman empire must have exceeded our estimated minimum gross product considerably."[37] Raymond W. Goldsmith's analysis of the available data leads him to the conclusion that "from the late first centuries B.C. to the mid-second century A.D." the actual figure was approximately 20 billion sestercii annually.[38] Goldsmith estimates that "the top three percent of income recipients [received] in the order of 20–25 percent of total personal incomes," leaving three-quarters of all income to be divided among 97 percent of the population.[39] Limiting himself to the senatorial families—some six hundred in number—he estimated that they garnered 0.6 percent of all incomes earned within the empire.[40]

Hopkins's minimalist population approach yields a figure of 10 percent of the gross product being collected by the Roman government in taxes.[41] Working from an empire-wide collective income of a bit more than double that of Hopkins, Goldsmith reduces that figure to 5 percent of gross product.[42] (Either figure looks nostalgically attractive to late-twentieth-century residents of Western nations.)

These taxes were collected from a number of sources. There was an empire-wide sales tax of 1 percent.[43] If you bought a slave, you paid 4 percent tax; if you freed that slave, you paid a 5 percent tax.[44] There were import taxes of 25 percent for everything brought into the empire from outside.[45] Export fees were presumably set at the same level.[46] These border fees were effectively increased by the fact that an *additional* tax was imposed at each provincial line that was crossed.[47] At every port an additional 2 1/2 percent tax was levied.[48] One French scholar estimates that the various taxes doubled the price of articles between the Asian cost and their arrival on the Roman marketplace.[49]

Harbors of the empire required that a ship carry 70–80 tons of cargo in order to utilize their facilities. This was lowered under Claudius to a 65–70 ton range.[50] Although vessels were common that carried as many as four hundred tons or more, the typical vessel was generally in the range of 120–150 tons.[51] While sea trade could move large amounts of goods at one time, there was the constant danger of adverse weather that could shipwreck both the vessel and the sizable financial outlay invested in the effort.[52] In addition to ocean-going vessels, barges carried internal trade down major rivers to regional ports.[53]

Intra-empire shipping was a major moneymaker for those involved in the trade. The wealthiest locals in both Asia and Egypt were those involved in shipping produce and manufactured goods abroad.[54] At least some Christians found their way into the business and into personal fortune. Marcion of Pontus (located northeast of Asia) was a second-century heretic who accumulated a massive personal fortune. When he went to Rome around A.D. 139 he bestowed upon the church there an impressive gift of two hundred thousand sesterces. Although his opponents pursued him for his unorthodoxy, they did not criticize him for his occupation of tradesman and shipowner.[55]

Rome exported items such as pottery and wine as far away as India and China.[56] There is at least limited evidence that Chinese-Roman trade was large enough to result in the creation of a permanent colony of Roman expatriates in

China itself.[57] Be that as it may, the more common exchange of oriental and western goods probably took place in either Persia or India, which would have been a convenient meeting place for long-traveling merchants from the two regions.[58]

In the second century Aelius Aristides hyperbolically describes the immense volume of imports into the empire, "Cargoes from India and, if you will, even from Arabia the Blest one can see in such numbers as to surmise that in those lands the trees will have been stripped bare and that the inhabitants of these lands, if they need anything, must come here to beg for a share of their own."[59]

In the days of Pliny a pound of cinnamon typically cost ten times the price of a pound of wheat. In times of scarcity it skyrocketed from its typical five denarii price to fifteen hundred denarii per pound.[60] Silk also brought a high price. The ancient writer who describes it as being sold for its weight in gold was surely exaggerating, but that doesn't gainsay its exorbitant price.[61]

The major revenue producer was the *produce tax.* Set at a fixed percentage of the annual crop, it could vary dramatically from year to year. In order to eliminate this factor, the Romans introduced *tax farming.* Groups of wealthy Romans joined together in massive corporations to buy the right to collect taxes in various parts of the empire. In exchange for a percentage of what was collected, they assumed the risk of shortfalls, while the government got its cash ahead of the actual collection of the taxes in the field.

The farmers of Asia were victims of this system in at least six ways. First of all, the crop yield and tax burden were predicted for a *five-year* period, even though the actual figures would vary from year to year. Second, farmers were obligated to pay the *full* tax *regardless* of actual crop production.[62] Third, they were faced with field representatives more interested in results than justice. Fourth, the central authorities in the system had minimal or no contact with the region. In Sicily tax-gathering rights were purchased for each individual city, permitting the local wealthy to become involved.[63] With their local base, they might at least be sympathetic with the local farmers' problems and difficulties. In contrast, "the Asian *publicani* were rich Romans and Italians of equestrian rank, inevitably, as the contract for the Asian tithe was sold at Rome, for five years, and involved the pledging as security of land worth millions of sesterces by the successful bidders."[64]

Fifth, with the vast sums pledged as security and with the yearly taxable total paid *in advance* to the emperor, those who financed the collection system were themselves in a massive bind: humanitarian instincts (assuming they were present) would inevitably be at war with personal financial survival. It was a system guaranteed to produce injustice and one with minimal impediments to prevent injustice. Finally, the publicans were effectively independent of the local governor's judicial power. The equestrian-based syndicates usually had great influence if not outright control over the courts in Rome where charges of financial misconduct were judged against former governors. Vigorous action could expose governors to fraudulent accusations of extortion, charges that would be tried before courts controlled by those they had tried to curb. Hence governors shunned confrontation lest their action come back to haunt them.[65] (Since governors often enriched themselves from their posts, there was probably an implicit sense of mutual non-opposition: I won't oppose your chicanery if you don't expose mine.)

The field representatives of these vast syndicates (publicans) gained a nefarious reputation for maximizing corporate (and personal) income at the risk of fairness and justice. If they were to make a profit—especially in times when agricultural production fell below estimates—friction with the public was inevitable. With the power of Rome and the corporations behind them, the local publicans found it tempting to increase their yield even further to make their own private fortunes.[66] The collection of customs duties was also in their hands.[67]

When regional excesses grew so numerous that delegation of the tax-gathering power to the municipalities was considered prudent, injustice could still occur. The Romans were interested in revenue; how the locality obtained it was secondary. Hence when cities collected the taxes, the urbanites commonly shifted the heaviest part of the burden onto the farmers within their region.[68] Farmers did have one ultimate retaliatory threat, however: if pushed too far they might abandon the land and flee, totally eliminating their taxes and harming the local economy.[69] This was certainly a common occurrence in Egypt,[70] and presumably in Asia as well, whenever the tax load became too heavy for too long.

Just as taxes were an ongoing concern, the cost of living was as well. The most fundamental cost was for bread and/or the grain purchased to make that bread. Five *modii* of grain was a reasonable monthly ration for most workers under most circumstances.[71] A price range of four to six sesterii per *modius* of wheat would have been recognized as reasonable both in Asia itself and throughout the empire.[72] Just before a new harvest came to market, one could count on a substantial increase as the grain reserve reached its lowest ebb. In at least one case the price jumped as high as twenty sesterii per *modius*.[73]

In time of famine[74] the sky was the limit. The price cited in Revelation 6:6 translates into thirty-two sesterii,[75] at least 500 percent above the normal price range. In one first-century B.C. famine Asian prices soared to an even more exorbitant forty-eight sesterii.[76]

Living in an urban location resulted in higher fundamental living costs than residing in a less developed area:

> Evidence from the East suggests that prices for grain might be substantially higher in large towns than they were outside. The normal price for wheat in the mid-fourth century at Syrian Antioch, one of the biggest towns in the empire, was apparently double the normal cost in Egypt (Julian, *Misopogon*, 369). Cicero indicates that grain prices at Ephesus, a great city on the coast, were substantially higher than those at Philomelium, a town in central Asia Minor (*Verr.* 2.3.191).
>
> A series of inscriptions show extremely high prices for bread at Ephesus at different times during the Principate....Dio Chrysostom claimed that the famine price of wheat at Prusa in northern Asia Minor was no higher than the price which prevailed in some other towns when prices were at their lowest.[77]

Passage of time produced higher prices for essential items as well. Wheat prices in the breadbasket of the empire, Egypt, jumped 25 percent between the end of the first century and the end of the second century.[78] Bread prices in Asian Ephesus doubled in that same period, though we are left uncertain whether the same type of bread is under consideration or whether the higher prices refer to a superior quality product or were the result of "local conditions, such as seasonal scarcity, war, or other factors" that may have disproportionately increased the figure.[79]

Inflation and heightened dependence upon the imperial legions presumably influenced army pay: During the reign of Augustus (27 B.C.–A.D. 14) pay was set at 900 sesterii. Under Domitian (A.D. 81–96) this was increased to 1,200 sesterii a year, and under Severus (A.D. 193–211) to 1,800–2,000 sesterii.[80] Hence there was a doubling in a two-century period, which may well have been below the actual inflation in prices. Overall, Richard Duncan-Jones estimates an empire-wide inflation rate during the second century of 4.0–4.9 percent annually. This was not a steady increase but proceeded on an irregular basis and may have varied dramatically in different sections of the empire.[81]

The Roman economy involved the transportation of countless tons of commodities over distances that ranged from a few miles to hundreds and even thousands of miles. In turn, this involved the annual movement of thousands of individuals for commercial purposes; people also traveled out of personal interest and inclination.

Roman roads were built and maintained primarily for quick military transit and secondarily for swift governmental communication throughout the empire; they were also used for short-range travel by both animals and wagons.[82] Although they were traditionally (and proverbially) built in an arrow-straight line, the engineers were quite willing to bend or twist or whatever else was necessary to balance directness with the necessities imposed by the local terrain.[83] In many places they preserved and improved already existing road systems rather than replacing them with new ones of their own.[84]

Most produce was consumed in nearby cities.[85] The high

cost of long-distance transportation by road made sales to distant localities generally impractical.[86] The most one could usually hope for (and not always that) were sales in other parts of one's own province or the adjoining ones.[87]

The situation was improved when one was dealing with cargo. It was sometimes possible to ship large quantities a great distance and still turn a profit. Hence seagoing vessels were the preferred method of long-range transport because they could carry more material and move faster than their alternatives.[88]

Even here, however, there was the difficulty of obtaining a sufficient quantity of product from the surrounding region. Although one was able to move large quantities by ship, the costs (raw product, taxes, the danger of loss at sea, and profit) inevitably escalated the sales price at the destination.[89]

The relative speed made seagoing vessels the preferred mode of transportation for travelers. Since passenger ships were an invention of a much later age, travelers had to seek out a vessel heading to their destination or to a major port where they could make the necessary connection.[90]

Major cities often had what we might call trade offices in various seaports to assist their merchants. These could provide information to travelers as to what ships were likely to be available in the near future.[91] Obtaining transportation was only the beginning. Travelers had to carry their own bedding as well as food and methods to prepare it—or pay the way for their servants to do so.[92]

If one traveled by land (whether on business, pilgrimage, or other reason), one wore sturdy shoes, a hat, and carried a variety of clothing for various weather conditions. A small sundial would be a useful accessory to tell the time.[93] Those carrying products had to decide what type of animal to utilize. An ox had ideal weight-carrying capacity but only modest speed. The best compromise between weight and speed was provided by the mule, which could carry its load some fifty miles on a typical day.[94]

For a multi-day trip one had to consider accommodations. A tent was one option.[95] On the other hand, "the major roads had inns about every 25–30 miles (40–56 kilometers;

average day's travel). They varied in quality from those which could accommodate high government officials in comfort *(cursus, mansions* or *stationes)* to those of minimum standards *(mutationes),* generally set between the *stationes.*"[96]

The quality of the establishment depended upon its intended clientele. The best ones provided all the services wealthy travelers might require—decent food, fresh animals (or shelter for the ones brought along), and available craftsmen to fix any damage that might have occurred to gear or equipment.[97] Both the best and the worst establishments could provide company for sexual entertainment.[98]

## Military

If one were not already a Roman citizen, citizenship was automatically granted upon entry to active duty service as a legionnaire.[99] In contrast, those who served in the auxiliary units of the army or in the imperial fleet were granted citizenship only upon discharge back into the civilian population.[100]

The official length of army service was twenty years,[101] divided into sixteen as a full legionnaire and four in an attached but separate unit of veterans. The financial costs of mustering out the soldiery caused the emperors to delay releasing active-duty forces who had fulfilled their term of duty. In the second decade of the first century this caused a mutiny in Pannonia and Germany,[102] which resulted in a temporary improvement but not a permanent one. It was not until Vespasian that an abiding commitment was finally made. Under Domitian this took the form of an every-other-year mustering out of all eligible veterans.[103]

Retired military officers are known to have made their homes in Ephesus and other places in Asia.[104] Presumably these were individuals who were either born in those regions or had done service there.

During the first century A.D. Asia and the other eastern provinces constituted an invaluable source of manpower for the Roman legions. At the time of Claudius, 23 legions were staffed with eastern manpower. By the end of Vespasian's reign this had increased to 110 out of the 334 legions then in service.[105] Asia, at least, provided far more military manpower than it devoured military resources: during the first century it appears that the Romans normally maintained only a modest military commitment in the province,[106] a marked tribute to the relative peacefulness of the region and the lack of any serious danger of insurrection.

Throughout the first and second centuries most Roman military units were based in the countryside rather than in the major cities of the day. The exceptions were those locations (like Jerusalem and Alexandria, Egypt) where there was an ongoing prospect of serious disturbance.[107] In the second century Aelius Aristides wrote of this policy and how prevalent it was:

> Thus [because Rome served the interests of both rich and poor] the cities can be clear of garrisons. Mere detachments of horse and foot suffice for protection of whole countries, and even these are not concentrated in every household but are dispersed throughout the rural area within bounds and orbits of their own. Hence many nations do not know where at any time their guardians are.[108]

Even in Asia there were exceptions to this policy of basing units in the countryside. A unit of the VII praetorian cohort appears to have been stationed at Ephesus sometime during the second century.[109] A cavalry unit was based there in 223–24.[110] A unit of the VII praetorian cohort is also known to have been based in Smyrna in 212.[111]

Around 300 a distinct shift to urban basing began to occur. At least one contemporary considered the policy reversal a major mistake. Zosimus criticizes one emperor for "removing the majority of the troops from the frontiers and stationing them in cities which had no need of auxiliary forces, thus...subjecting the cities to the scourge of the military."[112] By the late fourth century, ancient writers clearly state or imply that such urban basings had become common and even dominant.[113]

In addition to a rural setting, the legions were broken into substantially smaller units for actual posting purposes. It was normal practice for a large minority of personnel to be serving far away from the legion headquarters. Although such a dispersion of forces is known to have existed in various places throughout the empire, two surviving duty rosters from a legion stationed at Dura provide some specific figures. One roster speaks of 42 percent on such assignments and 46 percent at another date. They were divided between nine outposts, one as far as 155 miles from headquarters.[114]

An army is essential in wartime and in periods of great international stress. On the other hand, an army is expensive to maintain, and it must be preserved in times of peace for those inevitable periods of conflict. So how does a society obtain its money's worth during such periods of at least relative tranquillity? The Romans did it by using military forces for a wide variety of tasks beyond the realm of making war.

They were prime resources in maintaining civic peace against the forces of lawlessness that exist in any society. Legion peacekeeping was more often police work than war-style blood-shedding. Here the dispersion of troops over the countryside provided an invaluable boost: by stationing the forces this way, they covered a wider area, in greater depth, and far more knowledgeably than if they rarely saw the region where they were supposed to function. Tertullian spoke of the practice in his day when he noted that "military posts are stationed throughout all the provinces for tracking down brigands."[115]

There were additional regional non-legion peacekeeping forces as well. Each province had a frontier militia composed of upper-class horsemen.[116] Their responsibilities included such police duties as handling cases where sheep were discovered grazing in vineyards owned by other people.[117] As with any position of public trust, it was one that could be abused. A decree from Hierapolis (near Laodicea) prohibited them from demanding more supplies from the villages they passed through than was fair and equitable.[118]

Distinct from these units were the rural mounted constables. They pursued bandits and examined those accused by the locals of various specific crimes. They did not, however, have the authority to punish; they had to pass on to the provincial governor both their prisoners and the evidence they had accumulated.[119]

Likewise, each city in Asia had a parallel group of magistrates with the responsibility to put down disorder and threats to the peace. It follows from this that each community had its own jail—not so much as a punishment in itself as a place of confinement until trial. Government-owned slaves normally ran these jails.[120]

Legion personnel played a major role in providing manpower for the royal governor. Because their salaries were already being paid by the government and because they existed as a force to serve the government's purposes, the legions' resources provided a natural source of manpower for provincial governors anxious to secure quality personnel and, perhaps equally important, to keep their operating expenses at a minimum. "As many as 100 legionnaires could be seconded to the *officium* of the governor at provincial headquarters, to assist him in his military, administrative, clerical, judicial, and religious functions."[121] Quasi-judicial duties came their way: interrogation, transport of the accused on the way to a higher authority, and execution of decreed sentences.[122]

Military forces were coopted for civic improvements and government-run businesses as well. In quarries and mines they were used in all ways (varying according to their personal skills, the local needs, and the location): for skilled technical leadership, for guarding convict labor, and even for personal manual labor.[123] Both their technical skills and their physical strength were utilized for harbor dredging and other public construction projects.[124]

"On post" noncombat personnel were required, as in every army of every age. Literate clerical record-keeping personnel were common not only at headquarters but also, it appears, at least one such individual was routinely assigned to each century (100 men) within a legion. At one legion post whose records have survived, some 6.7 percent of personnel were involved in record keeping and other support functions, such as arranging and providing a steady supply of food for the troops.[125]

It is not certain if there was the concept of a "medical corps" as a distinct body of personnel. Unquestionably the

Roman army encouraged at least certain soldiers—whether regarded as professional medical men or not—to become deeply versed in how to care for the wounds and health needs of their comrades-in-arms.[126]

For purpose of analysis we can divide army religious activity into official and unofficial. Official refers to those activities endorsed, approved, and carried out as part of the official Roman or army calendar. Unofficial refers to the private and usually supplemental religious activities of individual soldiers and officers. The Romans offered great latitude in the performance of individual acts of religion; potential conflict came only when one neglected or rejected participation in the official religious rituals because of these private loyalties.

Throughout the year, various pagan religious activities were routinely carried out in the camp. Essentially these ceremonies duplicated the civilian religious calendar.[127] One of the most important occasions—due to its direct military relevance—was the annual early January repetition of the enlistment oath, an oath that was also repeated each year on the date the reigning emperor had come to power. It is likely that "the third of January was a festival day which included as well the burial of the preceding year's altar overlooking the parade ground and the dedication of a new altar for the current year."[128]

The standards carried by the legions were themselves objects of reverence and worship and of central importance to the official side of army religion. They were emblems of their calling and symbols of their triumphs. Hence it was easy for the cult of the standards to outweigh the significance of the various civilian-orientated cults. In the third century the Christian Tertullian argued that, "the camp religion of the Romans is all through a worship of the standards, a setting the standards above all gods."[129] In a different place he spoke of how, in legionnaire camp religion, the participants "adore the standards, they swear by the standards, they prefer them to Juppiter [sic] himself."[130]

Among the nonofficial religions that came to have a special place in the hearts of many legionnaires, the Romanized form of Mithraism deserves special emphasis. Although only beginning its penetration of the army during the first century, by the second it had found many adherents, and by the early decades of the third had probably reached its greatest degree of influence.[131] Samuel Laeuchli speculates that the cult of Cybele and similar cults significantly altered the nature of existing Mithraism during its early spread into the Roman sphere of influence. As a result of these changes in the cult while on Asian soil, it took forms more amenable to the temperament of the Roman West.[132] Certainly there were substantial regional variations in the cult's popularity within the legions. Inscriptional evidence from Italy indicates a modest 4.3 percent rate of soldier-participants. In the provinces the figure reaches 25 percent in Spain and Germany, over 30 percent in north Africa, and in excess of 50 percent in England.[133]

Its imagery of light overcoming darkness was of obvious psychological appeal to the self-esteem of any army that believes its cause to be just. The exclusion of women from its ranks also fits in well with the masculine emphasis inherent in the military service of the age.[134]

Church writers as early as the second century (Justin Martyr) and third century (Tertullian, Origen) waxed indignant at the similarities between Christianity and Mithraism. They explained these on grounds of Satanic influence.[135] These similarities fall into three categories: those caused by the development of beliefs and doctrines after the first-century formative period;[136] those where the New Testament itself claims even earlier Old Testament precedent;[137] and those where there are superficial parallels that disappear when examined in more detail.[138]

Enthusiasm for the cult of Juppiter Dolichenus also peaked about the same time as Mithra. Since his worship was connected with turning irons into weapons, the professional soldier would find within it a natural appeal.[139]

The Syrian cult of Sol Invictus began to be popular among soldiers in the second century. Unlike Mithras (from Persia), which had attracted greater interest among military personnel than among other sectors of the population, followers of Sol Invictus enjoyed a wider base of support, one that also included women.[140]

Not all "private" religions could be so easily incorpo-
rated: Judaism and Christianity provided demands of exclusive loyalty to one deity that made participation in the official
religious activities of the army extraordinarily difficult, if not
impossible. The conflict was partly resolved by the fact that a
monotheist was unlikely to *enlist,* for he knew all too well the
practical and spiritual difficulties he would be facing. The
problem was most likely to occur among those who were con-
verted to either of these faiths while serving on active duty.

In regard to utilizing Jews, at least two other major difficulties existed. From the army standpoint the special dietary
restrictions of the Jews imposed logistic and planning difficulties.[141] Even more dangerous was the Jewish opposition to
any labor (much less fighting!) on the Sabbath.[142] However,
not all Jews were unwilling to fight on the Sabbath, and even
those who were opposed would sometimes make exceptions
to this prohibition in time of outstanding peril.[143] Even so,
refusal had been manifested on sufficient occasions and was
demanded by a sufficiently large proportion within the Jewish community, so that one could not count on the uniformity
of practice that might have made incorporating Jews on a significant scale (or entire Jewish units) an enticing possibility.

Asia played an important role in the recognition of the
right of Jewish nonparticipation. Although the legions went to
a purely voluntary service system decades before the birth of
Christ, in times of grave emergency the empire retained the
right to "draft" Roman citizens. Hence an important precedent was established in 49 B.C. when the Roman citizen–Jews
of Asia received the right of exemption from involuntary service—even in periods of emergency.[144]

Biblical texts demanding peacefulness have often been
interpreted as requiring pacifism and as explaining minimal
Christian participation in the Roman army during the first
two centuries. In 173, Christians in the "Thundering Legion"
are referred to. Before then, the only documented case is that
of Cornelius, a convert, found in the book of Acts.[145] Some
have tried to minimize the example of Cornelius because the
text does not state that he remained in the military.[146] On the
other hand, there is nothing to suggest that he left, and one

can't help but wonder what acceptable grounds he could have presented (in the eyes of the government) for seeking to resign his position. Be that as it may, polytheism in general and emperor worship in particular were deeply rooted in normal military procedure. Even assuming willingness to accept the military as an honorable profession, fully compatible with Christian ethics, the pagan religious elements would have presented immense obstacles to any who embraced monotheism with commitment and conviction.[147]

## Social Affairs

Under this broad heading it is useful to examine three categories of the population: the gladiators, the physicians, and the women. The first group plays a disproportionate role in our image of the Roman Empire, and the last, until recent decades, was often totally ignored. The middle category accumulated and codified the body of medical knowledge that ruled European thinking for over a millennium.

### Gladiators

J. P. V. D. Balsdon points out that culturally the Greek East (including Asia) had far greater impact on the western part of the empire than vice versa. There was one exception. "Gladiatorial fighting was the only large interest which started in the West and spread eastwards. It was beginning to spread in the second century B.C. and in the Roman Empire gladiatorial fighting was every bit as popular in the Greek East as it was in the West."[148]

Buildings constructed exclusively for gladiatorial fights were not required. The custom of using other facilities as temporary amphitheaters was common in the first and early second centuries.[149] Theaters were sometimes utilized; less often stadiums were adapted to the purpose.[150] Temporary amphitheaters were erected in some communities.[151]

Under Lucullus's reign as provincial governor of Asia (71–70 B.C.), the first gladiatorial fights were introduced into the province.[152] Some twenty years later they arrived at Laodicea.[153] From the days of Augustus on, the imperial priesthood sponsored these contests in the province.[154] Although the Asiarchs occasionally sponsored other forms of entertainment, such as human-animal fights, festivities that included gladiatorial combats were the overwhelmingly preference.[155] Whether they sponsored only the contests or the teams of combatants as well is harder to determine. Various inscriptions erected by groups of gladiators praise specific Asiarchs but leave unclear the answer to this question.[156]

Individual municipalities also held gladiatorial combats as part of their locally initiated efforts to honor Rome.[157] Nor did the imperial cult have an exclusive franchise upon offering the entertainment as part of its quasi-religious calendar. The priesthoods of various other deities freely sponsored their own mortal-conflict games as well.[158]

Although there were gladiator schools at Philadelphia, Smyrna, and Pergamon,[159] only Pergamon had an amphitheater as such (that is, a facility erected with the specific purpose of holding armed combats).[160]

What special types of fighting appealed to the Asian enchantment with this pseudosport? Arnold, a scholar with special interest in the athletic interests of the region, writes:

> The favorite types of gladiators seem to have been the heavy-armed "Thracian" and myrmillo, but the light-armed "net-man" (*ritarius*) also frequently participated in combats, and even horsemen and drivers of war-chariots are mentioned. Among animal combats, bull-fights were the most frequent, but African beasts were also used. These spectacles were sometimes very elaborate. At Ephesus as many as 39 pairs took part in the course of a thirteen-day celebration, and there were hunts at Ephesus lasting five days during which 25 African beasts were killed.[161]

There were two basic types of gladiators: those consigned to the combats in place of official execution, and those who were professional combatants. The former category consisted of certain individuals sentenced to death and selected prisoners of war. These were turned over to the gladiatorial schools for short-term training for the arena in place of immediate execution.[162]

Professional gladiators were generally slaves, yet slaves who intended to serve well and long. (After all, the alternative was death.) If they did, fame and fortune might well come their way—even freedom.[163] Natural ability and the skill of their trainers (and physicians) played important roles in obtaining success in this most dangerous of all athletic careers. Two additional factors increased the possibility of living out a decent life span.[164] First, gladiatorial contests were on neither a weekly nor a monthly basis. The typical gladiator would fight only about twice in any given year. Second, the contests were rarely to the death. If a person fought skillfully and well—even if ultimately defeated—the prospect of being spared death was great. What has probably created the image of repeated contests and inevitable death are those infamous exceptions when these customs were consciously ignored.

Some report that the night before a combat, the gladiators would hold a lush banquet.[165] The account probably exaggerates, since great excess would have undermined their fighting edge. Effective combat required that they be on a healthy diet that would maximize their strength.[166]

The gladiator schools attempted to obtain first-class doctors to tend to the health of their students and to mend their wounds after the public fights. The famous Galen served as one such doctor in Pergamon before going on to greater fame as the dominant medical authority of the age. In retrospect, Galen took pride in how the general health of his fighters prospered under his guidance and how serious wounds were so successfully handled that the mortality rate dropped substantially.[167]

Although private individuals occasionally sponsored the games where gladiators exhibited their talent, the vast majority of such fights were provided as part of a civic-religious occasion.[168] Imperial ego may well have played a major role in this; the emperors wanted to be recognized as the preeminent providers of such entertainment for they believed it garnered vast public appreciation among those who attended.[169]

Hence it seems that those on a lower level might use such entertainments to rally local public opinion behind an

individual or official and thereby effectively shield that person from retribution from Rome for any misdeeds. It was on this official ground that Nero banned the provincial governors from holding such festivities.[170] The expense of such entertainment was great, but if it provided protection from scrutiny over purely personal financial irregularities it was well worth the effort and cost.

These trained fighters posed a potential security risk, if not against the emperor personally then as a potential fighting force to support revolution in the provinces. Hence in A.D. 200 the prohibition on moving gladiators across provincial lines was strengthened even further: henceforth not even the provincial governors themselves could authorize it; all permission had to be by special permit issued in Rome itself.[171] If Rome had such distrust of its own governors, how much *more* reserved were Roman authorities about private individuals sponsoring such armed fights!

*Physicians and Medicine*

At least three of the outstanding physicians of the first and second centuries had major connections with Roman Asia and one (Galen) became the preeminent medical authority throughout the Roman Empire.

Rufus of Ephesus (c. A.D. 110–80) wrote over a hundred treatises on various medical issues. He practiced in various places in Italy and in the eastern half of the empire. He emphasized the need for careful symptom gathering so the doctor would be better able to understand the causes and results of various illnesses.[172] He was a very practical man who warned that theory should never be permitted to overrule actual evidence: "I advise anyone who wants to arrive at correct knowledge of everything, not to take a position over against inquiry."[173]

Soranus of Ephesus came into the maturity of his skills about A.D. 98 and flourished through the entire first four decades of the following century. He was a firm advocate of "methodism" or "methodist" school of thought. This medical ideology asserted that there were only three underlying causes of physical disease: the humors were not in balance;

humidity was excessive; or dryness was extreme. He was the last prominent physician in the ancient world to uphold this approach. He wrote widely and fluently on many subjects, including gynecology. In light of the custom of child exposure (which, with considerable justice, might be considered a postpartum abortion technique), he sought to make the live/perish decision a more rational one. Hence his volume *How to Recognize the Newborn That Is Worth Rearing.*[174]

Galen was born in A.D. 130 and died seventy-one years later.[175] About age sixteen or seventeen he began his medical training at the Asklepieion in Pergamon, where the god Asclepius was believed to use both natural and supernatural means to heal devout health-seekers. He was never a member of the priestly apparatus of the sect, however. Instead, he served as a medical therapist or consultant for those using the facility.[176] Galen was convinced that upon one occasion Asclepius intervened and saved him from an otherwise fatal disease. This cemented his loyalty to the cult.[177]

Dreams played an important role not only in the cult in general but in particular in Galen's relationship to it. His father was reported to have sent him to the Asklepieion because of an instruction received in a dream.[178] Furthermore in his later, fully developed medical career he remained convinced that Asclepius directly communicated with him through dreams concerning matters related to his medical work. His critics accused him of receiving the cures he gained through this means rather than through the application of personal skill. A modern psychological explanation would be that the dreams were expressions of his unconscious tangling with the difficulties of a case and presenting its conclusions under the authoritative image of the god himself.[179]

Galen found a contradiction between such "revelation" in specific cases and adherence to the strict doctrines of the "dogmatic" school of medicine. Members of the dogmatic school, convinced that they were the exclusive possessors of medical wisdom/insight/truth, found no room in their thinking for those who did not give allegiance to their medical orthodoxy.[180]

Galen reached the height of his career when he served as an imperial physician. This began under Marcus Aurelius and continued through Septimus Severus.[181] He composed a mammoth body of writings that influenced both contemporaries and those who came afterward, literally for a millennium or more. Those that have survived would exceed twelve thousand printed pages if published in one collection.[182] Through the translation of his works into Latin, Galen eventually became the dominant authority in medicine throughout Europe during the Middle Ages and Renaissance. Ironically—thanks to Syriac and later Arabic translations, he exerted a similar preeminent influence during the same centuries in what became the Islamic world.[183]

In spite of his deep insight and great success as a physician, Galen did not, of course, possess the knowledge of the modern physician. Indeed, he intentionally neglected what a later age would have considered an invaluable means to deepen his knowledge of the human body: his human dissection work was limited to two corpses, though he examined the innards of many monkeys in his efforts to expand his knowledge.[184] Nor did he work out the implications of certain important facts that he *did* know. Although Galen detected that blood moved in human arteries he never developed this into a theory of blood circulation.[185]

Men like Rufus, Soranus, and Galen represented medicine at its ancient peak.[186] Their science was full of misunderstandings and misconceptions, true,[187] but it was still the best the ancient world could produce. There were many lesser known but capable talents as well. Unfortunately, they were outnumbered by a much larger body of unlearned and ignorant individuals who only looked upon medicine as a tidy way of turning a profit. Galen himself once conceded that the bulk of would-be doctors weren't worth anything: "Between robbers and physicians lies this difference only: that the misdeeds of the former are buried in the mountains, but those of the latter in Rome itself."[188]

Galen used his pen to try to convince the reader of his day that it took much time and effort to become a trustworthy physician. He warned against the self-serving claims of physician trainers who assured everyone the necessary skills could be learned virtually overnight.[189]

The first-century doctor Epiketios (A.D. 50–120) engaged in this imaginary dialogue with an individual who considered mere possession of the correct medicines as equivalent to knowing how to treat a patient:

> You have a doctor's practice even though you have nothing but the medicine. You don't know, nor have you tried to learn, when and how to use these medicaments. "Look!" you say, "He has these eye ointments and so have I." Yes, but do you also know whom they will help, and when, and in what ways?[190]

No festival of the eastern world (or western, for that matter) would have been complete without a traveling medicine show. Plutarch refers to those who acted "like sophists, putting on a show in the theater to attract patients."[191] They would display their tools and deliver a spiel of "scientific" knowledge.[192] Slick words were used to gloss over minimal knowledge. Hence, when one discovered a physician who truly knew his business, one was well advised to hold on to him.

The medicines obtained from doctors or from the marketplace in any town were likely to be of some good. "Imported" drugs carried a certain superior status, even though their quality was just as likely to be dubious. Cynical Romans bemoaned the passing of effective rural herbal cures and their replacement with overpriced or more easily obtained but less helpful imitations.[193] Emperor Claudius (A.D. 41–54) spoke respectfully of those humble rural practitioners of herbal medicine who could almost "instantly free the sick from all pain and danger, as if by divine intervention, by administering efficacious drugs."[194]

Quality health care was encouraged in many Eastern cities in two important ways: by the employment of official civic doctors, and by the bestowal of tax exemption upon those who practiced the craft.

It was customary in cities with a Greek ancestry (such as Ephesus) to maintain a number of doctors on the public payroll. Although it seems that they were permitted to receive fees from their patients, their de facto obligation was to accept those unfortunate enough not to be able to pay at all or those who could only render token reimbursement.[195] The civic physicians also examined individuals who claimed they had been assaulted by others in order to verify the true extent of their wounds. Another function they fulfilled was to examine corpses where the cause of death was suspicious and to provide the authorities with their expert judgment as to what had happened.[196]

Asia also encouraged the medical profession by granting exemption from taxes to practicing physicians. (Grammarians and rhetoricians were also attracted in large number by the same generous offer.) Those enjoying the exemption reached their greatest number by the fourth decade of the second century. At that time the emperor decided that far too many individuals had gained exemption and that this had unjustly shifted the tax burden to the population at large. Henceforth, he decreed, there were to be strict limits on how many could be granted the privilege. The small towns were permitted three tax-free doctors, larger communities seven, and the biggest ones only ten.[197] Nor did this modified approach guarantee a *permanent* exemption: the community that granted it had it within its prerogative to revoke its earlier grant.[198] One assumes that such a dramatic step would have required considerable provocation.

Doctors receiving tax exemption, either before or after these drastic restrictions, were under obvious implicit moral pressure to bestow a degree of free care upon the needier citizens of the community. There is no way of determining how much was considered necessary either by the doctors themselves or their respective communities.[199] Human nature being always variable, it is probable that a wide range of conduct was exhibited, varying according to the practitioner's own inclinations and local conditions and expectations. Certainly the doctors were permitted to charge fees and were no more immune to avarice than other members of the human species.[200] Although competition among physicians over rates would seem a natural result of the lack of formal municipal regulation, this was not always the case. A partially preserved inscription from Ephesus seems to imply that in at least that major metropolis physicians had agreed to a common set of charges for their services.[201]

*Women*

Although worthy of prolonged examination, we can only consider a few areas of female behavior, especially as it was manifested in the culturally Greek-dominated eastern part of the empire and in Asia in particular. Socially acceptable attire represented a subject of obvious concern to all women of that day and will be our beginning point.

Plutarch observes that "it is more often the custom for women to be veiled."[202] Tertullian speaks of how younger women were veiled "throughout Greece," but that it was less common in African cities.[203] Veiling in Greek areas covered the head only; one had to go to Arabia to find the custom expanded to include covering the face as well.[204] Mosaics from the eastern section of the empire universally depict women with *uncovered* faces and *usually* with uncovered heads as well. "Terra cotta statuary from Smyrna of the first and second centuries"[205] also reveals that going bareheaded in Asia was commonplace, at least in *artistic* representations. This has been interpreted, by some, as at least partially a result of upper-economic-strata women being depicted far more often than typical citizens.[206] Although there is sometimes, even today, a gap between acceptable attire for the social and economic elite and their lower-class sisters, the fact remains that the attire of the upper class tends to become the standard to be imitated, where and when feasible. Hence one would expect the more liberal bareheaded standard to result in many if not most adopting the same style.

A similar phenomenon of social liberalization through the imitation of Roman and upper-class conduct was also at work in regard to women dining with men. This was a Roman rather than a Greek custom. It began with the Romans and was imitated by the elite in the provinces. Although there was a great deal of resistance to the practice, many Romans not only felt comfortable with it but were startled that there was a different approach in the East. Cornelius Nepos wrote of these regional variations in the first century A.D.:

> For what Roman is ashamed to bring his wife to a banquet? What matron does not appear in the front room of

the house and go about in the throng of guests? Things are quite different in Greece. For women are not brought to meals except in the presence of close relatives, and they stay in the interior of the house, which is called Women's Quarters, where no male goes except a close member of the family.[207]

An area of possible major deviance from what might be assumed of the era lies in women's utilization of the public baths. Although women certainly took advantage of their availability, the actual operating arrangements seem to have varied with the time period and, quite probably, with local custom and preference. In some places the physical construction of the bath argues that the two genders utilized different sections. In other cases the design did not permit this; such baths may have been open to women at different times than the times for the men. On the other hand, in at least some documented cases, simultaneous use of the same facility definitely occurred. This became more common in the second century A.D.[208]

Women were under severe social and practical constraints in their activities outside the home. The ideal of being a keeper at home was easily read as functioning *only* in that role, though a husband's home duties were never interpreted in such exclusive terms. From the practical standpoint, a preindustrial economy also severely limited opportunities (outside agriculture) for *both* genders: there was simply no need for the complicated and massive infrastructure developed in any advanced economy. Even so, a minority of women did make a significant impact upon the public mind—not just for being ideal in their roles as women or wives but in other realms as well.

Perhaps the most socially acceptable area of influence was in religion. Because of the Greek impact on Asia and the surrounding provinces, a similar cultural definition of "women's role" in religious worship would normally be followed. Although there are few cases of a priestess serving a (male) god in Greece proper, there was near equality when it came to serving the (female) goddesses. In a survey of 348 cultic leaders serving various deities, 171 were discovered to have been female and only a slightly larger 177 were male.[209]

A few women became respected philosophers during the early centuries A.D. In the mid-fourth century, for example, Sosipata of Sardis gained an impressive reputation for her accomplishments in the field.[210]

Although women doctors were not common, they did exist, more so in the Greek eastern provinces than in the West.[211] In the second century Panthia of Pergamon was honored with this glowing inscription:

> Farewell, lady Panthia, from your husband. After your departure, I keep up my lasting grief for your cruel death. Hera, goddess of marriage, never saw such a wife: your beauty, your wisdom, your chastity. You bore me children completely like myself; you cared for your bridegroom and your children; you guided straight the rudder of life in our home and raised high our common fame in healing—though you were a woman you were not behind me in skill. In recognition of this your bridegroom Glycon built this tomb for you. I also buried here the body of [my father] immortal Philadelphus, and I myself will lie here when I die, since with you alone I shared my bed when I was alive, so may I cover myself in ground that we share.[212]

### Slavery

As of A.D. 100, Ramsay MacMullen estimates that slaves represented less than 10 percent of the total population in each region of the empire.[213] Raymond W. Goldsmith (without a specific date in mind) places the figure at between 10 and 15 percent of the population.[214] William V. Harris puts it as high as 20 percent.[215] To this must be added the ex-slave element in the population.[216]

Slavery existed primarily in an urban rather than a rural context. In larger and more prosperous cities (such as Pergamon) it easily included 25 percent of the population.[217] Household slaves would be the numerically dominant group, with the remainder engaged in various types of labor for the businesses of the town.[218] T. R. S. Broughton reasons in this way, working from the estimate of forty thousand slaves in Pergamon derived from Galen: If one grants the assumption that half of the slaves in Pergamon were women, then with rare exceptions one would expect the entire grouping of that gender to have been engaged in domestic service.[219] (However odd this may seem to a gender-conscious late-twentieth century, it rings true for the period we are discussing.) This would leave twenty thousand predominantly male slaves to divide among "the occupations of domestics, personal agents, clerk or secretaries, civic servants including clerks in the public offices, and the menial laborers used in the cleaning of baths and streets, or in private services where rough, unskilled work would do."[220]

The percentage of slaves is believed to have dropped dramatically as one moved to smaller and less wealthy towns and villages.[221] Agricultural slavery existed, but there was considerable skepticism as to its general effectiveness. Varro wrote that "it is better to work unhealthy land with hired labourers than with slaves, and even in healthier districts, for the more important agricultural operations like bringing in the produce of the vintage or the harvest."[222] Quite likely the rationale was that, though you could make a slave *work*, "work" did not automatically translate into efficient and productive labor.[223] Regardless of the specific rationale, the fact that such reservations were common can be seen in the fact that the limited available evidence from the "imperial estates of eastern provinces" indicates a dominant reliance upon free labor. If any element of the population was in a position to avail itself of slave labor, it was certainly the emperor and his local estate agents—yet they conspicuously did so only to a limited extent. A similar pattern of limited usage appears throughout Asia Minor.[224]

Depending upon the year or decade under consideration, slaves came predominantly from one of several sources. After a successful war, prisoners were commonly taken to be sold as slaves.[225] Although this provided a sporadic influx of new slaves, it was obviously not one that could be counted on on a regular, predictable basis.

Among the Greeks (and that sizable section of Asia and Asia Minor influenced by the Greek colonization/acculturation efforts) it was considered permissible to "expose" an unwanted or sickly newborn, leaving the infant to perish at the hands of nature. If rescued, that child could be raised as the rescuer's slave. If the child were the offspring of a slave (and it could be proved), then the owner of the mother had the right to claim the child as his own property.[226] Of course, if the child of a slave was retained, the child automatically was a slave.

Based upon inscriptional evidence of slave names, 70 percent bore Greek names.[227] This was subject, as always, to significant local variations. A study limiting itself to southern Italy produced a figure of 53 percent and one of Cisalpine Gaul 46 percent[228]—still high percentages. Two significant limitations on these surveys should be noted: Greek names were popular among many people not of that actual ethnic ancestry,[229] and the percentages may be skewed by their necessary reliance on *inscriptional* data. By their very nature inscriptions would relate to specially honored slaves and successful freedmen and not necessarily represent the much broader category of slaves in general.[230]

Greek names only indicate a probable origin in the eastern half of the empire, including Greece proper and Asia and beyond. Roman writers commonly spoke in terms of Asia Minor as representing the most abundant source for new slaves.[231] This raises an interpretive problem for us: if Asia itself—as part of that major slave-exporting region—was such an ongoing source of slaves, why is it that the data indicate that *resident* slaves in Asia represented such a modest percentage of the population?

There was no set pattern that a purchaser had to follow in naming his new slave. The ancient writer Varro speaks of how a master might select his slave's name from any of several sources, "If three men each bought a slave in Ephesus, one might take his name from that of the seller Artemidorus and call him Artemas; another from the region in which he made the purchase Ion from Ionia; the third names his Ephesius from Ephesus."[232] The nation of the slave's origin played no role in the selection.[233] Indeed, there were few distinctly "slave" names at all; almost any name selected would be borne by many freedmen and citizens as well.[234]

Slaves could be treated in a most despicable way. Seneca

(who rejected such callous treatment) spoke of such an extreme case when he wrote that "the poor slaves may not move their lips, even to speak. The slightest murmur is suppressed by the rod; even a chance sound, a cough, a sneeze, or a hiccup, is met with the lash. There is a terrible penalty for the slightest breach of silence. They must stand all night, hungry and dumb."[235]

Whatever legal right that an owner might have to abuse his slave, by the first century there was a general rejection of the *exercise* of that right.[236] In addition to abstract concepts of right and wrong and the virtue of restraint versus the evil of excess of any kind, advocates of temperate treatment also expressed the case in terms of utilitarian self-interest. Quintilius Varro, for example, spoke of how "men go to work with a keener will if they get better treatment or larger rations, more clothes or holidays or remission of work or permission to graze some of their own cattle on the farm, or other things of this sort. In this way and by this sort of kindness, you can restore their feeling of loyalty to their master after heavy work or even after punishment."[237]

When speaking of slaves *as a class* rather than in terms of a *particular* individual, one would most naturally expect a heavy emphasis on the utilitarian element; considerations of sentiment would be far more likely to grow out of good will toward a specific, well-known individual. Indeed, a young person of talent, combined with an understanding master, could produce slaves of marked administrative skill, individuals who were given great responsibility above and beyond that of most freedmen. Even affection could grow out of such an emotionally altered legal relationship. We find Cicero writing to his brother concerning a recently freed slave whom they both had long appreciated: "I have just heard about Tiro. He ought never to have been a slave, and now you have decided [by freeing him] that he should be our friend instead."[238]

One should neither glorify the Romans for practicing a "benevolent slavery" (though it was sometimes that) nor condemn them for "barbaric slavery" (though at its fringes it was certainly sometimes that as well). The modern reader needs to recognize that the treatment of slaves represented a continuum, and the treatment of individual slaves could fall anywhere on it. By the first century excesses were in ill repute, and preservation of one's own reputation required responsible and reasonable treatment of those under one's charge—including slaves.

Furthermore, slaves of this period had more real and de facto rights than those in the eighteenth and nineteenth centuries. Varro's reference to allowing slaves "to graze some of their *own* cattle on the farm" refers to certain property-owning rights they retained. *They* might be the property of their owner, but that did not totally exclude them from exercising certain ownership privileges of their own.

Slaves had at least the de facto right to exercise whatever religion they wished. Paul refers to Christians in Caesar's household (Phil 4:22), a term that seemingly must include not only freedmen but slaves as well.[239] A slave presence in a wide variety of ancient cults is well documented. In some (such as the cult of Dionysus), they were even accepted as full equals.[240]

Slaves were also accorded certain elements of *respect.* Legally "their oaths were binding, their graves were sacred and could not be violated without penalty, and their curses were regarded as efficacious."[241] If their owners were renowned, a certain element of that respect would rub off on them as their owners' functionaries. If an individual displayed initiative and ability, his own responsibilities (and perceived status) could easily grow as well—even for slaves owned by Rome itself.[242]

Such legal and social recognition argues that the extremes of dehumanization tended to be avoided. Perhaps this is the reason that ancient writers—even former slaves—limited themselves to the denunciation of the excesses of slavery rather than attacking the institution itself.[243]

To be a freedman was a natural aspiration of the slave: whatever one's own virtues, talents, and attitudes might be, they could still be contemptuously ignored by an embittered or vile-minded owner. On the other hand, being free was no panacea. It provided no guarantee of a job nor adequate financial income to live a tolerable life. In contrast, slaves *had* to be fed and if they were employed in the household or immediate retinue of the owner, they had to be attired in a way in keeping with that owner's status.

Although slaves might well gain status from being important functionaries of their masters, poor freedmen were just as likely to be viewed as the equivalent of twentieth-century "white trash." Juvenal once described the popular attitude this way:

> If you're poor, you're a joke, on each and every occasion.
> What a laugh, if your cloak is dirty or torn, if your toga
> appears a little bit soiled, if your shoe has a crack in the
> leather. Or if several patches betray frequent mending!
> Poverty's greatest curse, much worse than actually being
> poor, is that it makes men objects of mirth, ridiculed,
> grumbled, embarrassed....Sons of freeborn men give way
> to a rich man's slave.[244]

Although being granted freedom automatically bestowed Roman citizenship, *if* one had been the slave of a Roman citizen,[245] it did not provide the full benefits that went with being born free. Criminal accusations against a former master were permitted only when the charge was treason; civil accusations could be tried only with the former master's approval.[246] At the time of being granted freedom, slaves were traditionally required to make an oath committing themselves to a specified number of days of labor on behalf of their former master—and the ex-master had the right to let that work-obligation be exercised in service to a third party.[247] Ex-slaves had the moral obligation of doing anything and everything necessary to relieve the distress of the former owner. This included providing for that owner if he himself became impoverished and accepting the guardianship of the surviving children if that became necessary.[248] Unlike previously existing Greek forms of slavery—where these continuing obligations might end in as few as ten years—Roman law made these lifelong obligations.[249]

Although it would be natural for former slaves to be appreciative of the gift that had been given them, Roman law was written in a way to assure that they could never fully forget their former status. John G. Gager argues that because of these limitations on personal freedom "it is not surprising that most freedmen continued in the same jobs which they had held as slaves: chief of the household, supervisor of the master's business and financial affairs, foreman in his factories," or such like.[250] On the other hand, why would one feel obliged to reject a secured and honored position for the potential dangers of an unknown and uncertain future in a yet unoffered position? Prudence for one's own interests reinforced existing ties in such cases.

The status of much farm labor—in the empire in general and Asia in particular—is unclear. Varro writes of "those persons whom the Romans used to call 'debt-bondsmen' *(obaerati)* and of whom there are *large numbers* even today in Asia Minor and Egypt and Illyricum."[251] Varro, in context, seems to distinguish these individuals from both slaves and true free labor. This would point to a substantial body of individuals either permanently or temporarily in forced labor, presumably to their creditors to pay off past debts.

One's *practical* and *actually exercised* freedom may be far different from one's *theoretical* and *official* status as a free person. Hence some speak in terms of a first century *developing quasi-serfdom* (as distinct from the fully developed medieval form with which we are more acquainted).[252] Part of this was self-imposed: individuals normally chose to dwell in one specific location or in one particular village year after year throughout their lives. Barring necessity, most humans are inherently conservative, hewing to the path that has been walked a thousand times before. Reinforcing these natural instincts of human nature, those utilizing their farm labor or on whose estates they dwelt would seek *stability of work force* in order to preserve their own economic interests and to maintain a regular, predictable (more or less) level of income. These forces acted together to make *voluntary* decisions *semi-obligations,* which could be avoided only with the risk of personal and societal censure. Although this phenomenon is most easily seen beginning in the third century,[253] the frame of mind that led to it was operative at a much earlier date.

# 2

# Rome and Its Asian Province

In studying the relationship of Rome to the province of Asia, the discussion falls into two categories: the historical and the political. The first involves the *historical,* the development of the relationship between the two and Rome's ultimate dominance over the province. The second involves the *administrative,* how Roman power was actually exercised on an ongoing basis after the province came under her control.

## Evolution of Roman Involvement in Asia

Attalus III ruled a mere five years over his Pergamonese kingdom (138–33 B.C.), which ultimately formed the heart of Roman Asia and the basis for ongoing, permanent Roman power in the region. Yet after this short reign his written will brought it under direct Roman control.

On the positive side, Attalus successfully beat off a military foe (identity unknown) and provided respectable donations to the religious cults of his day.[1] On the other hand, the mildest epithet that can be given this ruler is that of "eccentric," and depending upon the credibility one attaches to the literary evidence critical of him, he may well have crossed the line into being outright demented.[2] When both his fiancée *and* mother died within a suspiciously short period of time, he passed on most actual administrative powers to others. He shifted into a research mode and zealously sought curative powers in the plants of his day, or so he wished others to believe. The dominant negative evaluation in his own age was that he was more interested in discovering the *lethal* powers of these substances to use against real and imagined foes.[3]

The bequest startled his own kingdom and the Romans

themselves. He had visited Rome as a youth in 152 B.C. and was greeted with conspicuous enthusiasm by the senate.[4] But no one could have anticipated that such friendly sentiments would translate into his later drastic action. Hence there have been a number of suggestions put forward to explain his conduct. A few nineteenth-century scholars suspected that the original will was a Roman forgery. A contemporary inscription was then discovered that refers to the will, and this effectively undermined the thesis that the Romans made up the "gift" out of whole cloth.[5]

Others sought a psychological explanation—perhaps *psychiatric* explanation would be more appropriate in a case this extreme. Attalus hated his subjects so much that he vented his wrath in the ultimate act of giving them and his kingdom not to a native-born ruler but to a foreign power.[6]

Whatever psychological predispositions may have existed, most analysts see in the decision a strong streak of political *realism*. If Attalus despaired of the ability of the kingdom to hold together, Roman control offered the best alternative. If his primary goal was to guarantee that Aristonicus did not gain the throne, this was the best preventive. If he simply saw the advancing power of Rome as inevitable and wished to secure favoritism for his people, this undemanded and purely voluntary action guaranteed at least minimal *emotional* ties, which would not exist toward a conquered people and which could not but help predispose Rome to favorable policies and attitudes.[7] Certainly the question was not so much *whether* Rome would gain dominant influence in the region but how much *explicit control* would accompany that dominance. Indeed, the most recent expansion of the borders of the Pergamonese kingdom had been at Roman insistence, as the reward for supporting Rome in the war against Antiochus.[8]

In attempting to explain what occurred, there is no need to limit ourselves to one explanation. In real life the decisions an individual makes are usually produced by several factors of varying importance. Why should Attalus's decision have been any different?

Will or no will, the transition did not come easy. Attalus's suspicions of Aristonicus as a would-be ruler proved true when

Aristonicus grabbed for personal power rather than permitting an unopposed Roman takeover. At first the rebellion went his way, with significant early victories. Even after the Romans reversed his early triumphs in the nearby islands of Asia, he remained a power to contend with on the mainland. He seized Thyatira, assaulted Smyrna, and endangered the capital of Pergamon itself. That Aristonicus had successfully tapped into a deep reservoir of resentment at the established political system (commonly interpreted to mean that he successfully appealed to the frustrations of the lower classes and the slaves) can be seen in the fact that even his capture did not result in the complete collapse of the rebellion. A determined mopping-up operation by Roman legionnaires was required to accomplish the final suppression.[9]

With the Pergamonese kingdom securely in their hand, other acquisitions were obtained over a period of time to flesh out the new province of Asia. In 116 B.C. Phrygia was added;[10] Pompey's successes in the middle sixties B.C. brought in the remainder.[11]

Before these last additions, however, local rage at Roman taxation broke forth when Mithridates seized Asia from the east. Resentful local citizens lashed out at the Romans in general, slaughtering thousands, whom they lumped together with the tax farmers who were bleeding the region.[12]

Not only were the massive casualties in Asia horrifying in themselves, but word of the defeat and atrocities brought economic chaos in Rome itself. The catastrophe represented not only a massive Roman humiliation but also the (temporary) loss of many properties and the destruction of yet others. Cicero later referred to "how payments of debts were stopped at Rome and credit shaken when so many had lost their property in Asia."[13]

Although Mithridates provided Asia a pleasing temporary revenge against the Roman occupation, he could not make it permanent. Acting under minimal restraint by their officers, the reconquering Roman soldiers were permitted to enact virtually any revenge they wished. To these individual tales of retribution was added a provincial one: when the reconquest was completed, Sulla announced that the Asian cities would have to pay a twenty-thousand-talent fine for their participation in the revolt.[14]

During the Roman civil wars the region became a cash cow to be milked by both sides. The fact that the taxes had already been paid counted for nought, for they were to an opposing regime. Now they must not only be paid for the current period but for years ahead—immediately! Brutus and Cassius demanded that the Asia cities pay *ten years'* worth of tribute—ahead of schedule, within the following year. Although Antony was convinced to reduce his demands to nine years' worth of tribute, he still demanded one-third in each of the following years and was angry at having to be this "generous."[15]

The triumphant Caesar's demands seemed light in comparison to the previous short-term extortion by the others. Even so, his demands were far beyond what the province could reasonably bear, and he was convinced to reduce the tax level by a third. It is widely doubted that this was anything more than a "paper" generosity and that all that was done was to reduce the taxation level to that *already being received.*[16]

Caesar certainly removed one major cause of grievance by withdrawing the publicans from Asia. Henceforth the tax-tithe was to be paid by each community's treasury on behalf of the entire municipality.[17] It has been speculated that the reduction was that which would have been the publicans' share of the gross.[18] A third seems more like triple the official return they were guaranteed,[19] but their excesses would certainly have run up the percentage far above the recognized one.

Negatively, the administrative costs were now borne by the municipalities, and unlike the publicans, they received no reimbursement. The "reduced" ongoing taxation level remained burdensome—indeed, overwhelming—especially when inflicted upon a province economically crippled by the terrible extractions of the civil wars. The province sank into a sea of bankruptcies, which Augustus met by foregoing taxes and by widely canceling other debts in the province.[20]

The renewed internal peace was the vital prerequisite for Asia's natural resilience to express itself. As we will see later, soon Asia was again renowned for its prosperity. Roman military power discouraged domestic insurrection and foreign intervention. As Cicero had argued at an earlier date, "Let Asia consider this, that no calamity of foreign war or internal discord would have been wanting to her if she were not protected by this Empire."[21]

Yet the potential for becoming an international battle-ground was always present. Not far to the east lay the kingdom of Armenia. The rival desires of Persia and Rome to control that kingdom created a dangerous flash point for conflict, one that would quickly have spread to include all of Asia Minor. Fortunately for Rome, throughout the first two centuries A.D., the rulers of Persia were usually weak or hindered by the danger of internal civil war. A united Persia would have represented a major threat to the continuation of Roman power in the East.[22]

### Roman Administration of Asia

When Rome took over Asia, the capital was at Pergamon. A few centuries later it is certain that the capital was Ephesus.[23] What is more controversial is where the capital was located during the first and second centuries A.D. Many say it remained at Pergamon.[24] Others just as confidently refer to it being located at Ephesus.[25] Yet others refer to the disagreement and decline to express a judgment.[26]

J. P. W. Sweet notes that Pergamon "is usually held to have been the Roman provincial capital, though the evidence is not quite clear."[27] Perhaps it is the ambiguity of the evidence as to *when* the transition occurs that leads yet another group of individuals to use *bridging* rhetoric, which says, in effect, "yes, the capital was at Pergamon *but...*," with some type of comment that simultaneously backs away from the assertion. An extreme example of this is Francis Lyall, who simultaneously calls Pergamon "the capital of the province" yet adds, in the very same sentence, that Ephesus was "a main seat of government."[28] Others use the distinction between de jure and de facto, making Pergamon the former and Ephesus the latter.[29] In this reconstruction Ephesus becomes "the virtual capital,"[30] "the practical capital,"[31] or "the real, though not the titular capital."[32] In a somewhat similar vein, others distinguish between Ephesus as the "chief city" of Asia[33] and its "most important city,"[34] and Pergamon as its capital.

Assuming that the capital *did* change during the period, when did the move actually occur? Some date it explicitly[35] or implicitly[36] during the life and reign of Augustus. Others prefer a date later in the first century[37] or during the reign of Hadrian (117–38 A.D.)[38]

Since there is no explicit evidence with which to settle the issue, we must deal with inferences and careful reasoning. The Augustan period is an especially weak claimant. Steven J. Friesen dates the transfer in 29 B.C., but in that *same year* the first imperial temple was established in Pergamon, as he himself admits.[39] He argues that to have established the provincial cult anywhere else "would not have helped consolidate the authority of Augustus in Asia."[40] By the same logic, would not the Romans have felt the need to retain the *official capital* in Pergamon as well?

The strongest basis for inference comes from the clear presence of provincial governmental functions in Ephesus. Yet even here we do not know when this took place and whether it preceded the official move or was simultaneous with it.[41] On its own merits we would expect Ephesus's inherent importance to attract considerable preferential treatment and the equivalent of "branch" offices that, over time, would easily tend to become the "main" offices of provincial administration. Furthermore, as a much larger cosmopolitan city than Pergamon, Ephesus would probably be the residence preferred by the governor, regardless of where the official capital was located.

Furthermore, the Asian cities were engaged in vigorous— "vicious" would be more accurate—competition for prestige and acknowledgment. In light of such intense feelings, it would be natural for the Romans to nibble away at the official prerogatives of Pergamon and allow the public acknowledgment of Ephesus's superiority to long precede official action. Hence a date no earlier than Hadrian would make the most sense for the change.

What seems to have happened is that Ephesus's dominance in *public opinion* ultimately led to it being *officially* recognized as the capital.[42] Roman action was *re*active rather than initiatory. Since the Romans could rule from either city equally well, there was no need to risk antagonizing the locals when it was not needed.

Because Asia was a senatorial province, the Roman Senate was responsible for the selection of its governors (called proconsuls because their powers paralleled those exercised by a consul in Rome). (This did not, of course, rule out considerable or even decisive input by the emperor.) Senatorial proconsuls differed in two key ways from governors directly appointed by the emperor. Proconsuls were normally limited to one-year terms, while imperial governors were not. Second, proconsuls rarely had as large a military force under their authority as imperial governors did. On the other hand, provinces such as Asia tended to be more peaceful than those retained under direct control of the emperor and, therefore, less in need of the stabilizing power provided by stronger military forces and multi-year continuity in leadership.[43]

Yet multi-year assignments did, upon occasion, occur. Under Augustus, Publius Petronius remained governor of Asia for six years.[44] Another served three years.[45] One factor involved in such prolongations was concern for both efficiency and *relatively* honest government. Tiberius argued that once a governor had gained his fortune from his posting, he was unlikely to inflict any further serious harm during the remaining years he retained the post.[46] A second justification given by Tiberius for not maintaining the official one-year term required by tradition lay in the fact (at least, so he claimed) that many refused to accept the post of provincial governor. In other words, a uniform application of one-year terms was both impractical and impossible.[47] What further complicated the picture was the fact that regardless of whether a governor was dishonest or not, and regardless of whether he in fact sought self-aggrandizement, he would certainly be *accused* of such by his critics and quite possibly have to face formal accusations.[48] Corruption was notable not so much for its existence as for its excess. For example, Gaius

Silanus was tried before Tiberius and the senate on the charge of committing massive theft while serving as proconsul of Asia. So abundant was the evidence against him that he waived his right to present a defense.[49]

The Asian governorship and that of Roman Africa were considered the two highest posts to which an individual could aspire.[50] One was supposed to have served as a consul in Rome and five years were to have passed before one could be posted to either location,[51] but the time delay requirement was waived upon occasion.[52] The annual change in office in Asia occurred during the middle of summer, with July the most likely date.[53]

Various tax collecting and proconsul offices were centralized in Ephesus, certainly by the second century A.D., and, at least with a smaller number of personnel, in the first century as well. This would have required a substantial number of record keepers and administrative personnel to run the actual tax-collection mechanism.[54] The number of personnel would have been further increased due to the city being the center of an assize district and by whatever permanent staff the proconsul maintained in the city.[55] (The substantial reliance of the governor on military personnel for his staff was discussed in chapter 1.) An unknown number of personnel of various types would have had to be maintained in other cities as well. Among these would have been skilled individuals to run the regional coinage mints that existed at both Ephesus and Pergamon during the first century.[56]

Not everyone working for Rome reported to the proconsul. Many operatives retained direct links back to the capital city of the empire.[57] They administered the royal estates. They served as officials attached to various military commands. These and others working under independent commission enjoyed both the right of direct correspondence with Rome and, the flip side, direct responsibility if their decisions were not acceptable. Although by current standards their numbers were modest, judged by the standards and expectations of their own day they represented a considerable body of individuals. During the third century their numbers increased dramatically, and by the end of the fourth century they numbered as many as two or three thousand,[58] a figure that mushroomed again in the following century.[59]

The foundation of imperial land ownership in Asia lay in the possessions of the previous Pergamonese kingdom: the royal lands possessed by that emperor automatically passed to the Roman ruler when control of the province changed hands.[60] Some of these Pergamonese possessions may have been ones seized from the religious cults of the day—either in a display of naked power or by leaving technical ownership in the hands of the sects while confiscating the profits. The once popular assumption that such procedures were common appears to be ungrounded.[61]

Several factors produced a further increase in imperial ownership under Roman rule. For one thing, the exact boundaries between imperial, city-owned, and privately owned estates were open to maximizing claims by all parties concerned.[62] Since the emperor's representatives would make the final determination, it is probable that much or all of the benefit of the doubt went in the direction of expanding the borders of imperial property. Bequests would naturally come from appreciative locals and those seeking favor with the current regime. Unscrupulous confiscation also would have been a readily available tool, especially if one could maintain that the property had been abandoned or was owned by a real or imagined foe of the emperor or his local representatives. In spite of these opportunities, the direct imperial holdings remained a subsidiary element in the total agricultural economy rather than the dominant element in it.[63]

For administrative ease and convenience, Asia was broken down into a number of smaller judicial districts, each known as a *conventus*.[64] A proconsul writing about 50 B.C. spoke of nine such districts in Asia.[65] Pliny the Elder (working primarily from an Augustan-era document) speaks of ten such districts, though not in a way that necessarily excludes the existence of additional ones.[66] An inscription at Didyma has been interpreted to imply the existence of thirteen assize districts in A.D. 40.[67]

All three of these sources refer to Ephesus, Sardis, Smyrna, and Pergamon as being the seat of a conventus.[68] An Ephesian inscription of Vespasian's reign mentions five by name (including Sardis and Pergamon) but omits Ephesus and Smyrna.[69] In the second century A.D. Philadelphia was split from the jurisdiction of Sardis and became an assize city in its own right.[70] After the Emperor Caracella visited Thyatira in A.D. 215, he promoted that city to conventus status as well.[71]

Given the size of Asia, it seems inherently probable that local courts enjoyed sizable jurisdiction in local cases, though with the right of appeal to the governor. Likewise, it seems inherently probable that the governor reserved to himself the right to appoint a judge when citizens were involved who resided in different cities and when a case involved one or more Roman citizens.[72] Furthermore, the governor traveled on a circuit, stopping periodically in each of the assize cities to hear cases.[73]

The entire region was joined into a province-wide consultative assembly that helped alleviate potential tensions between the local population and the Roman government. The provincial assembly was attended by representatives of the various "peoples" scattered throughout Asia. Its annual meeting provided a regular forum whereby the governor could present the empire's policies and wishes. Although these political functions were important, so were its religious duties, for the provincial assembly bore the responsibility for preserving, celebrating, and encouraging the worship of both Rome and its emperor.[74]

During the last decade B.C., the Roman proconsul Paullus Fabius Maximus convinced the local authorities to alter the traditional calendar. Henceforth the new year would begin with Augustus's birthday on September 23.[75] The new first month was called Kaisarios (or Caesareus), and the first day of the new year (that is, Augustus's birthday itself), Sebaste.[76]

*3*

# Characteristics of Life
# in Roman Asia

Having surveyed Roman life and attitudes in general and how Roman power developed and was exercised in Asia, let us turn our attention to what it was like to live in that province. This will involve an examination of topics as diverse as urbanization, farm living, the regional economy, and the role of Judaism in the province.

## Physical Description and Problems of the Region

The province of Asia varied in size at different points in its history. At the maximum it occupied about one-third of the western and southwestern portion of modern-day Turkey. To the extent that Europe met Asia in the ancient and even medieval world, it was primarily through the land corridor of Turkey. A prominent nineteenth-century specialist on the region wrote:

> Across this bridge, the religion, art, and civilization of the East found their way into Greece; and the civilization of Greece, under the guidance of Alexander the Macedonian passed back again across the same bridge to conquer the East and revolutionize Asia as far as the heart of India. Persians, Arabs, Mongols, Turks, have all followed the same route in the many attempts that Asia has made to subdue the West.[1]

The same authority described the physical characteristics as well:

The great mass of Asia Minor consists of a plateau, 3,000 to 5,000 feet above sea-level, around which there is a fringe of low-lying coast-land. The plateau is like a continuation of Central Asia, vast, immobile, monotonous. The western coasts on the Aegean Sea are full of variety, with a very broken coast-line and long arms of the sea alternating with prominent capes.[2]

A more recent traveler to the region provides this word picture:

Approaching the country from any direction, it has the appearance of a massive mountain range backed up against the horizon. While this massive aspect is most conspicuous on the south and east, it applies equally to the north and west, where the ranges are frequently broken by abrupt passes issuing in extensive lowland areas, as along the coasts of Sicily and southern Italy. In the territory of the Carian, Lydian, and Mysian provinces on the Aegean littoral, particularly in the vicinity of Miletus, Ephesus, Sardis, Thyatira, Pergamum, and Troas, the hills recede to create fertile basis extending into the interior from twenty to one hundred miles....

A journey into the interior of Asia Minor proves very quickly that the massive backgrounds are more than appearances. Proceeding inland from any direction, one is impressed with the marked change in elevation, which reaches, on the average, about 3,000 feet above the Mediterranean. While the greater part of this ascent is gradual, at some points, especially the narrow mountain passes, it becomes sharp and tortuous. This is an indirect way of stating that the whole of interior Asia Minor is an immense plateau with a variety of topographical features—open spaces, fields, upland levels, and a few valleys originally characterized by great fertility.[3]

The coastal regions and the less elevated sections of the valleys leading into the interior have a climate that is thoroughly Mediterranean and is more warm and temperate than Greece.[4] "The valleys rarely suffer from frost or snow, and the worst of the summer heat is relieved by the west winds which blow steadily up them almost every day. Rain falls in considerably less volume than in the north and is very differently distributed, since there is practically none during the summer."[5] Even so, twentieth-century Smyrna receives ten inches more rainfall a year than Athens.[6]

The conditions naturally shift as one moves westward into the plateau and as the various valleys influence local climate and agricultural conditions. For example, along the Caicus valley as far inland as Pergamon, environmental conditions are virtually identical with Smyrna. Yet as one proceeds further inland, the rainfall drops four inches or more a year and usually comes year-round rather than disappearing during the summer.[7]

Figs, grapes, and olives grow abundantly in the coastal valleys and hills, such as those that lead to Smyrna.[8] Figs disappear as one proceeds inland beyond the coastal valleys.[9] Olives disappear as one passes eastward beyond Thyatira.[10]

The most frightening physical phenomenon of the region are the recurring earthquakes. Erzincan (in Anatolia) was wiped out a minimum of eleven times during a nine-hundred-year period.[11] Antioch in Anatolia was similarly devastated seven times within two millennia. The last massive earthquake in that city (now called Antaka) was in 1873.[12] Hierapolis, near Laodicea, was ultimately abandoned because of earthquakes.[13]

Beginning its list with the first century, a 1952 study listed 750 major quakes as having occurred in Turkey.[14] A 1967 list of quakes with Turkish or near-Turkey epicenters recorded almost seventeen hundred occurrences.[15] Of course, these studies relied heavily on literary sources, which would normally have mentioned only the worst cases.

In light of these substantial figures, it is not surprising that massive quakes ravaged first- and second-century Asia. In A.D. 178 a large earthquake and accompanying fire destroyed Smyrna.[16] A huge quake wreaked damage throughout much of Asia and surrounding provinces in A.D. 115.[17] It appears that one damaged both Hierapolis and Laodicea in A.D. 144.[18]

To move backward to the first century, Colossae, Laodicea, and Hierapolis endured substantial damage in A.D. 60.[19] In A.D. 29 a major quake hit various points in Asia,[20] including Sardis[21] and Ephesus.[22] In A.D. 24 one hit Sardis,[23] and a wider-ranging one had also hit the province in the preceding year.[24] Thyatira and Laodicea were both hit by a quake about 20 B.C.[25] and even earlier, about 24 or 25 B.C.[26]

Of special interest is the mammoth earthquake of A.D. 17 that wrecked at least twelve cities of Asia and inflicted a major loss of life.[27] Turkish experts believe that Ephesus was near the epicenter, and that the earthquake would have registered a "10" on the modern Richter scale.[28] If so, Ephesus was extraordinarily lucky, for the Romans believed that Sardis "suffered most severely from the destructive visitation."[29] Tacitus described the horror this way:

> The same year twelve populous cities of Asia fell in ruins from an earthquake which happened by night, and therefore the more sudden and destructive was the calamity; neither did the usual mode of escaping in such events, by rushing into the open space, avail now, as those who fled were swallowed up by the yawning earth. It is related, "That immense mountains sank down, that level places were seen to be elevated into hills, and that fires flashed forth during the catastrophe.[30]

Taxes were suspended for five years—an action that had been taken in the past, when Roman governments realized that the taxes could not be collected anyway.[31] Tiberius, however, went beyond this and provided a sizable government grant in order to assist the region; he also appointed a senator to oversee the rebuilding program.[32] Suetonius—determined to paint Tiberius as the ultimate miser—struggled to find a way to explain this assistance and could only assert that this was an exception to the pattern.[33]

In 12 B.C. another wide-ranging earthquake decimated the province. In that case Augustus had provided assistance from his *personal* fortune, rather than utilizing the financial resources of the empire.[34] Tiberius's action of tapping the treasury of the empire can be read as recognition that "if the provinces paid tribute in time of prosperity, they were entitled to assistance in the hour of misfortune."[35] Hence one can find here evidence of imperial *obligation* being added to the traditional concept of imperial *rights*. The cynic, however, can conclude from the same data that Tiberius was willing to be generous with the empire's money—at least in an extreme case, such as this—but was unwilling to do so on a personal basis, as Augustus had done.

## Regional Characteristics

Although Asia was influenced by both Greece and Rome, that never ruled out the existence of variants upon the patterns found in other parts of the world. Even in the modern world different regions of the same country tend to have distinctive attitudes and practices somewhat at variance with those dominant elsewhere. In the ancient world, where travel was slower, regional variations tended to perpetuate themselves longer and be more pronounced. Several areas of life and conduct exhibit this phenomena.

Not only were the Asians far more under the influence of the Hellenistic heritage than mainstream Roman, but they developed a continuing reputation for quality sculpture that was in such demand that not only the finished product but the sculptors themselves were enticed to faraway locales to practice their art.[36] In common with other regional artisans (such as Aphrodisias in Caria) they "developed their own style of carving, which contrasts with the modeling of the classical tradition, preferring deep drillwork and angular shapes producing strong effects of black-and-white. As the empire develops we can see the influence of this new technique in many places, in Rome already in the time of the Emperor Trajan."[37]

Even the method of glorifying the emperors in the civic sphere varied between the East and the West. In Italy and that region mammoth triumphal arches symbolized the power and success of the Romans. Few such arches were constructed in Asia. "Instead the medium of imperial propaganda is the imperial portrait statue in all its forms, especially those based on the traditions of classical religious sculpture. Groups of the Roman emperor and his family took the place of cult statues in temples and in public buildings."[38]

In Asia, architecture tended toward the *massive*. As George M. A. Hanfmann writes:

> Inspired by the Roman use of concrete, the builders of Asia Minor developed a new building system which permitted adaptation—but not complete imitation—of Roman vaulted architecture. The new material in Asia was mortared rubble laid to form very thick walls (six feet are common); a variant with intervening bonding courses of brick was fully developed by the second century. (At Sardis, the victory of mortared rubble over traditional Hellenistic masonry seems directly connected with the Roman-sponsored renewal program after the earthquake of 17.) In the fully developed Asiatic system, strong masonry piers linked by heavy stretches of rubble-and-brick walls carried the major loads....Quite sizable spans were achieved with a sophisticated distribution of loads and stresses, as indicated by the 40-foot vaulted span over the swimming pool unit of the gymnasium at Ephesus.[39]

Layers of marble were commonly hung from the walls to increase the beauty of the building.[40]

Sculpture and architecture are designed to serve the living. Yet in regard to burial customs there were also unique regional patterns:

> Unlike their counterparts in other areas of the Greco-Roman world, the Jews and non-Jews in Asia Minor were accustomed to purchasing burial sites and erecting funeral monuments in advance of the death of even one family member. The phrase "So-and-so erected this monument for himself and his family while still living" is a common feature of both Jewish and non-Jewish grave inscriptions throughout Asia Minor.[41]

It was common among both Gentiles and Jews to have formal inscribed curses engraved on their burial monuments. These invoked temporal discomfort or disaster upon the disturber of the site. The invocation of divine wrath essential to make the threat credible is often implicit, although at other times the divine intervention is explicitly stated. Some also demanded the payment of a substantial financial penalty to some specified organization if the site were altered or used for any other purpose.[42]

## Cities and Civic Affairs

William M. Ramsay describes Asia as the Roman province "fullest of great cities."[43] A few centuries after the first–second century period we are primarily interested in, it was known as the province of five hundred cities.[44] Aelius Aristides wrote, "For when were there so many cities both inland and on the coast, or when have they been so beautifully equipped with everything?...The coasts and interiors have been filled with cities, some newly founded, others increased under and by [Rome]."[45]

All cities in the Roman province had the right of self-government, subject to the veto of the proconsul.[46] Seven cities—none of which was one where any of the seven churches was located—possessed the right of changing their governing constitution on their own authority, without gaining the concurrence of the Roman government.[47]

Like its modern-day counterpart, Asian cities secured funds from a number of sources, some of which sound a bit odd to the modern ear. One they did *not* use (but which was popular in other regions) was a charge for the use of public water (in the baths, for domestic use, etc.).[48] A wide variety of other revenue sources was fully utilized, however.

Individual cities customarily charged a modest percentage of the value of all products transported across their boundaries for sale.[49] Cities often charged license fees based upon the specific occupation being practiced.[50] There is abundant evidence of local governments renting sales space to merchants in civic buildings and porticoes.[51] Admission fees were common at both theaters and the public baths.[52]

Municipal-wide per-person direct taxes were sometimes imposed upon all free citizens. (Sometimes these are called "poll taxes," a misleading term for modern readers who tend to think in terms of fees required before an individual can vote.) These inevitably aroused pleas of poverty from the citizenry.

Due to the inevitability of ill-will resulting from their imposition, cities avoided imposing such fees whenever possible.[53]

In contrast, renting municipally owned lands aroused no such protest. Only those directly involved had to pay the fee, which was paid out of the revenues generated by the property. If a municipality utilized local publicans, the situation was further simplified: the municipality received the fees in advance, while the publicans were stuck with any difficulties involved in actually collecting the rents.[54] These rental fees—if collected directly—might be either in coin or in produce.[55] Sometimes the property's revenues went to the city as an entity; in other cases the bequest of property to the city had been set up as a trust for the benefit of certain institutions or activities located within the community, and the city simply served as the administrator.[56] Even in this indirect fashion, government was able to avoid expenditures that it might otherwise have been held accountable for by the public, resulting in an *effective* decrease in taxation, even if not an official one.

In the pre-Roman period, individual cities had accumulated the estates of convicted felons, a practice the Romans generally prohibited.[57] Limited voluntary gifts of land continued to be made, as did periodic purchases of additional properties with monies contributed to the city.[58] If the city had extra cash on hand, it often loaned it out as mortgage money.[59]

Small and modest fines existed for violation of local civic codes governing house, road maintenance, and related topics. Much of the code of Pergamon has survived. The modest penalties these codes provided would likely have been of only marginal value in meeting any city's actual operating expenses.[60]

Although coming from a variety of sources, the *cumulative total* of city income still fell far short of civic expenditures. In this context of limited urban income and substantial urban expenditures, being a civic leader was an expensive proposition. First there were the expenses of being appointed. Throughout Asia Minor those seeking to hold various public posts were expected to provide substantial "donations" in advance.[61] As it became customary to provide such a "gift" to the community, the same amount—or more—was expected of each and every individual who later occupied that position. In the second century, when Pliny studied Bithynia, he was startled not by the existence of such fees but by their lack of uniformity. The same post could require a dramatically different outlay from city to city. Hence he attempted to create a uniform schedule of fees for all communities, an effort the emperor Trajan proceeded to veto.[62]

Substantial *ongoing* expenditures also came out of the pocket of important magistrates. Major public works—and even significant minor ones—represented a substantial civic expense that was passed from the community at large onto the shoulders of its would-be leaders. These could take the form of aqueducts, fountains, theaters, or any other project that would enhance the appearance and reputation of the city.[63] Foreign service on behalf of the city was, of course, at the diplomat's own expense.[64] Cost of domestic (city) service also came out of his own resources. Furthermore, he was expected to cover the payroll and expense costs of anyone serving directly under him when the municipality itself did not cover the costs.[65]

When one considers all the various ways that a magistrate contributed to the expenses of the community, one can understand why these semi-voluntary expenditures may well have constituted the bulk of any city's revenues.[66] At least in the time period we are considering, these societal expectations had not reached the point of neutralizing the desire to serve. The increased respect leaders received still outweighed the financial costs.[67] In addition, it was the primary method of expressing their solidarity with their community: in this period Asians continued to define their central/core political and social loyalties *not* in terms of their province or the empire as a whole, but in terms of their native city.[68]

In addition to the construction of public works, civic expenditures took a number of other forms, including the repair and maintenance of these public works. Indeed, this was one of the "down" sides to such heavy reliance upon the well-to-do; since they had great control over which specific project they undertook to better the city, it was easy for them to choose those with the maximum possible reputation-building effect regardless of what ongoing maintenance expenses later magistrates and the community at large might be called upon to bear.[69]

Salaries represented only a minor urban outlay. As already noted, leaders were expected to serve gratis. Lower-echelon posts, however, were sometimes filled by individuals who received either a salary or fees for the work they performed.[70] The least respected jobs were commonly allotted to municipally owned slaves or to criminals as part of their punishment.[71]

In contrast, religious/cultic activities constituted a major expense for the municipality. These embraced both strictly religious activities and public entertainments carried on in the name of a specific cult as part of a quasi-religious celebration. When a cult was prominent and possessed substantial holdings of its own—such as the cult of Artemis of Ephesus—the sect itself could underwrite much or all of the activities it sponsored, rather than letting the burden fall mainly on the city.[72] Like the medieval merchants who flocked to religious celebrations many centuries later, the first centuries' religious and quasi-religious rites attracted many individuals who were far more interested in turning a profit than in anything else. Celebrations could provide a significant financial boost to the sponsoring local community,[73] thereby providing an incentive for continuing public support in spite of whatever financial and administrative difficulties might occur.

The public games carried out in connection with emperor worship were different. Being sponsored by the *province* of Asia, the province had to provide the financing.[74] It is probable that being an Asiarch not only provided one with the honor of being the titular leader of emperor worship in the province, but also the financial obligation to assure that the costs of these associated athletic events were fully covered.[75]

In contrast, local gymnasiums were a local obligation and these carried a substantial double burden to the city. The city was obligated to provide the oil that was rubbed on the bodies of those utilizing the facilities[76] and also to provide the large amounts of firewood required to maintain the heated pools.[77] Some ancient cities set up special funds to finance the providing of the oil, while others provided a direct public subsidy.[78]

Elementary male education was a common phenomenon in Asia, but the degree of government support is unknown.[79] Publicly appointed physicians are known to have existed in such cities as Ephesus and Pergamon. They appear to have received a certain amount of financial support from the government in return for not charging poor patients for treatment.[80] Government-run welfare for the poor (that is, direct financial or food grants) was unknown in the region,[81] but city governments commonly *did* appoint an official to expedite the receipt of grain into the community[82]—an activity that helped protect the physical well-being of the community at large in time of scarcity.

The communities engaged in civilly supported street-cleaning and firefighting. By utilizing government-owned slaves, the costs of such activities were kept to a minimum.[83]

In spite of tapping into the financial largesse of the local aristocracy, city expenditures could easily get out of hand. Although lavish local spending on public facilities and public games and shows contributed to the local sense of well-being, they also represented a financial danger to the Roman government. Unless a tight rein were maintained, the localities could find themselves unable to meet the tax demands imposed upon them by Rome itself.[84] Indeed, to permit major cities to collapse financially could not help but dangerously affect public confidence in the financial stability of other cities and of the empire itself.[85]

About the end of the first century A.D. *correctores* were imposed upon the Asian cities; these officials had the power to impose an *additional* tax if local spending seemed too high. As direct representatives of Rome they were not answerable to the local authorities, and this intensified the local aggravation at their independent taxation authority. Under either Trajan or, possibly, Hadrian, the Asian cities were given the option of selecting their own tax overseers. This local option was conditional, however, upon the establishment of a substantial financial reserve that would be forfeited if the locality were unable to meet its required tax obligations to Rome.[86]

Asia was not the only region to receive such overseers. Trajan appointed *correctores* in Greece (c. A.D. 108) and two years later for Bithynia-and-Pontus (with senatorial concurrence, since this province was not normally under direct imperial control). Pliny was given the responsibility of setting the affairs of this province into a responsible and solvent form. He reported that it was typical for cities in the area to be "in a state of disorder."[87] He promptly imposed corrective measures to remedy the worst abuses.[88]

## Life Outside the Urban Centers

Although cities were common in Asia and the larger ones had populations reaching the hundreds of thousands, the majority of the population lived in smaller towns and villages and in the countryside. In the smaller communities and the countryside the predominant source of income was farming. On an empire-wide basis the percentage of workers involved in agricultural pursuits has been estimated to have ranged from 75–80 percent[89] to a high of 80–90 percent.[90] Most were involved in subsistence farming; that is, they "produced most of what they themselves consumed and consumed most of what they produced."[91] In a highly urbanized province such as Asia, one would expect a bit lower farm-based percentage than in other regions.

Just as twentieth-century Americans often looked down upon small towns as educationally and culturally inferior to major cities, the Romanized urbanites of the first century treated with scorn the rural villages scattered throughout the empire. Villages (some of which were very large) deeply resented the snobbishness and took great pride when their own local or provincial elite advanced to prestigious positions, such as Asiarch.[92]

Nor were even the most rural villages totally bereft of the social-collective interaction that brought joy to urban citizens. Writing of the more isolated communities of northwest Asia and Bithynia, Ramsay MacMullen recounts:

> Inscriptions speak of village wine parties to which the
> inhabitants or their rich patron contributed food and
> drink and wreaths, hiring a little orchestra and providing

lamps and candles to carry the rejoicing through the night. If the costs proved too heavy or the occasion honored a deity of wide cult, several villages would combine. Religious festivals brought the greatest crowds together, of which traders naturally took advantage. And traders, along with traveling craftsmen, kept even isolated hamlets in touch with each other.[93]

It has been argued that fewer gods were worshiped in the countryside than in the city.[94] If so, this may have been due, in part, to a lack of acquaintance with them.[95] (A modern-day parallel would be lack of acquaintance in rural areas with the latest theological fads.) Realistically, however, the far more restricted financial resources of the countryside would never have permitted the elaborate multiplicity of temples found in urban areas. There would have been an inevitable concentration of resources on those deemed most important and neglect of those considered secondary or of marginal significance.

The worship of long-established regional deities such as Sabazios, Ma, and Angdistis was more common in the countryside than in the cities.[96] This phenomenon fits in well with the conservative attitude normally dominant in rural areas, where the known and traditional are far more respected and embraced than the new, little known, or unknown.

Although Asia was agriculturally prosperous, great effort was required to overcome the negative effects of the physical geography. Speaking of the entire Asia Minor region, William Ramsay writes:

> The low grounds are frequently marshy; there is an oversupply of water. The great level central plateau is arid; for, although abundant rain falls, it must be stored.
>
> The sloping grounds and hillsides are liable to be swept clear of soil at certain seasons by too abundant rains, which run down and stagnate in the marshes of the low lands. It is necessary, therefore, to conserve and distribute the water-supply.
>
> On the hillsides an elaborate system of terracing is required to retain the rain or the melting snows, and so prevent devastating floods. In the low ground the marshes must be drained and transformed into highly fertile soil.[97]

Farmers preserved and stored their produce so it would last throughout the year. For poor farmers these measures were primitive indeed; some Asia Minor peasants are known to have simply dug crude pits to store their grain.[98] Evidence from other areas shows that jars were also used and, if there were a sufficient need, large storage buildings were erected that could hold several thousand kilograms of grain.[99] Galen of Pergamon refers repeatedly to the use of pickling and drying as standard techniques to preserve food in his day.[100]

In spite of the abundant produce of the province, there was no absolute protection against scarcity, especially in an off-season or just before a new crop came in. Although food could be imported, this was always expensive and time-consuming and hinged upon the availability of an exportable external crop. Rome enjoyed an official monopoly on receiving grain from Egypt—and Egypt, with justice, can well be called the granary of the empire because of its massive production. When supplies were available for Asia the *first* priority was feeding the resident Roman troops.[101]

In the second century the situation improved. During a visit by the Emperor Hadrian in A.D. 129, the Ephesians requested and received permission to import grain from Egypt for their domestic use.[102] Since additional inscriptions at Ephesus and other sites in Asia Minor and Greece refer to such importation without any mention of advance imperial permission, this argues that prior approval was not required[103]— though such imperial endorsement obviously added political clout to the request. What made Hadrian's action significant is that it gave a *priority status* to Ephesus's request,[104] a status that was presumably intended to continue indefinitely.

Be that as it may, the prefect of Egypt had authority to consider any request for food that he received.[105] His first priority had to be the needs of the city of Rome; after that was assured, he had freedom of choice in regard to selecting other markets—but also answerability to Rome for his decisions.[106]

One way of producing a more comfortable margin of survival was to increase the amount of Asian acreage devoted to grain production. The problem was that the cultivation of grapes had a higher priority in Asia in those places where they could grow well because of the cash value of wine sales domestically and in export form. (These sales represented a challenge to native Italian wine production as well.) Hence, in A.D. 92, Emperor Domitian attempted to serve both his own domestic political interests (by appeasing the Italian wine industry) and simultaneously compel greater interest in domestic grain production, by requiring Asia and other provinces to destroy *half* of all existing vineage.[107]

It is known that in approximately the same year there was a major famine in Antioch-near-Pisida. It has been speculated that this famine may well have affected a large part of Asia Minor as well.[108] If so, this would have further inflamed Asian indignation: It was bad enough that they lacked food; now Rome was going to deny them the profits from their vineage, which they could use to buy the food they lacked!

Although the importance of the grape crop varied from one Asian city to another, Philadelphia was especially dependent.[109] The grievance ran wide and deep, however, and the Asian assembly selected Scopelianus of Smyrna, a respected orator, to take the regional case to Rome. So successful was he that he not only convinced Domitian to reverse the policy but to fine those growers who did not *increase* their vineage![110]

Sometime between A.D. 91 and 94, a major famine struck nearby Galatia-Cappadocia, while L. Antistius Rusticus was its imperial legate. The governor took an inventory of available food stocks and ordered all grain not needed for seed or personal consumption to be sold to the public under strict price controls. Although these "controls" yielded a hefty profit, the permitted price was still far below what unrestrained price gouging would have yielded.[111] The chronological linkage between this and the famine in Antioch-near-Pisidia is unknown. If they occurred simultaneously, both reinforced Asian misgivings about the emperor's policies. If either or both occurred before the policy was decreed, they spurred a determination not to be vulnerable. If they came afterward, they reinforced the provincial wisdom in opposing the policy. Or so it would have seemed to the people at the time.

One thing was certain: the danger of famine was always present. Money crops would not prevent them from coming

but might well help the province survive the crisis. Help in
times of crisis would be repeatedly called for during the second century, when a serious grain supply crisis hit Asia upon
several occasions.[112]

## The Asian Economy

Both ancient and modern historians agree that at the
time Rome took over Asia, that area and the entire Greek
world were effectively bankrupt.[113] Cicero boasted to the
Roman senate: "There is no place in the whole world to rival
the Province of Asia for the sheer wealth and fertility of the
land. Asia is Rome's most valuable overseas asset."[114] Once tax
farming was reined in and the Roman civil wars ended, the
province began to bounce back to become once again "the
richest part of the Roman Empire."[115]

In spite of the glowing tributes to Asian prosperity, there
remained an undercurrent of skepticism among at least a
minority: Asia might be prosperous but nowhere near as
much as would have been the case without the Romans. The
Sybelline Oracles (6:142–43), predicted about A.D. 80 the dramatic end of this situation: "Great wealth shall come to Asia,
wealth which once Rome, having gained it by rapine, stored
in a house of surpassing riches, but anon she will make a two-
fold restitution to Asia; then there will be a surfeit of strife."[116]

Whatever the collective wealth of the region, certain
individual cities prospered above others. Having a seaport
was always an economic bonus, and two of the seven churches
were in communities that possessed major ones. Ephesus lay
at the mouth of the Cayster River, and Smyrna at the mouth
of the Hermes. The port at Pergamon on the Caicus River
allowed that city to provide a link between vessels traveling by
sea westward and caravans traveling eastward on the internal
trade routes. A fourth major seaport in Asia was that of Miletus, which lay at the seaward end of the Maeander River.[117]

An Asian economic decline began a few centuries after
Christ, but it was more gradual than precipitous and
occurred on an uneven basis throughout the province.[118] As

Stephen Mitchell has written, "When the Empire effectively broke into two in the fourth century and the imperial capital was transferred to Constantinople, Asia Minor continued to serve as the main source of strength and economic resilience to the Byzantine Empire until it eventually fell to the Ottoman Turks in the fourteenth century."[119]

In a non-technologically advanced economy—subject to abrupt disruptions in supply—price gouging was an ever-present danger. Hence *agoranomi* were appointed in various cities to set official prices. If persuasion and requests could not gain compliance, they had the authority to force merchants to lower their prices if they thought the situation were extreme enough and the circumstances justified such action.[120] In Pergamon, evidence survives from the second century indicating that they established the regular price structure on a number of products.[121] An inscription in Ephesus lists the names of several of these individuals and claims that due to their actions "there was plenty and fair dealing."[122]

This regulatory approach functioned best with locally produced merchandise. When a product was imported from abroad, all the *agoranomi* could do was to curb the worst extremes. Though they couldn't make an importer reduce a possibly outrageous price, they could at least prevent him from taking advantage of a local shortage by imposing an even higher figure after the product reached the open market.[123] They could also demand that the importer sell directly to the retailer, thereby cutting out the middleman's price markup.[124]

As in later centuries, worker groups (*craft guilds* would convey the idea better than the more recent term *labor unions*) became discontented and took organized action to press their grievances. In the mid-second century A.D. the proconsul of Asia appears to have intervened in a building dispute that had inordinately delayed the construction of a government building in Pergamon.[125] Toward the end of the same century the proconsul in Ephesus came down vehemently against the bakers. He was reluctant to jail the offenders because it would cut off the bread supply needed by the city. Instead, he ordered a ban on baker guild meetings and ordered the bakers to return to work. The time for toleration had passed. Warned the proconsul,

"When from this time forward any one of them shall be caught in the act of attending a meeting contrary to orders, or of starting any tumult and riot, he shall be arrested and shall undergo the fitting penalty."[126]

Much later—in A.D. 495—we find in Sardis the actual text of a lengthy pledge by the construction workers to produce quality work and the spelling out of procedures to assure that promised work was actually performed. This commitment grew out of the "divers accusations against divers persons of our craft, to the effect that they take in hand pieces of building work, leave these unfinished and obstruct the employers."[127]

Numerous types of exports flowed from Asia westward into the heart of the empire. Among these was pottery.[128] Perfumes were exported from Sardis, Smyrna, and Ephesus to markets throughout the Roman Empire.[129] Smyrna enjoyed a reputation for the dyes it made[130] and for the carpets it produced.[131] Both draperies and tapestries were produced in the province for a market elsewhere in the empire.[132]

Of the Asia region, the ancient Strabo contrasts the "good wine" of many offshore islands with the fact that "most of the whole of the adjacent mainland produces the best of wines." Ephesian wine is described as a modest "good," in contrast with "Smyrna and other less significant places [which] produce exceptionally good wine whether for enjoyment or medicinal purposes."[133] Hence it is not surprising that quality wines should occupy a place on the list of major Asian exports.[134]

When available, grain was exported.[135] On an ongoing basis, one could count on salted fish being shipped as well as dried fruit.[136]

Horses were exported live.[137] Animal products were exported both in their unprocessed form as hides[138] and wool[139] and in the form of parchment[140] and finished garments. (Laodicea had special fame as a garment-manufacture center.)

Natural resources were also exported. Metals and minerals[141] and valuable gemstones[142] were sent westward, as was timber.[143] Both sculpture[144] and the marble that could be utilized for either sculpture or building purposes were similarly sent abroad.[145] Regardless of where marble originated in the empire, slaves did the hard labor under overseers, who were often freedmen.[146] The same techniques of extraction were common from one quarry to another.[147] Among the various Asian quarries was one only about six miles northeast of Ephesus.[148] The scale of such shipments can be seen in the fact that one late-second-century shipwreck off southern Italy left behind some 170 tons of marble.[149]

## Asian Jews

No introduction to Roman Asia could be complete without a discussion of the Jewish community, the attitudes toward it, and the various crises and turmoil it underwent as it attempted to survive and prosper in a Gentile environment.[150]

It is common to assume that the Jewish presence in Asia Minor dates from the time when Antiochus III moved some two thousand exiled Jewish families from Mesopotamia into Lydia and Phrygia.[151] Ellen Saltman, however, makes a very powerful case for an ongoing Jewish community(ies) from a much earlier date.[152] Although she does not use the term, the existence of a "*commercial* diaspora" would certainly summarize her argument.

For example, 1 Kings 10:29 refers to Israel's role as middleman in the import of chariots into the nation and their exportation to "all the kings of the Hittites." (What remnants then remained of the once powerful Hittite empire were in Asia Minor.) Setting aside this strict "political" use of the term, the "ethnographic" one embraced people in a wider area of Asia Minor as well.[153]

We know that there were joint Israelite-Phoenician trading missions from Ezion Geber (1 Kgs 9:26–28), which went on trading missions eastward that took three years for completion (1 Kgs 10:22). Saltman conjectures that it would have been quite natural for joint trading expeditions to have been launched northward and westward as well, and for the Israelites to have joined with the Phoenicians in the colonizing that was—and remained into the twentieth century—the quite natural outgrowth of expanded trade.[154] Furthermore, if Solomon backed international trade as much as the biblical text indicates, "it is difficult to believe that he would have [avoided making] arrangements to obtain the valuable and essential metals available in northern Asia Minor. Old, established trade routes, instituted by the Hittites, would make such commerce feasible."[155]

Regardless of *when* ethnic Jews first came to Asia Minor in general and Asia in particular, by the first century they were unquestionably widespread in the region. In addition to their presence in "every important city of Asia Minor,"[156] especially large and important communities existed in such Asian cities as Sardis, Laodicea, and Pergamon.[157]

Estimates of the first-century Jewish population vary from a minimal figure of two million worldwide to a maximum of nine million.[158] It has been estimated that the total number of Jews in the entire Asia Minor region numbered about one million[159] and represented about 20 percent of the local population.[160] Speculative as such figures must be, they provide some indication of the numerical importance of the Jewish community in the region: loved or hated, they could not be ignored.

Indeed, anti-Semitism was common and ranged from a relatively restrained rejection to vigorous contempt and hatred.[161] Such a strongly negative public image made overt persecution a credible option when resentments and specific issues pushed the hostility beyond a certain threshold. To the extent that Christians were lumped together with Jews—and their shared monotheism made a great deal of this inevitable, even after the obvious schism between the two groups—Christians became natural targets for these negative attitudes as well. They lacked the legal protections of Judaism and provided a safer outlet for venting anti-Jewish feelings, especially since many early Christians were Jewish ethnically.

Although intense anti-Jewish feelings and outbursts can be documented in various parts of the empire, Asia Minor stood out in the first century A.D. due to the conspicuous *absence* of such incidents.[162] This does not mean that local incidents may not have occasionally occurred, just that they represented a departure from the general atmosphere present in Asia and surrounding provinces. *Tensions* remained, but both sides

avoided actions that would break the mutual understanding. This peacefulness continued into the second century as well. Even the Bar Kochba–led Second Jewish War in Palestine in the second century did not destroy the relationship;[163] nor did the various provincial Jewish revolts in A.D. 115–17 result in Asian Jews rising in arms, as did many of their brethren in Egypt, Cyprus, and Cyrenaica.[164]

The precedents for the Asian Jewish-Gentile detente had been established after intense debate and opposition in the century before Christianity. Being a monotheistic minority in a polytheistic world, the Jews were naturally concerned that they be granted the right to practice their religion without undue restriction, harassment, or retaliation. Josephus reproduces at length the decrees adopted in various places to grant and preserve these rights.[165] There was a marked lack of local enthusiasm for adopting such a policy.

Ephesus made plain that it was reacting to Roman pressure, the Jewish community having requested the proconsul to protect their rights. "Accordingly, it was decreed by the senate and people, that in this affair that concerned the Romans, no one of them should be hindered from keeping the Sabbath-day, nor be fined for so doing; but that they may be allowed to do all things according to their own laws."[166]

In Pergamon the local decree explicitly refers to the demand of the Romans for a cooperative policy toward the Jews. The presence of a delegation from Israel itself is also referred to as encouraging local cooperation with Roman pressure. After hearing the high priest and reading the official Roman request, the Pergamonese "made a decree ourselves, that since we also are in confederacy with the Romans, we would do everything we could for the Jews, according to the [Roman] senate's decree."[167]

In the case of Laodicea, Roman pressure is again specifically mentioned. In this case, pressure to *reject* the pro-toleration demand is also explicitly referred to—and rejected. The Laodicean decision refers to how the Jewish request was "that the Jews may be allowed to observe their Sabbaths and other sacred rites, according to the laws of their forefathers, and that they may be under no command, because they are our friends and confederates; and that nobody may injure them in our province." The Laodiceans pledged that they would accept the Roman demand and adopt the tolerance policy so "that no complaint be made against us."[168]

Sardis, the final church-city of Asia quoted by Josephus, is also the only one that manifests any degree of real sympathy or enthusiasm for the Jews:

> Whereas those Jews who are our fellow-citizens, and live with us in this city, have ever had great benefits heaped upon them by the people, and have come now in the senate, and desired of the people, that upon the restitution of their law and their liberty, by the senate and people of Rome, they may assemble together, according to their ancient legal custom, and that we will not bring any suit against them about it; and that a place may be given them where they may have their congregations, with their wives and children, and may offer, as did their forefathers, their prayers and sacrifices to God.
>
> Now the senate and people have decreed to permit them to assemble together on the days formerly appointed, and to act according to their own laws; and that such a place be set apart for them by the praetors, for the building and inhabiting the same, as they shall esteem fit for that purpose: and that those that take care of the provisions for the city, shall take care that such sorts of food as they esteem fit for their eating [i.e., ceremonially "clean"], may be imported into the city.[169]

The guarantee of a meeting place is especially interesting and may help explain how the second to seventh century A.D. synagogue was located not only in the heart of the city but in a former public building as well.

Why were the Romans willing to go so much further than the Greeks and to use pressure to temper the severe non-toleration attitudes of the East? Peter Garnsey suggests, in effect, two motives. The first is Jewish support of Rome against her adversaries; even in the civil war itself, Herod astutely and quickly moved to support Julius Caesar at the critical moment immediately before the battle of Actium. This sense of due reward was reinforced during the following century by "shrewd, energetic and on the whole effective diplomacy, built on a close personal relationship between Jewish and Roman leaders."[170] A commitment to the abstract idea of religious toleration played no role in their support.[171] Yet the *practical* effect was to effectively broaden the tolerated range of religious conduct, regardless of the explicit motives that lay behind the decision to tolerate at least Jewish monotheism.

So free did many Asian Jews feel and so broadminded were many Gentiles of the province that they found it possible (hopefully without compromising their moral and religious integrity) to play active roles in government. "We know from inscriptions that three members of the Jewish community were in the Roman imperial administration [of Asia] and that at least nine were city councillors."[172] These figures are, of course, always subject to upward movement by future discoveries.

The road to this tolerant relationship was not an easy one, as we have already seen in the remarks of Josephus about local Asians opposed to such a broadminded relationship. One area of repeated conflict lay in the temple tax, because here concrete monetary matters reinforced the religious difference. The temple tax was a half shekel (equivalent to two Greek drachmae or two Roman denarii)[173] that was given annually by all Jewish males from age twenty to age fifty,[174] males beneath this age being exempted, as were all women.

In 88 B.C. a large sum of Jewish money was seized by Mithridates when he raided the island of Cos. Since Josephus calls it "God's money," it was presumably the temple tax, though he does not explicitly call it such. Since Josephus claims that the sum was all of eight hundred talents large, there has been speculation as to how it could have reached such an impressive amount. H. Mary Smallwood considers the number either a manuscript error for a more modest eighty talents or as including "large voluntary gifts for the Temple" above and beyond the temple tax itself.[175]

The temple tax again comes to the forefront in Asia in 62 B.C., when Flaccus seized it on behalf of the Roman provincial government. When, in Rome, Flaccus was brought on trial for the action, Cicero described the incident this way:

When every year it was customary to send gold to
Jerusalem on the order of the Jews from Italy and from
all our provinces, Flaccus forbade by an edict its exportation from Asia. Who is there, gentlemen, who could not
honestly praise this action? The senate often earlier and
also in my consulship most urgently forbade the export
of gold. But to resist this barbaric superstition was an act
of firmness, to defy the crowd of Jews when sometimes in
our assemblies they were hot with passion, for the welfare
of the state was an act of the greatest seriousness....

Where, then, is the ground for an accusation
against Flaccus, since, indeed, you never make any charge
of theft, you confess that there was judgment, you do not
deny that the business was openly proposed and published, and that the facts showed that it was administered
by excellent men?

At Apamea a little less than a hundred pounds of
gold was openly seized and weighed before the seat of the
praetor in the forum through the agency of Sextius Cae-
sius, a Roman knight, an upright and honourable man; at
Laodicea a little more than twenty pounds by Lucius Ped-
ucaeus, our juror. At Adrayttium a hundred pounds by
Gnaeus Domitius, the commissioner; at Pergamum a
small amount. The accounting for the gold is correct. The
gold is in the treasury, no embezzlement is charged, it is
just an attempt to fix odium on him.[176]

On the one hand, Cicero concedes that this exportation
had been done "every year"; on the other, he stresses that
exportation of gold had been prohibited on more than one
occasion. Established precedent is weighed against sporadi-
cally enforced law. It may not have been the wisest thing to do,
but it was at least technically legal. In light of the chronic
problem of proconsular fraud, it was useful for his case to
stress that Flaccus was *not* personally enriched by this case. At
worst, his action was merely intended to uphold past precedent rather than fatten his own pocket. Hence the action was
well intentioned, understandable, and excusable. Implicit in
the argument is a core of anti-Semitic hostility, for Cicero
begins his oration by stressing that he would need to speak to

the jurors in a soft voice lest others hear and use his remarks to turn the Jews against him (28.66).

If this were the sum total of the evidence, Cicero's anti-Semitic aside was hardly needed. On the other hand it may have been intended as rhetorically throwing dust into the air to distract the audience from inconvenient facts. As to exportation of gold outside the empire, the confiscation was far less defensible than in the past, when the action went unhindered. Although Flaccus may well have been motivated to the seizure by the forcible resistance to Pompey's expansion of the empire into Palestine,[177] the *inclusion* of the region in the empire was clearly inevitable. Hence, the shipment of the temple tax was quite arguably transportation of gold *within* the empire.[178]

Furthermore, Cicero is conspicuously silent in regard to the large centers of Judaism in Sardis and Ephesus. Menahem Stern suggests that Cicero may have cited the particular four cities he mentions by name because *there* the best face could be put on the situation. It may well be that in *those* communities the proper legal forms and procedures were observed, but what of those that had large Jewish communities but which go unmentioned? Could it be that these could have undermined his case?

Be that as it may, in the case of Flaccus's confiscation of the temple tax, we once again find that the reported amount is unusually large. A. J. Marshall suggests several possible explanations. For example, the amount could have been inflated by the inclusion not just of the temple tax but of the "entire community funds" from each of the involved Jewish communities.[179] Marshall also speculates (quite logically) that the sum represented not only that from individual cities, but also that of the "surrounding areas for which the named cities served as natural centers."[180] Furthermore, the military conflicts going on in Judea at the time (as Rome gained control) could have resulted in a multi-year backlog in the size of the seized funds.[181]

Although a generation or so later local Asian officials again stirred up trouble over the temple tax, Roman officials never did so again in the province. Indeed, one must go to the period of A.D. 37–38 in a completely different country (Egypt) to find the next case of a Roman prefect attempting to abort the Jewish privilege of sending their temple contribution to Jerusalem.[182]

When the Jewish revolt ended with the destruction of the Jewish Temple in A.D. 70,[183] the Roman government saw a readily available new source of revenue in the long collected temple tax that was sent yearly to Palestine. The *didrachmon* or *Ioudaion telesma* was substituted for the earlier ethnic/religious obligation and demanded in an identical amount. However, the revenue was vastly increased because "Vespasian did not limit liability to free and adult male members of the various Jewish communities as had been the case with the temple-dues. His Jewish tax fell also on women, slaves, and children, with a lower age limit of three years becoming established in due course."[184]

This resulted in a *double* taxation for Jews in Asia, since a fixed-sum per-person tax was also imposed upon all citizens of that province by the same emperor.[185] This likely resulted in double taxation for Christians in Asia as well, since many Christians were Jewish ethnically.[186] Their common belief in monotheism would have made Romans skeptical of any claim of not being "real" Jews, while it would simultaneously have exposed them to possible prosecution as members of an illegal sect if their claims of a difference *were* accepted.[187]

The Capitoline Temple had been destroyed during the Roman civil wars and the Jewish revenue was officially used to rebuild and maintain it.[188] The temple was destroyed by fire yet again in A.D. 80, requiring yet another rebuilding.[189] This official rationalization of the tax as subsidizing pagan worship was doubtless designed to be humiliating to the Jews. But even if this polytheistic religious purpose had not been utilized, the very idea that a *sacred* tax could be expropriated for *any* purpose—especially on an ongoing basis—could not have removed the inherent insult in the action.

That the revenues were actually used for purposes far beyond the official, pagan religious purpose is clear from the zeal with which the *fiscus Judaicus* (the agency assigned to collect it) broadened its application. It pushed to broaden the coverage beyond practicing Jews to all those who, with the least excuse, could conceivably be rationalized as owing the yearly payment.[190] These actions became so excessive under Domitian that they undermined the emperor's reputation. Emperor Nerva reined in these excesses. So widespread had they become that a coin of the time praises him for "The Abolition of the Vexatious Exaction of the Tax on the Jews"—an exaggeration, for the collection continued. But *in comparison* with what had happened under Domitian the threat of having the tax indiscriminately imposed *had* been removed.[191]

Having examined the relationship of the Jewish community of Asia to its pagan environment, let us consider certain of its internal characteristics and its relationship to the "mother" community in Palestine.

It has been argued that the Jews of Asia Minor were in such minimal contact with mainstream Pharisaic Judaism in Palestine that the regional variety was distinctly *un*orthodox if not explicitly *anti-orthodox* in attitudes and practices.[192] Some go so far as to assert a major difference between coastal and inland Judaism in the province.[193]

One would be unwise to exaggerate these differences, however. They are based upon inferences that may or may not be valid. For example, in the second century one Rabbi Meir discovered himself in a certain Asian city that lacked a copy of the book of Esther. As a result, he wrote it out from memory so they could utilize it in the Purim festival. Does this indicate the existence of a different canon, their poverty in lacking a complete set of scrolls of Torah, Prophets, and Writings, or hostility to the anti-Gentile attitudes that could easily be encouraged by Purim and "verified" by Esther?[194] What is *known* is an oddity; what it *means* is an uncertainty.

The theology and religious divisions and attitudes of the homeland clearly had a different impact upon those of Asia. (Just as the Catholicism of contemporary Italy, Poland, Ireland, and the United States represents the same core of faith and organization yet exhibits manifest differences and contradictions in actual practice.) The differences in environment, culture, and political situation would inevitably have produced these variations. But the *forms* the differences took are hard to establish with certainty.

For example, in Palestine the monotheists were divided between such primary groups as the Pharisees, Sadducees, and Essenes. To what extent were these divisions duplicated in the Diaspora and to what extent did different regional movements exist? Certainly some of these were known in the wider Roman world. To give a particularly vivid example of this interaction of homeland and the external world, we have the case of John the Baptist. We know there was a body of his disciples in Ephesus (Acts 19:1–7),[195] which is surprising in light of John's short ministry, his extreme asceticism, and the distance of the group from the site of John's Palestinian work. Yet the group's presence (and existence) argues that even the more radical elements in Judaism could find an audience in Asia and *that*, in turn, implies an ongoing, rather intimate knowledge of religious affairs in the homeland.

These contacts were of several types. There may well have been "missionaries" sent out by one faction or another of Palestinian Judaism; Christians practiced such a procedure, and Jesus alluded to this phenomenon among other Jews of his day (Mt 23:15). Those rabbis sent forth from Israel either to collect funds or to ensure that the religious calendar remained synchronized[196] would be sources of up-to-date information regarding both events and religious trends. Likewise, the movement of tradesmen throughout the empire would have brought news to Asia not just from westward points (such as Rome) but also from other areas in the East, including Palestine itself.

Nor should non-written communications be minimized. Pilgrimage to Jerusalem for the various feasts was common. Both Philo and Josephus refer to the popularity of such pilgrimages. The latter claims that as many as 2,700,000 visitors flooded the city on such occasions.[197] In Acts 2:9–11 we find a lengthy list of those regions represented at the feast of Pentecost, including Asia. Nor is Asian presence presented as if it were some remarkable curiosity—it was *typical* for Asians to be there, along with those from a wide variety of other regions. *Inescapably* this created an ongoing communication channel between rank-and-file Judaism in Asia and that of Jerusalem.

Written communication supplemented these other sources. At the end of Acts (28:21), the Jews of Rome refer to

the information-carrying nature of both pilgrims and the written word, "We neither received *letters from Judea* concerning you, nor have any of the *brethren who came* reported or spoken evil of you." Jacob Neusner rightly takes this text to indicate that "letters or personal reports were sufficiently frequent so that a man of bad character would be so labeled in a reasonable time."[198]

These multiple sources of information would carry back word of religious issues, controversies, and disagreements. If Asian Jewry were in bold defiance of fundamental Judaism, the continued popularity of pilgrimages from the area would seem very odd. Indeed, the commonness of pilgrimage and written communication tends to introduce "corrective theology" by those exposed to the orthodoxy of Jerusalem and Judea.

This does not necessarily mean that the Judaism of Asia was *identical* with that in Palestine. The very existence of a predominantly Gentile population and a dramatically different socio-historical setting would automatically create variances, though not necessarily of a "heretical" nature. Whatever differences may have existed between Palestinian and Asian Judaism—and within Asian Judaism, for that matter—*culturally* the Jewish communities of the province fit in well with the surrounding community. Perhaps this grew out of a desire to "fit in" in a society in which the line between Jew and Greek was always present by minimizing the "social" differences that made the cleavage even more apparent. The rigid social chasm that an earlier generation of scholars believed existed in the region has gradually been discovered to be a misinterpretation of a far more fluid relationship.

Among Jews, Greek—not Hebrew—was the dominant spoken and written language outside of Palestine.[199] The types of flasks and lamps that would be considered distinctly "Jewish"— and found in abundance in Palestine—are few and far between in Asia.[200] In Sardis there were Jews who not only enjoyed Roman citizenship but city citizenship as well.[201] In Hierapolis the heads of both the tapestry-maker and the purple-dyer associations were, at least at one point, members of the Jewish community.[202] This argues that at least in some places there were not only inter-ethnic trade guilds but that Jews were even acceptable as leaders. (This does not rule out the existence in other cities and even in the same city of ethnically segregated guilds, just as integrated and segregated unions coexisted in the United States at one time.)

The existence of a recognized, synagogue-based Judaism represented the type of Judaism Gentiles would most commonly come into contact with. The example of the Ephesian Johannine disciples (Acts 19:1–7) provides an example of how a minority movement could exist in Judaism *independent* of synagogue control: Paul speaking with them (verses 1–7) is clearly distinguished from his "going into the synagogue." True, they were Johannine *Jews,* but they were Jews *independent* of synagogue control and had a distinct, separate existence. The same was the situation of *Christian* Jews, at least after the passage of time.

Christian Judaism was introduced into Asia when the pilgrims referred to in Acts 2 returned to their home province. Somewhere in this process of expansion it became clear that most Jews were not going to accept Jesus as Lord and that Christians were not about to repudiate their own acceptance. This could only lead to the existence of Christianity apart from the synagogue. Since this conflict over the lordship of Jesus lay at the heart of the gospel message, the "organizational" breach into a distinct movement could only have occurred at a very early moment, however much a shared ethnicism and rejection of polytheism continued to maintain at least token ties between the two groups.

The *public* recognition of two semi- or openly hostile monotheistic groupings would likely have come about through the increasing acceptance of Gentiles in the movement. Although Judaism accepted Gentiles as converts and hangers-on, Christians began to affirm boldly that Gentiles could be openly accepted as social equals (Acts 10, 11) and that they could remain uncircumcised and live without any pretense of obeying the "ceremonial" laws of the Old Testament (Acts 15:1–2, 5–6, 22–23). Even the most traditional Jewish-Christian, at this point, was forced to recognize that one was no longer speaking in terms of a *Christian* Judaism but, increasingly, in terms of Christianity *or* Judaism. Especially is this true in places like Asia, where living in an overwhelmingly

Jewish environment would not have existed as a partial counterbalance. Paul's fervent missionary work among Gentiles throughout Asia (Acts 19:26) and proclamation of their independence of the Jewish Law played a vital role in *shifting the proportion* of Jews and Gentiles in the church, and this reinforced the image of Christianity as a separate religious system.

However important Christianity was to its adherents and to its closest rival (Judaism), the movement made little impact on the general public consciousness in the first century. True, it was *there*, but it did not play a pivotal role in society; it was, at best, an annoying facet of life that seemed best ignored. At least this seems the most convincing generalization based upon the widespread silence, even among those one might expect to have mentioned the movement. Timothy Barnes summarizes this pattern of ignoring Christianity when he writes:

> Even in Rome, where there had certainly been Christians since the reign of Claudius, the varied epigrams of Martial and the satires of Juvenal make no identifiable allusion to the new religion, though both authors deride Jews and Judaism. There is equally no hint of Christianity in the voluminous and variegated ethical and theological writings of Plutarch and Chaeronea (c. 50–c. 120). Plutarch's silence is all the more significant since his work contains so many coincidences of thought and diction with early Christian literature. Similarly, the guide to dreams which Artemidorus of Daldis composed in the middle decades of the second century has no Christians in its everyday world. Moreover, as late as the 230s Cassius Dio could complete a history of Rome down to 229 in eighty books without ever mentioning Christians. Dio's silence, however, betrays itself as both deliberate and forced when he makes Maecenas recommend the persecution of religious innovators—a covert but undeniable allusion to the newly won respectability of the Church in the early third century.[203]

Hence, Christians are ignored by most writers and barely mentioned by others for more than two hundred years after Christ's death.[204] The most obvious exception is Celsus's assault on Christianity as a religion[205] and later pagan theological opponents who similarly rebuked, critiqued, and assailed their monotheistic rival.[206]

Of special interest to us is the famous doctor Galen, who grew up in the Asian city of Pergamon. He mentions Christians in four places.[207] Although he sees them as capable of exercising great self-control, he has no use for them intellectually. They have a contempt for argumentation and "accept everything on faith." They are stubborn and mule-headed and refuse to change, admittedly a harsh judgment, but one he also applied to the philosophers and physicians of the day! How much of his negative opinion grew out of his acquaintance with Christians in Asia—or later, for that matter—is unknown.

In a world where most people were poor or close to poor, one naturally assumes that most Christians were of a similar background. Not because they were *different,* but because they *reflected* the economic situation of the society in which they dwelled.[208] Yet there were also those who were prosperous and, in at least a few cases, even rich. As a New Testament scholar from Sweden sums up the evidence:

> 1 Corinthians 1:26 and the letter to Philemon indicate that certain of the Christians belonged to the upper classes (see Matthew 27:57 and Luke 8:3). This impression is confirmed by the observation that some of the parishioners held high office (Erastus, Romans 16:23), and were in a position to perform special tasks (Phoebe, Romans 16:1–2; Stephen, et al., 1 Corinthians 16:17; Gaius, Romans 16:23; Aquila and Priscilla, 1 Corinthians 16:19, Romans 16:3–5, Acts 18:26; and Titus Justus, Acts 18:7), and travelled about (some of these individuals [just mentioned], together with Chloe's household, 1 Corinthians 1:11, who, however, may have belonged to the lower classes). Of 17 persons named in 1 Corinthians, nine seem to have been members of the upper classes.[209]

It is reasonable to assume that Asian Christians also reflected the cross-section of provincial society: some destitute, most poor but not desperate, others prosperous—and maybe even a handful of the truly wealthy.

# 4

# John, Patmos, and the Recipients of His "Revelation"

That deep similarities exist between John's Revelation and traditional, non-biblical apocalyptic literature is clear. They are all given in the form of "visions," symbolism is used as key to communicating the message, and some of the word pictures are startling and even defy meaningful pictorial presentation. Yet there are also profound differences that separate John's work from others in this type of literature.[1]

Non-biblical apocalyptic (if dating schemes are anywhere near correct) was written by individuals injecting themselves under a fictitious persona *into the past* and "predicting" events that actually had happened in the years between the time when that fictitious individual had died and the then-current world came into existence. In contrast, John firmly roots himself in the *present,* reviews events of the past, and speaks of events clearly not yet having occurred. Hence there is a clear shift in *authorial viewpoint* between John and non-biblical practitioners of this form of writing.[2]

He also differs regarding the time frame in which events are to occur. Although some may occur in the far-distant future, the central emphasis is on the *imminency* of the fulfillment. The future history bulk of the book begins in the third verse of the book, "Blessed is he who reads and those who hear the words of this prophecy, and keep those things which are written in it; *for the time is near*" (1:3). Only ten verses short of the end of the work we find John commanded, "Do not seal the words of the prophecy of this book, *for the time is at hand*" (22:10). Whatever references to past history he makes and whatever allusions to future history he presents, his appointed task as author is to speak of things *in the near term.* In contrast, traditional, non-biblical apocalyptic speaks of events at some unspecified and far-distant point in history.[3]

Noncanonical apocalyptic tends to blame the existence of evil solely upon the unbeliever. The moral lapses of God's people are either glossed over or ignored. John's Revelation is well aware that evil is afoot in the world and sets out to portray its impact. Yet he is candid about the moral lapses and failures of God's people as well.

However different John's Revelation is from these other books, it is also virtually certain that John's contemporary readers were personally acquainted with the imagery and attitude of such works. Assuming they were religiously interested individuals of conservative religious or moral principles, many would have been acquainted by firsthand reading of such texts, just as modern Christians are often personally acquainted with a wide range of literature and religious advocacy moving in a similar direction as their own theology, though differing with it to one degree or another. So it would come as no surprise if John alluded to traditionally established imagery, even imagery mythological in origin; such images were part of the established religious folklore of his day and his ethnic background.

Yet it requires only a modest acquaintance with the text of Revelation to recognize that John's *primary* and *dominant* rooting is in *biblical* literature. Hence any use of mythological language is modified, molded, and adjusted into a framework acceptable to one raised in the Judaic works of the Old Testament. *These* are authoritative, and the other *supplementary.* Likewise, in interpreting John's meaning, the biblical precedent is central, however it may be broadened by concepts and ideas from other sources.

The same is true of the historical, cultural, and religious allusions John makes in the first three chapters of the book to the conditions in his seven selected churches and cities of Asia. Because they have not been adequately brought together, they are the subject of this book; but however much one understands these matters, unless one *also* has an understanding of the Old

Testament allusions and references, one will not be able to understand fully the mind of the author.

Regardless of the specific John who wrote the Revelation, we may safely reject the theory that it was an individual falsely utilizing that name to add authority to his work. If he is doing so, he amazingly *understates* his credentials: we would expect an *explicit* claim to apostleship; after all, there were many named John who were alive and well in his day. If one did not cringe at adopting another's name, would one hesitate to directly assert an apostolic position that would make unmistakable one's claim to acceptance?[4]

There are other major difficulties in the pseudonymity approach as well. First, there is the *ethical dilemma* inherent in such theories. Were the early Christians so gullible and their "prophets" so unscrupulous that a liar could feel guiltless in palming off his work as that of another? Were early believers so naive that they "fell for it" to such an extent that they even accepted it in their body of sacred literature, keystone to their faith? A *doctrinal* problem also undermines such theories. Since early Christians believed that miraculous revelatory gifts (prophecy, for example) could exist outside the apostolic circle, there was no reason for the genuine possessor of such gifts to make a false attribution. A *chronological* problem derives from the fact that many of the apostles lived for decades after the birth of the church (and their immediate disciples into a yet later period), thereby making a successful imposition extraordinarily difficult to accomplish.

For our purposes, it does not matter whether the John who wrote the book was the apostle (to whom it is traditionally attributed), John the Presbyter of Ephesus (the main secondary choice), or some other unknown individual who bore the same name. More important is whether one accepts the book's claim to have been given by *divine intervention,* that God did indeed reveal to him this book that purports to be *prophecy/prediction* of both near and (in fewer cases) far-distant events. It is not unfair to note the general correlation between a denial of apostolic authorship and the denial of the volume being genuinely inspired by that external outside revelatory power we call God. If one wishes to dispute the *apostolic* rather than *prophetic* origin of the book, that is one thing. If one is simply using the authorship question in order to attack the volume as genuine revelation, that carries one into a far more serious realm of controversy, far beyond the subject and framework of the current work.

Two ancient writers[5] provide the factual (and speculative, if you will) basis for attributing the book to John the Presbyter (or John the Elder), with one of them building upon an assertion of a yet earlier writing. Papias lived from about A.D. 70 to A.D. 140, and what little has survived of his writings has come down primarily through Eusebius's *Church History*. According to that source, there had been two prominent Johns in Ephesus, the evangelist (apostle) and the presbyter. Although Papias did not personally attribute the Revelation to either of these individuals, this restrained statement was the basis for Eusebius's own speculation that John the Presbyter was the real author.[6] The second ancient authority to suggest the alternative authorship was Dionysius of Alexandria (writing c. A.D. 265), who did so, not upon the basis of Papias's remarks, but on the basis of stylistic differences between the gospel of John and the book of Revelation.[7]

Although there are a number of objections to the apostolic authorship of the work, three deserve emphasis in the present context: (1) The self-designation of the writer as a "prophet" rather than "apostle"; (2) references that can be read as *distinguishing* the writer from the office of an apostle; and (3) linguistic difficulties.

The word *apostle* carries with it connotations of position and authority. Although Old Testament prophets also possessed such, the traditional emphasis in prophetic writings was on the future, on prediction, on events that would occur as the result of present behavior and conduct. In Revelation the emphasis is not so much on moral exhortation but on painting the near-term *consequences* of current world conditions. Hence the self-description of prophet makes far more sense in *this* context than would a claim to apostleship.

Of more concern is the description in Revelation 21 of the heavenly city being lowered to earth, in which the author seems to distance himself from the office of apostleship,

"Now the wall of the city had twelve foundations, and on them were the names of the twelve apostles of the Lamb" (verse 14). Would this not be terribly self-congratulatory if the writer were himself one of those twelve? Does not the wording argue a *dis*sociation from that group?[8] The central explanation may rest in the time frame in which John is working. This occurs *after* the "thousand years" of chapter 20—he is speaking in the context of the then-distant future, after he is long dead. In *that* context, the reference is stripped of all possible ego overtones. And it is presented in just that unemotional, bare-facts approach that would be expected in an individual who is not interested in building up himself but in simply and accurately presenting what he has seen in his vision. Because of that distant future context, the only real *personal* relevance it has to John as an apostle is to *encourage* him to remain faithful so he will be counted *worthy* of being counted as part of that heavenly foundation. If John is narrating an actual vision, is he to censor out this reference because it carries a reference to the position he holds? Would he not be guilty of an even greater egoism?

The above arguments are ones in which the individual can easily judge whether the pro or con side is the most convincing. The most difficult argument for English-only speakers to evaluate is the linguistic one, for it involves the writing style and narrative peculiarities accessible in detail only to those with an able knowledge of the Greek language. Yet the advocates of John the Presbyter as author and of the anyone-but-John-the-Apostle school of thought find here the most convincing evidence for their case, and it *is* of such a magnitude that even the strongest advocate of the apostolic authorship feels the need to explain the differences.

As noted above, Dionysius of Alexandria concluded that Revelation *had* to have been written by a non-apostle because the two texts *sound* so different in the original language. A World-War-I-era scholar summed up much of the opinion of his own era (and ours) when he wrote: "The internal evidence is decisive that it is not from the same author that wrote the Fourth Gospel. The language and idioms of the two books are fundamentally different."[9] (Unlike Dionysius, many who take this approach deny the apostolic authorship of *both* books.)

Some explain this by arguing that John used two different amanuensis or that Revelation "reflects [John's] own rough Hebraic Greek," while John represents the same author utilizing a skilled secretary/amanuensis.[10] Revelation's primitive Greek and the gospel's far more fluent and impressive flow could also be explained if one assumes that Revelation was written relatively early and John relatively late in the same author's lifetime. (Most commentators still hold to a Domitian-era date for Revelation, ruling out this option.) Even assuming Revelation was written later than John, the physical and psychological results of John's imprisonment (especially if harsh or preceded by brutal conditions) could well have caused him to revert to a more primitive style as he presented his case against the pagan world.

More important is the question of "intent" in the author's mind: would he be *expected* to write apocalyptic the way he would an epistle or a gospel? In other words, does he violate "the rules of Greek grammar" not out of ignorance but in order to create the *effect* he wishes?[11] In the Old Testament writers the imagery and style can change dramatically as a writer shifts from historical narrative to predictive imagery. As *New* Testament apocalyptic would we not expect a similar divergence when the same writer shifts from one subject (the life of Jesus) to another (the apocalyptic triumph of Jesus over a hostile world order)?[12]

The dominant dating of the composition of Revelation remains late first century, while a growing minority holds to a Neroian/post-Nero composition. Although the early date approach is the most convincing to this author,[13] the points made in our analysis are rarely, if ever, affected by the choice of date.

The repeated use of Old Testament imagery (and specific Old Testament textual quotations and allusions) argues that John was writing primarily for an ethnically Jewish audience. This Jewish audience was, however, a Hellenistic Jewish audience due to its very geographic location, one living in a Gentile environment and with full access to Gentile ways of thinking and acting. This does not exclude the presence of Gentile Christians as part of his targeted audience, but the style and heavy textual allusions make best sense with Jewish Christians being the numerical majority. (This also argues for an earlier rather than later date for the volume.[14])

When did John write Revelation? Can we make a distinction between the time when he "saw" it (remembering that it was a *vision*) and the time he took pen in hand to record it? John says near the beginning of the book, "I, John, both your brother and companion in tribulation, and in the kingdom and patience of Jesus Christ *was* on the island that is called Patmos for the word of God and for the testimony of Jesus Christ" (1:9). This has been used to prove that John saw the vision at one point and actually wrote it down at a distinctly *later* point in time.[15] The theme of *immediacy* in the first three chapters—the urgent need to set aright whatever the local weaknesses might be—argues strongly against any major postponement. One might deal with this, in part, by arguing that the mini-epistles in this epistle were sent out first and then, after the imprisonment, the bulk of the work was penned. Yet having gone *that* far, one wonders why John would hesitate before recording the rest of the vision. The most generous approach would be that he wrote it *as quickly as possible* after the exile was over, "while [the visions] were still fresh in his memory."[16]

It is highly questionable whether even this concession is necessary. He could have said, "I am on the island of Patmos," but he avoids the present tense in the text of the vision of the future (chapters 4–22), and it would seem more natural to have that approach in his opening remark as well.

Some have argued that there is clear textual evidence for an intra-exile composition of the work that would allow us to settle this matter. Earl F. Palmer sees the strong possibility that the "hidden and cryptic language" of the book was motivated by the need for caution in what the author said since he was still in exile.[17] However, if later commentators can so easily detect the anti-Roman allusions, is it likely that the Roman officials of that day would have missed them? Hence, the veiled remarks provided only the most token of protection for John and his audience—*regardless* of when he wrote the book.

Moses Stuart may be on stronger ground when he argues that "intervals between the visions [are] noted in the book itself during which we may very naturally suppose that to be written which had preceded [it]."[18] If so, it would be quite natural to write "was" on Patmos, because the composition took whatever number of hours or days or weeks during which the vision was revealed. In other words, these reflect "pause points" to give John the opportunity to record the specific parts of the vision.

As to actual evidence of the multi-day composition he points to Revelation 4:1, "*After* these things I looked and behold, a door standing open in heaven." This would certainly constitute a logical breaking point. Putting two breaking points in a single chapter, however, seems rather unlikely: "After these things I saw four angels standing at the four corners of the earth" (7:1); and, "After these things I looked and behold, a great multitude" (7:9). The next proposed stopping point is a more realistic eight chapters later, "After these things I looked, and behold, the temple of the tabernacle of the testimony in heaven was opened" (15:5). Similar "after these things" phrases then become indications of the revelation of new segments in 18:1 and 19:1. Stuart argues that further indications of distinct revelations may reasonably be found in 12:1, 20:1, 20:11 (again twice in one chapter), and 21:1. Looking at this overall, we see an inherently feasible theory undermined by the pure number of breaks, and twice two breaks even occurring within the same chapter.

If one is to see intra-text evidence for pauses from the vision for John to write what he had seen, more logical ones would seem to be the commands "to write." Before each of the mini-epistles he is commanded to write, perhaps suggesting a pause at the end of each to do just that. Certainly on *at least* one occasion between the last of these and chapter 10 he has paused to record the vision, for we read that "I was about to write"—an intention that was interrupted by the command to avoid recording what the "seven thunders uttered" (10:4). In 14:13 he is again commanded, this time to write rather than to abstain. Twice again he is commanded to write (19:9; 21:5). After the visual image mentioned in each case was completed, it would have been logical to do so. Whether we read too much into these cases or not, the reference to "I was *about* to write" in 10:4 unquestionably indicates that the writing was contemporaneous with the vision. What we *don't* know is at what specific points one ended, the writing began, and the vision continued.

## Patmos

The New Testament does not tell us how John ended up in Asia Minor. The only data that may be relevant concerns the fact that John had been deputized as a "substitute son" (if you will) for Mary when Jesus died (Jn 19:26–27). From this it follows that *if* Mary was still alive at the time of the move, it is virtually certain that she accompanied John when he moved permanently to Asia. Since later church tradition insists that John spent many years in Asia, it is quite possible that he did so. However, the timing of his move is more open to question. It is quite possible that the multi-decade stay included several temporary evangelistic visitations before making the province his permanent home.

Major non-biblical sources of information about this period are contained in the so-called Acts of John and an account attributed to Prochorus (a Johannine disciple) called the Travels and Miracles of St. John the Theologian. Since both are apocryphal and are of a late date, one is far more likely to encounter mythology rather than fact. They represent "history as it *might* have been" rather than "history as it really was."[19]

Regardless of this background to his exile, John ultimately landed upon Patmos. Patmos itself it located some forty miles southwest of Asian Miletus[20] and twenty-eight miles south-southwest of the island of Samos.[21] Patmos is an irregularly shaped island, larger at both ends with a narrow neck connecting the two parts. Beyond this, there is no simple way to describe the island's shape. A nineteenth-century visitor found difficulty in doing so, even at greater length:

> In shape Patmos may be roughly described as forming a crescent, the horns of which face eastward; but its outline

is broken up by innumerable promontories enclosing land-locked creeks, so that, when seen from above, it presents somewhat the aspect of a strange polypus....Its area is rugged and broken; but the most marked peculiarity is that it is almost divided in two in the middle, for in this part, within a distance of little more than half a mile from one another, are two isthmuses only a few hundred yards wide, and rising but slightly above the sea level....The soil of which the island is composed is everywhere volcanic and very barren, and its coasts are flanked by red and gray rocks, which ever and anon break into quaint pinnacles.[22]

Because of the island's odd shape, different authors pro-vide conflicting statistics for its size. About six miles wide and ten miles long is the most common, though a goodly number provide figures at variance with this.[23] Its irregular shape pro-duces an actual area of not over twenty-five square miles.[24] At its highest point, it is only eight hundred feet above sea level.[25]

Like dozens of other small and obscure islands in the Aegean Sea, Patmos has little to attract outside attention—except for its linkage to John's exile. Archaeological work on the island has uncovered potsherds dating as far back as the fourth century B.C.[26] By two hundred years before Christ it had a sufficient population (though numerically modest) to justify the erection and maintenance of a gymnasium.[27] Apollo is known to have been worshiped on the island in the late first century A.D.,[28] and an inscription referring to the cult of Artemis dates from the same period.[29] One may safely assume the presence of other contemporary cults as well. Indeed, their absence would be more noteworthy than their presence.

In the seventh century the island began several centuries without permanent inhabitants. The presence of active Arab pirates in the region discouraged the creation of any new, small (and inevitably vulnerable) community.[30] In 1088 the first monastery was erected on the island. Because of the con-tinuing danger of attack, it was moved to a high point and carefully fortified.[31]

From this point on Patmos became an important religious center in the Aegean and was subsidized by the Byzantine emperors. Even after the collapse of Byzantium, the popes extended protection to the Greek monastery, and it continued to prosper though it was a Turkish territory. The Turks retained legal control of Patmos until 1821, when it gained temporary independence. In 1832 it was returned to Turkish jurisdiction by the Treaty of Constantinople. In 1912 Italy annexed it, and it only legally became Greek territory in 1947.[32]

Some have challenged the claim that John was on the island because of persecution. At first glance this seems to fly in the face of John's assertion at the beginning of the book, "I, John, both your brother and companion in tribulation, and in the kingdom and patience of Jesus Christ, was on the island that is called Patmos for the word of God and for the testimony of Jesus Christ" ["because of the word of God and the testimony of Jesus," NRSV] (1:9). Some have argued that a non-persecutionary interpretation is the most natural reading of both the English text[33] and the Greek.[34]

Those denying the persecution basis of his Patmos residence suggest one of two alternatives to explain his presence. Perhaps the most obvious alternative is that he was there to preach. Wilfrid J. Harrington argues that the words "was on" render the Greek *egenomen en,* "literally, 'I found myself'" and that this "bland" expression fits well with the theory of John being on Patmos specifically to preach.[35]

Of course, isolated words should not be used in a way that undermines other words in the verse or the general thrust of the entire verse and context. The references to tribulation and patience (the even stronger "endurance" in the translation he utilizes) both point to a period of adversity. These certainly are not "bland" words (his term) but are suggestive of conflict and difficulty, and it is *within this context* of conflict and difficulty that he "found himself" on Patmos.

Although a missionary may well go anywhere, there is normally a *rationale* for doing so. What was the rationale for Patmos? "The insignificance and location of the island" make it an unlikely target for an apostolic missionary journey.[36] It was so off the beaten path that it was hardly likely to become a jumping off point for further expansion of the gospel. The island was of little importance in its own right. Again, why go? This doesn't *rule out* his having passed through there on the way to somewhere else, but it makes it very improbable, barring strong textual evidence in behalf of the theory—which there isn't.

Others believe that John was there to receive the book we call Revelation.[37] The expressions "for the word of God and for the testimony of Jesus of Jesus Christ" (1:9) have been introduced in support of both the preaching[38] and revelatory receiving alternatives.[39] Richard C. Trench[40] points to other Revelation texts as proving a persecutory context for the phrases. In 6:9 we read of those "who had been slain" and then find very similar terminology to that of the first chapter, "for the word of God and for the testimony which they held." In Revelation 20:4 we read of those who had been "beheaded for their witness to Jesus and for the word of God." Henry Alford refers to these two passages as well and concludes that "for" or "on account" of "in this connection [means] 'because of,' 'in consequence of.'"[41]

Although one conceivably could make a parallel with Moses being sent to Mount Sinai to receive the tablets of the law, that Revelation was never intended to be on a par with *that* event is clear: Revelation is an element *inside* a broader body of existing religion, not the initiating event of that new religious system. Furthermore, there was nothing unique to the book that seemingly would require such a physical distancing from Asia proper. The same Spirit that could inspire him in Patmos could inspire him in Ephesus or anywhere else the Spirit so desired.

Having examined these alternatives, the soundest reading of Revelation 1:9 is that John's presence on Patmos grew out of anti-Christian persecution. This could have occurred in either of two ways: he could have been sent there as punishment, or he could have fled there, counting on Patmos's very obscurity to protect him from prosecution and possible death from temporarily outraged public opinion or threatening public officials or prominent citizens. Hence, if John was on Patmos temporarily to escape persecution, the demands of the text would be amply meant. (The very obscurity and insignificance of the island would provide protective coloration.) This would also remove the entire controversy about under what conditions John could legally have been banished. If he was on

the island to escape danger, none of these procedures would have been required.

On the other hand, the traditional interpretation is that he was on Patmos as *punishment* for being a Christian, and this is also quite possible. Yet here again certain cautions must be made: There is a difference between a site being used as an ad hoc rather than ongoing place of exile, and there is an even more profound difference between exile and brutal, prison-camp-style punishment.

The Romans used a wide variety of sites for exile,[42] including what Suetonius calls "rocky islands."[43] Hence Patmos would be a very convenient dumping point for a religiously and politically inconvenient apostle. Yet the choosing of Patmos only argues its appropriateness rather than it being some type of site specially set aside for such a purpose. (Indeed, it is rather odd that a Christian would be punished this way at all. In Revelation, John warns of the danger of governmental wrath in general and death in particular, but never of exile. Hence some unusual circumstances must have entered the picture—or else John was on the island to escape persecution rather than to be punished.)

We need to take this one step further. One common understanding of John's exile is that he existed on the island under extremely brutal conditions: he was engaged in forced labor,[44] either in mines or marble quarries.[45] If so, this could help explain the harshness of the rhetoric and imagery found in the book and its difference in emphasis from the writings of Paul[46]—himself a victim of unjust imprisonment, though under "only" inherently demeaning rather than life-threatening conditions. Assuming he was a true prophet (rather than merely a predictor controlled by his passions), there is no need to assume that book's ongoing warning of future conflict with Roman power represents a fundamental break with the attitude of the apostle Paul, who had done much labor in the same region.

Even so, the *form* the message of each would take would most naturally reflect the unique history of suffering he endured and personal reaction to what he had survived. In both testaments, revelation is presented to the reader not as an abstract message, but as God using the unique life-experiences of the individual to present the message most needed by his contemporaries.

Although exiles *could* be punished in a physically arduous and even life-threatening manner, whether they were so punished depended upon their status, the attitude of the authorities prosecuting them, and the nature of their offense. There was no inherent necessity for John to have existed under such terrible conditions.

Of the variables, economic status was the most important. Emil G. Kraeling writes that "deportation to an island, for those of the lower social level, was essentially life imprisonment at hard labor. The individual wore chains, was poorly fed and clothed, slept on the bare ground and worked under the lash of a military overseer."[47] Sir William Ramsay, pioneer investigator into the Roman rule in Asia and its biblical context, endorsed such a view of John's treatment while in exile.[48] Leon Morris argues that John's social insignificance as a preacher would have resulted in his receiving the most rigorous form of banishment, such as "hard labor in quarries or the like."[49]

Earl F. Palmer insists that "scholars of the first-century period have found evidences that the Roman government maintained rock quarries on Patmos to which prisoners and banished troublemakers were sent to live out their lives."[50] Whether archaeological or literary he does not state and provides no citations to support his assertion. Others have reached the opposite conclusion, that though the island may have occasionally been used for exile purposes, there was nothing approaching an ongoing "penal colony" or "prison settlement."[51] Hence there would not have been the involuntary manpower available to mine those quarries that is assumed.

Furthermore, the literary evidence does not back up a prison-camp type of situation on the island during the first century or the preceding ones. In the fifth century B.C. Thucydides reports that the vessels of Alcidas spread terror, for though they did not have the strength to hold permanently any place they seized, they had more than enough power to "fall upon the cities and plunder them." He recounts that an opponent "eagerly gave chase and pursued him as far as the island of Patmos, but, seeing that he was no longer within reach, he returned."[52]

In the first century the geographer Strabo also mentions the island but tells us nothing about it, "Nearby are both Patmos and the Corassiae; these are situated to the west of Icaria, and Icaria to the west of Samos." He then briefly mentions that Patmos lies within the Icarian "sea," named after another "deserted" but "famous" island.[53]

Pliny only discusses Patmos as one of the many islands in the area and limits himself to the concise remark that "Patmos [is] thirty miles in circumference."[54] Yet this brief mention of the island has been cited to prove that in his day Patmos was being used as a penal colony, in spite of the fact that there is no reference to it being used for any such purpose.[55]

Whether John's exile was punishment for his faith or self-imposed because of the great dangers to his freedom and life, we still must be careful about exaggerating its harshness and severity. Even a relatively unconstrained exile would have been uncomfortable and psychologically oppressive for a dedicated apostle: to be so near his people and yet so far; to know so many needed the gospel he preached but which he could not yet share with them. So whatever he endured would have been bad enough without magnifying it beyond what he claimed and what supplementary historical evidence can provide. He suffered, but that does not require that he was brutalized as well.

It has been speculated that the vivid imagery found in the Apocalypse may have grown out of the personal observations of John while on Patmos. Assuming an individual is the product of his life experiences, one would *expect* what John saw during his exile to have had an impact upon the way he expressed himself and the descriptions he gave of supernatural phenomena. Indeed, we would expect the very process of divine "revealing" to utilize those concepts, ideas, and attitudes rather than negating them and replacing them.

A visitor to Patmos in the 1970s found the visual impact still impressive. It automatically conjured up the images in certain Revelation texts:

The panoramic view from the roof of the Monastery of St. John is overwhelming. In the northwest appears the level line of the island of Icaria; further north are the peaks of Samos and the promontory of Mycale; to the southeast is the island of Leros beyond which rise the five summits of Kalymnos. To the southwest lies the island of Amorgos and the distant volcanic island of Santorini, or Thera. This was the view which, with frequent alterations during sunshine and storm, must have impressed John. I found myself wondering whether this scene might not be reflected in the imagery of such visions as "the sky vanished like a scroll that is rolled up, and every mountain and island was removed from its place" (Revelation 6:14) or "every island fled away, and no mountains were to be found" (Rv 16:20).[56]

J. Theodore Bent argues that John was on Patmos when the island of Thera exploded and that the heavenly phenomena it produced are the bases of the catastrophic imagery utilized by the apostle in chapter six and later.[57]

## The Targeted Audience:
## Why Seven Churches and
## Why These Specific Seven Churches?

It is certain that there were additional churches in the region beyond those written to by John. This would be a necessary deduction on the basis of Acts 19:10 alone, for there we read that during Paul's two years in Ephesus "*all* who dwelt in Asia heard the word of the Lord Jesus, *both* Jews and Greeks." It would be incomprehensible if this large-scale evangelism effort did not reap more growth than the establishment of Christianity in a mere seven communities. If the effort had been that unsuccessful, one would have anticipated the geographic width of Paul's work to have been downplayed rather than emphasized.

The evidence is far more direct than this, however. We know that there was a congregation in Hierapolis, for Paul refers to it (Col 4:13), not to mention Colossae, the recipient of a New Testament epistle (Col 1:2). In the context of describing his preaching in Troas, Paul writes, "A door was opened to me by the Lord" (2 Cor 2:12), a reference that implies a great deal of success and the existence of a substantial congregation in that city. Although we know little of the types of places met in by early believers (outside of the Temple in Jerusalem and individual homes), we do know that in Troas they were meeting in a third-story chamber (Acts 20:5–12). In the second century we read of letters written by Ignatius to congregations in Magnesia and Tralleis as well.[58]

Although usually lumped together, there are three distinct questions that need to be answered: (1) Why write to a multiple number of churches in the same epistle at the same time? (2) Why write to no more and no less than seven churches? (3) Why write to these particular seven churches?[59]

The most reasonable explanation for mini-epistles within the context of a larger work is that the *central* message each needed was the same (hence they all needed chapters 4–22), while the *specific details* that drove the point home for each group required a shorter supplementary letter. Hence John's approach linked together the greatest immediate relevance to each of the churches (his analysis of their own spiritual status) with the broad supporting theme of God's apocalyptic judgment upon the human race.

Even the seven mini-epistles are linked together by the fact that what is said to one is relevant to all: Each congregation is addressed with the admonition that it should "hear what the Spirit says to the church*es*," plural, not just to themselves (2:7; 2:11; 2:17; 2:29; 3:6; 3:13; 3:22). Hence each epistle had potential—even if not immediate—relevance to each of the other congregations being addressed. Although William M. Ramsay is specifically speaking of why Paul asked the Colossians and Laodiceans to exchange the letters they had, his point is relevant in this broader context as well:

> The wider application arises out of the essential similarity of human nature in both congregations and in all mankind. The crisis that has occurred in one congregation is likely at some period to occur in other similar bodies; and the letter which speaks direct to the heart of one

man or one body of men will speak direct to the heart of
all men in virtue of their common human nature.[60]

By addressing all of them in this public manner, he pre-
vents them from yielding to any urge to sweep their problems
"under the rug." The almost instinctive reaction of most institutions (governments, unions, corporations, etc.) is to pretend that problems don't exist; out of sight is out of mind.
Churches are tempted to do the same with their local problems. By not only committing his rebuke to writing but also
sharing it with other nearby congregations—and specifying
*their* faults as well—this tempting course was effectively
denied them. They could adopt the corrections demanded by
John or they could repudiate them, but there was simply no
way they could pretend that genuine problems had not been
pinpointed.

Having chosen to write to a multiple number of congregations, why did John select only seven from the list of those
available in the province? Many have believed that seven was
adopted because of its mystical connotations. The whole field
of biblical numerology is fraught with assumption and pre-
sumption, and one treads with great caution when discussing
the subject. Even so, seven is one of the few numbers where
there is a consensus and reasonable consistency from interpreter to interpreter: the central idea of seven is that of per-
fection, completeness, all-inclusiveness.[61] The use of seven
with this apparent intent in Revelation itself points in the
same direction.[62]

Furthermore in the ancient world, the number seven
enjoyed a special status of importance, uniqueness, and holi-
ness in a wide variety of cultures, nations, and religions. The
Babylonians built towers seven-stories tall as symbols of full-
ness and completion, of the universe as an entirety. Among
the Greeks and the Romans, seven was also granted status as
especially sacred.[63]

Although the seventh day as Sabbath (Ex 20:8–11) is perhaps the most obvious example of the sacred separation of
seven from other numbers in the Old Testament, the same
number is also used for other spiritually significant events. For

example, it was the number of days in the Feast of Unleavened Bread (Ex 34:18) and the Feast of Tabernacles (Lv 23:34). Every seventh year was also set aside as a sabbatical year (Ex 21:2).[64] In a book as deeply rooted in the Old Testament as the Apocalypse, it would not be startling to find John utilizing the number out of respect for its Old Testament usage.

We need to carry this a step further: Why should seven represent completeness in *this* case? Would it not be because it was a sufficiently large number to summarize the typical weaknesses and strengths of Christianity throughout Asia? If so, fewer churches would not have been sufficient and more would have risked redundancy.[65] In other words, seven is a natural choice of congregations because it grows out of the spiritual conditions in Asia rather than the need to satisfy a supposed mystical connotation. If one feels compelled to speak in such terms at all, it would be wisest to speak of how John utilizes mysticism *when it coincides with the truth he wishes to convey.* John controls the mysticism rather than the mysticism controlling him.

Although backing away from mystical excess, it is only fair to note that John found the number congenial to the type of document he was composing. According to William M. Ramsay, the number is used on fifty-four occasions.[66] In writing the clearly "apocalyptic" bulk of the book, seven may indeed be used primarily for its implication of completeness,[67] but in this far more down-to-earth introductory section it still seems most probable that any mystical aspects take second place to providing an adequate number of representative cases to illustrate the diverse spiritual conditions in Roman Asia.

Having decided to utilize only seven particular congregations, why were these specific churches selected from the longer list of those available? Different commentators and scholars have offered a variety of explanations. These can be divided into three broad categories: pagan religious explanations, Christian religious explanations, and socio-political explanations.

What we have called pagan religious explanations stress factors involving the importance of the pagan cults in these seven cities. One could theorize that the level of commitment to the pagan cults was higher than that found in other cities, but how and in what way one would go about proving this is highly questionable.

Paul W. Barnett sees the presence of emperor worship as the key reason these seven particular cities were selected: "Each of the seven cities/towns in the Revelation was located at a site of the imperial cult."[68] He reprints maps from another author who identifies "imperial temples," "imperial altars," and "imperial priests" as being documented in literally dozens of towns scattered throughout Asia Minor.[69] These facts may help establish reasonable grounds why emperor worship would (or could) represent a major motive behind the writing of the book, but the very abundance of evidence for the imperial sect undercuts the argument that its presence lies behind the selection of these seven particular cities. If emperor worship was that pervasive, the seven cities seemingly differed in nothing from literally dozens of other Asian communities.

One could argue that these cities regarded the cult with special zeal and enthusiasm, as manifested in their lobbying for the position of *neokoros* ("temple warden"): Smyrna, Pergamon, and Ephesus had earned the honor by the end of the first century; Philadelphia and Sardis were later added to the list.[70] This would still leave the problem of the inclusion of Laodicea and Thyatira. The fact that both communities "combined traditional and Imperial rites"[71] is of interest as reflecting the ecumenical, open-ended nature of polytheism but does little to make the cities sufficiently different from other Asian communities actively involved in the cult.

Others prefer to seek an explanation for the inclusion of these seven particular cities within the context of the first-century Christian experience. Doing this can take several different forms.

It could be that these congregations were either objectively the most important in the province or were so regarded on a subjective basis by those living in Asia or within their respective region of the province.[72] This might be called the conservative version of the view. Others believe that these congregations were *organizationally* the most important in the province: the one-bishop system over a geographical region (the "monarchical episcopate") was already in existence and each of these cities was the home church for such a bishop, presiding or ruling over his diocese.[73] Still others see the evolution of such a system already well on its way when John wrote even if its full-fledged development is open to question.[74]

When Ignatius passed through Asia about the second decade of the second century, his writings indicate that the system already existed in at least some places in Asia and he presents himself as a passionate defender of it.[75] It is commonly thought that Ignatius's fervor for the system (which, not coincidentally, exalted his own role in his Antioch home congregation) indicates that the institution had become well grounded and widely accepted throughout Asia. Some have *reversed* the argument, however, and argued that Ignatius's passion reveals not so much prevalent acceptance as concern that many in Asia did not share his enthusiasm. Thus it reflects his commitment to a new ideal not yet universally accepted in the region.[76]

Although it would be useful to know more concretely how widespread Ignatius's conception of the authority of the episcopate was, it is important to remember that even under the most generous reading of the evidence the vital leap from congregational to multi-congregational/regional jurisdiction was still in the future at that time. As W. F. Miles wisely observes, "The bishop is the all-important focus of the local congregation. There is no suggestion that he fulfills any such role in relation to the wider church."[77]

If the monarchical episcopate was of questionable prevalence in its limited congregational form in Ignatius's day, there is even less likelihood that it existed in the days of John's exile. Indeed, the apostle Paul used the terms *elder* and *bishop* as synonyms (1 Ti 1:5, 7), while the monarchical episcopate system was based upon the bishop having a higher, more authoritative position that ultimately involved the claim to be successor of the apostles.

Furthermore, if each of these cities (or its bishop) had control over other churches, would not John's rebuke have included references to the weaknesses and faults in the congregations

under their jurisdiction or at least a censure over having permitted such to have occurred? In other words, the way John presents his criticisms argues that it was these congregations
*independently and separately* that concerned him rather than
their alleged role "over" other churches in their vicinity.

But what of the more modest claim of greater prestige?
In regard to cities like Ephesus and Pergamon, their important status in imperial government would make any local congregation almost automatically be looked upon in at least a
vague way as important and significant, especially if the
church was large and prosperous. A congregation in Laodicea
would gain status from the wealth of the city, a wealth in
which many members of the church there shared (3:17).
There are, however, difficulties. Smyrna had historic pretensions of leadership in Asia, but any religious status this might
somehow gain for the church there seems more than compen-
sated for by the fact that poverty was the predominant economic status of its membership (2:9). Philadelphia also
presents difficulties, for it is described as a place where the
Christians have but "a little strength" (3:8).

William M. Ramsay tries to prove the existing status of
these seven churches as a kind of spiritual elite because "there
is no way of escaping the obvious implication in 1:4 and 1:11
that those Seven were *already* known to the world and established in popular estimation as 'the Seven Asian Churches,'
before the Vision came to St. John."[78] If so, why did John find
it necessary to specify in 1:11 the names of these churches
rather than allowing the introduction to each of the mini-
epistles to be sufficient? The most obvious reason would be
that no set group of churches yet had any such status.

Another explanation that falls within the confines of the
Christian experience concerns the spiritual importance of
the number seven in Old Testament usage and in John's own
Apocalypse. However, as already noted when we discussed the
significance of this phenomenon, we must also consider
John's desire to be *comprehensive*, to present a cross-section of
the wide variety of spiritual problems and difficulties that
existed in the province. If there were five or six that were
immediately obvious, it would be quite natural to add one or

two to make the total number fit in with the usage of the Torah. Even here the motivation would be the desire to be thorough rather than mystical, the latter serving as the tool of the former.

Yet another explanation lies in the relationship of these congregations to John. It could well be that the rationale for their inclusion or exclusion lies not just in their virtue or particular corruptions but in the probability that John's exhortation would be able to influence them in a positive direction. Walter Bauer reasons along this line when he suggests that "John selected the most prominent communities from those in his area which met the prerequisite of seeming to afford him the possibility of exerting a real influence."[79]

The third broad category of explanations roots the choice of these seven cities in socio-political explanations. We have already noted that certain of these cities *were* prominent and that this fact could easily enhance the perception of the importance of the local church, at least within the confines of the broader Christian community in Asia. But just as we encountered difficulties in counting certain of the congregations as spiritually prominent, we also encounter difficulties in counting certain of their communities as of special political-social-economic importance. Why do Thyatira and Philadelphia, for example, enter the picture? Some find the explanation in all seven being assize cities, where the Roman courts met. Unfortunately, as we saw in our study of the organizational structure of Roman Asia, this was not the case. With *most* of the seven church-cities, yes; with *all*, no.

Others see the explanation in all seven being on the Roman road system. The Great Road would carry one from Ephesus to Smyrna to Pergamon (and was the earliest Roman-constructed road in the province). The Imperial Post Road then carried one to Thyatira, Sardis, Philadelphia, Laodicea, and thence back to Ephesus.[80] Yet other cities, which are not included, were located on these roads as well, and surely faith communities of Christians were present in at least a fair number of them. (Hierapolis, for example, Col 4:13.) Following the major roads, one *would* come to each of the seven cities in the order John writes to them,[81] but isn't this an argument for why John writes in the order he does rather than to the places he selects?

Tied in with this is the fact that each of these towns would be logical jumping-off points for the Apocalypse, to be recopied and passed on to less significant communities in the nearby area. William M. Ramsay develops the point this way:

> The Seven Cities...were situated on a very important circular route, which starts from Ephesus, goes round what may be called Asia par excellence, the most educated and wealthy and historical pre-eminent parts of the Province. *They were the best points on that circuit to serve as centers of communication with seven districts* [emphasis added]: Pergamum for the north (Troas, doubtless Adramyttium, and probably Cyzicus and other cities on the coast contained Churches); Thyatira for an inland district on the northeast and east; Sardis for the wide middle valley of the Hermus; Philadelphia for Upper Lydia, to which it was the door (3:8); Laodicea for the Lycus Valley, and for Central Phryiga of which it was the Christian metropolis in later time; Ephesus for the Cayster and Lower Maeander Valleys and coasts; Smyrna for the Lower Hermus Valley and the North Ionian coasts, perhaps with Mitylene and Chios (if those islands had not as yet been affected).[82]

Examining the various interpretative options (most of which seem at least partially reasonable and likely), one may feel perplexed as to which to choose. Here we come face to face with one of the great problems of our age, the desire to oversimplify. We seek one reason when neither logic, reason, history, nor scripture requires that there be just one. The soundest course would be to assume that various churches were included for a variety of reasons, some for one, some for another, and yet others out of several causes. John has not spelled out what the considerations were; the most we can do is analyze the various specific factors that could have been involved and analyze their strengths and weaknesses.

## Writing to "Angels"

John's seven mini-epistles are characterized by the unusual immediate recipient who is addressed in each, "To the angel of the church of Ephesus [Smyrna, Pergamon, etc.] write..." (2:1; 2:8; 2:12; 2:18; 3:1; 3:7; 3:14). Who or what does John *mean* by these "angels"?

The terminology has been one of the prime pieces of evidence that the monarchical episcopate existed in the first century: The *angel* was the bishop, ruling over the congregation and/or other churches in the immediate region as well. As noted earlier, this system is a later evolution, developing from the pure congregationalism of the first century. A variant of this is to identify the angel with the minister, preacher, or evangelist working with the particular congregation.[83] Just as the episcopate interpretation would work well if the Revelation had been written in the Middle Ages, the ministerial interpretation would work well if the volume had been written in the twentieth century to a Protestant religious body. In neither case does the interpretation best fit the actual historical period involved.

Others see the angels as the messenger(s) carrying the Apocalypse to their Asian cities. Just as heavenly angels are presented in the scriptures as conveying God's message, these "earthly angels" perform a similar role. The way John switches, in each of the mini-epistles, from addressing the angel to addressing the congregation makes one wonder how a mere messenger "could be so closely identified with a congregation."[84] Furthermore, "one does not write to a messenger who is present in person: one speaks to him, or gives him a written message to carry back to the church."[85] Indeed, the harsher one regards John's exile on the island, the less likely that he would have been permitted visitors,[86] much less seven different ones. (Remember that he addresses not just one "angel" but seven of them.)

A literalist approach sees in the angels actual heavenly beings rather than some earthly parallel.[87] This could refer to guardian angels. Jesus seems to refer to such a concept in Matthew 18:10, but there the reference is carefully limited to children. Although the concept could quite consistently be expanded to all human beings (at least among those claiming discipleship) and even to congregations, the New Testament nowhere directly broaches such a claim. If John has in mind the concept of a *congregational angel,*[88] it represents the unique affirmation of the doctrine in the pages of the New Testament. The less explicit the sole reference to a doctrine or idea is, the more cautious one should be in asserting that it was what the writer intended.

Furthermore, how could writing a letter to a literal angel provide that message to the congregation being addressed? Of course if this was a way of instructing the angel to reveal that message to the congregation, then the obstacle would be met. Unquestionably, biblical angels are referred to as functioning in just such a capacity as revealers of the divine will. First-century Christians were warned, however, not to be credulous: a purported revelation might not be that at all (cf. Gal 1:6–9). Hence John's own written account would serve as verification that what had been received was not some subjective evaluation or criticism of the various congregations, but the actual divine revelation each mini-revelation purported to be. In such a case John is addressing not so much *guardian* angels as *revealing* angels, though the two concepts could easily overlap.

Another approach takes the "angels" as embodiments of the essential or core nature—the essence, if you will—of each congregation considered as a collectivity. William Milligan argues that "to St. John every person, every thing, has its angel. . . . The waters have an angel (16:5). Fire has an angel (14:18). The winds have an angel (7:1). The abyss has an angel (9:11)."[89] Milligan uses such texts to prove that "the active, as distinguished from the passive, life of the Church" is under discussion.[90] Hence other Revelation texts that refer to an angel *doing* various things don't disprove this view, since they exhibit angels as the symbolic incarnation of action and conduct.[91] Charles C. Whiting has a related idea when he suggests that each angel represents "the prevailing spirit of the church, or a personification of the church, and thus . . . the church itself."[92]

John's wording seems to best fit this type of approach. Note that in each of the mini-epistles John begins by addressing the "angel" and then *immediately* addresses the congregation as to its faults and virtues. Hence John seems to be using *angel* and *church* synonymously; and to do so, angel would need to represent that core essence of what the congregation really is and really represents.

5

---

# The Imperial Cult in Roman Asia
# and the Nature of Official
# Persecution

In light of the widely shared assumption that emperor worship played the central role in motivating anti-Christian persecution in the days of John and in view of the pervasive importance of the cult to Roman Asia, we need to examine in detail both the practice and organization of the imperial cult. This will involve both its activities and the assumptions (stated or unstated) that underlay its popularity and success in the province.

Few things seem more alien to the modern mind than emperor worship. Yet even in the middle of the twentieth century the industrializing nation of Japan made emperor worship pivotal to its culture. So there is no inherent reason why even an industrialized country might not adopt emperor worship if the cultural and religious factors found in the western world were lacking, repressed, or even abandoned.

Although emperor worship as an organized *institution* was an innovation, there were sufficient precedents in Roman thought and myth to provide an excuse if not a full justification. In the respected religions of Rome there was certainly precedent for a mortal becoming immortal. Both Asclepius and Hercules were examples of those who made the transformation.[1]

Roman political tradition provided a few examples of a popular cult springing up spontaneously to provide deification to a respected and admired leader. The sites where the Gracchi had been killed became sites for such worship among certain lower echelons of Roman society.[2] Romans of higher status did not permit class inhibitions to keep them from

112

embracing the apparently spontaneous cult that quickly developed around the assassinated Julius Caesar. Phenomena observed in the skies were cited as "heavenly" confirmation of the deification, and Octavian had sound political reasons to tolerate the movement and then to encourage it. After all, his uncle was now not merely a great general but a deity, thereby adding to his own prestige.[3]

This could be seen as exhibiting the robustness of polytheism; that is, it could still give birth to distinctive new sects. However, it can also be taken as a sign of despair, that the populace at large was "losing faith in the existence, or at least in the effectiveness, of their traditional gods."[4] They were willing to lower their standard of godhood because they were no longer convinced that the gods themselves were real. Regardless of how we interpret the significance of the movement, there can be no question that it was both popular and long enduring.

It should be remembered that there was a difference between worshiping *Rome* and worshiping a specific emperor. The former was practiced in Asia long over a century before Julius Caesar transformed the Roman government into the imperial system.[5] The pioneer was Smyrna, which erected the first temple dedicated to Rome in 195 B.C. About 170 B.C. another temple was erected in Alabanda, and about three years later one in Athens. In 98 B.C. Pergamon joined the number of municipalities with temples dedicated to the city of Rome.[6]

As individual emperors came to be deified, the concept of emperor worship tended to become merged with and (from a practical standpoint) virtually synonymous with worship of the city itself.[7] On the other hand, the actual worship ritual was normally either dedicated to the city *or* to the emperor, rather than to both at the same time.[8] One might see here at least some theoretical leeway for those who were appalled at the excesses of *specific* emperors yet still desired to show thanks for the benefits of peace and prosperity the empire had brought to the region.

Theoretically, provincials were supposed to offer their sacrifices only at altars for "Rome and Augustus" (that is, for

Rome personified); again theoretically, only Roman citizens were permitted to offer worship at cult sites dedicated to the emperors themselves.[9] There was a kind of implicit snobbery in this, that emperor worship was reserved strictly for the "better" class, those who had aspired to and obtained Roman citizenship.[10]

All empires need "glue" to unite widely disparate groups of people and to maintain that unity in spite of the inevitable stresses and pressures that occur over time. A shared language is one such thing. Just as English today serves as a "universal" second language, Greek united the widespread arms of the Roman Empire. Shared customs provide a second powerful "adhesive" to hold together disparate peoples, many brought into the empire by or under the threat of armed action. The glorification of Greek customs and cultures by Rome provided such a cultural basis for the governing and upper classes throughout the empire.

Religion represents a third powerful binding force. In the Middle Ages, Europe shared a common Catholicism. In the nineteenth and twentieth centuries Western Europe and the United States shared various forms of Protestantism. In each case it was a *substitute* for a different religious system. But Rome used the unifying power of religion very differently. Instead of trying to replace dozens of major cults (not to mention numerous hybrid and fringe movements), it simply *added* the worship of the emperor. In a polytheistic society this raised no local scruples and brought to bear the powerful stimulus of a common, shared religious element. (The Jews were the one annoying exception to this, and even there it was agreed that sacrifices would be offered *for* the emperor's well-being rather than *to* him.)

The imperial cult functioned on several levels. It functioned as a religiously garbed expression of political loyalty to Rome.[11] The presence of American flags in many modern religious sanctuaries and the inclusion of certain patriotic songs in church songbooks and worship—and sermons on the political consequences of Christian discipleship—represent contemporary efforts with a similar result, if not intent.

(This was true of the locally dominant religious cult as

well. In the 1960s and 1970s civic or secularized religion was pervasive; that is, the use of dominant religious terminology to rhetorically "flavor" the language of government and the people in all aspects of life.[12])

Furthermore, the emperor cult had the potential for bridging the psychological gap between political inferiority and self-respect, both individually and as a community. "They were not ruled by one who was remote and inaccessible to them, but rather by one with whom they had established a cultic rapport in the tradition of the cults of the benefactors."[13]

On an emotional and social level the cult's activities brought together in a shared experience pleasurable activities that could be engaged in with the entire citizenry, monetarily spanning the gap between rich and poor, aristocrat and plebeian. (A rough parallel is the late-twentieth-century experience of the church as the "poor man's country club" in which doctrinal and even religious matters become secondary to the sharing "fellowship" of having a good time together.) This bond of shared activity bonded the local citizenry into, if not strictly a unity of "faith," then certainly one of shared joy, happiness, and enthusiasm.[14]

Whatever Greeks in the time of Augustus may have thought or experienced in a sacrificial process in honor of the emperor,[15] such rituals were linked with parades, public meals, and lavish games. Imperial feast days became the high points of the entire year, times when the citizenry could experience a sense of community.

As part of the excitement, people streamed in from neighboring towns, markets were held, and self-important embassies came from distant parts. An imperial feast day was also a bright spot in the lives of the poor. Rituals performed for the emperor in faraway Rome blended with high spirits and pride in their own city. For prominent citizens it was an opportunity to show off their status and how much they could afford to lavish on honors for the emperor and enjoyment for their fellow citizens.

The emperors themselves had mixed feelings toward the cult. Some mocked it. Surely we see at least a touch of such an attitude in Vespasian's dying words, "I think I am becoming a god."[16] Emperor Caracalla was even prepared to decree the deification of the very brother he had killed, "Let him be a god, provided he is dead."[17]

And there was danger that typical Romans would be skeptical as well, if the emperor were conspicuously not deserving of special honor. After all, both the local power structure and freedmen "knew only too well the very human imperfections of *any* Emperor."[18] In many places outside Greece and Asia the concept of imperial deification was greeted with considerable skepticism. When Claudius wrote in A.D. 41 to the Alexandrians, this lack of credibility clearly played a major role in his rejection of their desire to bestow divine honors upon him, "I deprecate the appointment of a high priest to me, and the erection of temples, for I do not wish to be offensive to my contemporaries and I hold that sacred fame and the like have by all ages been attributed to the immortal gods as peculiar honors."[19] Hence it would be arrogance to improperly or unduly claim divine honors.

Several emperors accepted the *existence* of the imperial cult, but by their efforts to hinder its expansion indicated that they considered it more a fact of life than a desirable institution. They did not scorn those who bestowed the honor upon them but hindered others from joining their number.[20] The former is an expression of prudence; the latter reveals personal attitude.

For example, the actions of Caesar Augustus can be read as attempts to rein in the potential embarrassment of the cult to the sensibilities of the western part of the empire. Yes, you can have an imperial cult, but it must always be tied in with an existing sect, normally that of the worship of Rome. Yes, you may worship the emperor, but it should not be focused on the human being as such. Rather, it is the *Genius, Numen Augusti*, the divine spirit of the emperor, that is to receive the honor.[21] Rather than encouraging a cult of personality, the cult is, if you will, "depersonalized."

When Asia sought permission from Tiberius in A.D. 23 to erect a second imperial temple in Asia, precedent was on the side of permitting it, and Tiberius, therefore, supported the proposal. He was far less willing to encourage the expansion of the practice into other regions. In A.D. 25 he opposed the spread of the cult into Spain.[22] He also demanded that official sanction be obtained for the establishment of any new imperial cult anywhere—and persistently refused to grant it.[23] In spite of this official road block, various communities in the Roman East ignored the requirement of official sanction and proceeded to establish their own unofficial and strictly local cult centers and priesthoods.[24]

In his early years Caligula prohibited worship in his honor. But even in Greece he relented only enough to permit it at major festivals.[25]

As already noted, Claudius began his reign by prohibiting the citizens of Alexandria from erecting a temple in his honor and from creating a priesthood in his name. On the other hand, he did not attempt to discourage the cult where it already existed in Asia. Indeed, he is likely the emperor who first authorized the post of chief priest of the provincial Asian cult. (Unquestionably it was in existence by Nero's reign.[26])

Unbalanced or extremely insecure rulers could find in the cult a ready boost for their ego. Whether Caligula's early restraint was genuine or merely tactical is difficult to determine in light of his later extravagant claims to godhood. He even ordered the inflammatory act of erecting a huge image of Zeus in the Jewish Temple in Jerusalem. Zeus might have been the *name* of the image, but it was to bear the *face* of Caligula himself. The local authorities managed to avoid implementing his order until he was safely dead.[27]

Under Domitian, the cult was again taken in an extremely literal sense. Domitian even demanded that his servants address him as "master and god."[28] He created the practice of requiring that oaths be taken in the name of the "genius" of the emperor. He also initiated the requirement that a libation be poured out at his idol and a pinch of incense offered. These demands were retained by later emperors.[29]

The *koinon* (commune) of Asia was responsible for maintaining emperor worship throughout the province. The *koinon* held an annual meeting at varying spots in the province in order both to engage in joint worship of Caesar and to coordinate the work going on in the various cities and towns. Religiously, the top official was called the chief priest of Roma and Augustus; geographically, the post was called chief priest of Asia. The annual meeting chose this individual, and he served a one-year term.[30]

Although the evidence is not conclusive, the bulk of scholars read the evidence as indicating that the well-documented term *Asiarch*[31] is equivalent to that of chief priest (or high priest) of the cult[32]. A minority consider the position as primarily one of civic honor with no service to the cult implicit or required.[33] Others hold to a mediating position between these two views, that by the second century A.D. their priestly status had clearly evolved but that in the earlier centuries they merely *performed* certain religious functions rather than being viewed as formally ordained priests in the strict sense of the term.[34] Perhaps a modern-day parallel would be the distinction found in some religions between lay minister and ordained clergyman. Indeed, since the Asiarchs came from many other civic duties and returned to such duties after their very limited one-year term of office, they *inevitably* partook more of the former status than the latter, regardless of the official designation of their position.

A third view has the Asiarch as titular head of the cult but with the high-priest position occupied by a separate individual.[35] A potential variant of this is that the Asiarch may have been dominantly an administrative or supervisory post over the imperial temples.[36] Depending upon the particular advocate, this could be used to either link or delink the priestly and headship positions in the regional cult.

A related question involves how many Asiarchs/chief priests served at one time. In the late-nineteenth century the interpretation began to dominate that only one high priest served over the entire imperial cult in Asia. The alternative interpretation is that there was one high priest in each city that had an officially recognized imperial cult.

Two pieces of evidence have been introduced in behalf of this reconstruction. One is that we find the inscription "high priest of the temple in (with the city name)."[37] Of course, the actual *functioning* of the cult, on a day-by-day basis, was unquestionably local, and such references fit well with that reality.[38] Assuming that *Asiarch* and *chief priest* are equivalent terms, however, 90 percent of the time the term is used *without* such limiting descriptions.[39]

Second, in the approximately 320 years between the establishment of the cult in 29 B.C. in Pergamon and the changes imposed by Diocletian, at least eighty Asian high priests are known by name. This would seem a very high percentage of names to have survived if only *one* person possessed the honor at any one time.[40] Although the Asiarch might well have retained use of the term as a courtesy title long after his service had ended, the large number of individuals whose names are known argues that more than one individual functioned in the position at any one given moment.

Assuming there was more than one chief priest at a time, the question arises of what degree of coordinating power was exercised by the *koinon*. Was it in actual control of the local cults, or was it primarily the coordinating mechanism of basically independent movements? Logically, one would have to assume that one of these individuals (perhaps on a rotating basis?) headed the entire provincial cult, or that one of their number was accorded the annual honor, or that an *additional* appointment of a *provincial* (rather than city-only) chief priest was made. The data do not allow us to say. One would suspect that a provincial appointment was—from the practical standpoint—a far easier process than choosing between local claimants, whose own aspirations could far too easily be mere stalking horses for the excess civic pride that was so common.

The inscriptional references that have survived point to the Asiarchs being prominent members of the local aristocracy. Appointing them to such a prestigious post served to cement their loyalties to Rome. Their wealth also solved much of the financing problem of the cult; the Asiarch was responsible for paying for the annual festival and picking up the tab for the remaining expenses of the cult.[41] In a way parallel to the way city government functioned, those occupying the leadership were responsible for funding what could not be raised by other means. As a responsible aristocrat, the Asiarch was expected to provide administrative and financial support to his community both before and after serving in the position.[42]

The emphasis on the high priesthood/Asiarchs as at least local heads of the movement can easily obscure the fact that there were other positions in the cult as well. The hymnodies engaged in choral singing in honor of both Rome and the emperor.[43] "The gymnasiarch and agonothete were appointed to administer the annual festival, and the sebastophantes seems to have supervised the imperial mysteries, including the public display of the *imagines* of the imperial family in the provincial temple."[44]

The term *high priestess* was a courtesy title automatically given to the wife of the high priest of Asia.[45] This could, and sometimes did, serve as precedent for presiding over the worship of a goddess or over the worship of a female member of the royal family who had been deified.[46]

The most prominent sites of emperor worship were the official temples. The first was erected in Pergamon, the second in Smyrna, and the third in Ephesus around A.D. 89 or 90.[47]

However, it would be extremely misleading to assume that these were the only places where one found the cult. There were numerous less elaborate places of worship dedicated exclusively to the emperor; these ran the gamut from "special rooms in porticoes and gymnasia" to "free-standing buildings in their own sanctuaries." These, in turn, varied from extremely simple to extremely elaborate.[48]

If one were to participate in the athletic activities in the massive gymnasium complex in Pergamon, one found there what appears to have been the ancient equivalent of a chapel in which to venerate the emperor.[49] If one walked down the streets of Ephesus, one was unlikely to miss the large Antonine altar, which, though not located in a formal temple, was a place of worship.[50] The many statues of the emperor in the city served a similar cultic purpose for those so inclined.[51] Hence even the most devout monotheists could not live out their lives without running into manifestations of the movement.

Local priesthoods to promote the cult were numerous, though not necessarily officially recognized by Romans. One may exaggerate a little, but not much, by asserting that "there was scarcely a city without one or two imperial priesthoods."[52] We already saw the sporadic imperial effort to rein in the expansion of the cult and how it was unsuccessful, especially in the eastern provinces. It is quite possible that many of these priesthoods gained official acceptance during the extremist phases of the reigns of Caligula and Domitian. Unlike their more temperate predecessors, those emperors were hardly likely to make any such efforts at moderation.

In our study of the seven church-cities, we will find imperial worship being conducted (with no sense of incongruity) within the sacred confines of other polytheistic sects. We will also find specific emperors being blended in the popular mind with existing deities, creating a situation in which the worship of one of the traditional gods was transformed into being simultaneously the worship of the emperor. This process of intermingling a living emperor with a long-existing cult can be illustrated by Hadrian. He was an individual who loved Asia and the surrounding provinces, was generous toward them, and repeatedly visited them. During his fourth visit in A.D. 129, "everywhere, in inscriptions, dedications, statues, temples and festivals he was proclaimed Zeus Olympios and often assimilated to the other major gods of Olympus into the bargain. Ninety-one altars to him as a god have so far been found in Asia Minor, at least seventy-six cities there celebrated his personal cult and twenty-five of them took his name."[53]

The imperial cult utilized religious rhetoric that Christians believed could only properly be applied in a monotheistic context. In both a political and religious sense the emperor was considered the "father" of the entire population of the empire, a conceptual usage that was in clear contradiction to the determination of Christians to make the God of Israel the supreme father.[54]

Other religious rhetoric that Christians used exclusively in connection with Jesus was applied in the imperial cult to the emperor. Examples of this are the terms *epiphany, gospel, savior,* and *son of God.*[55]

Imperial worship involved a number of aspects. Sacrifices were offered both by individuals on their own initiative[56] and by the city or the province on behalf of its residents.[57] Sacrifices commonly took the form of liquid libations or ritual cakes.[58] Public festivals in the emperor's honor were more elaborate, involving not only the burning of incense but the offering of an animal, usually a bull.[59] (Pergamonese coins depict such a bull sacrifice.[60])

Hymn singing was not neglected; it represented a standard component of the worship.[61] In Judaism, sacrifices were commonly offered for the emperor, especially on the occasion of his accession, his recovery from illness, and when divine favor was sought for his efforts to defend the empire against its foes.[62] What is sometimes overlooked is that even the emperor's own cult overwhelmingly offered similar sacrifices, *for* him rather than *to* him.[63]

The same phenomenon appears in regard to prayer: people normally prayed on his behalf rather than seeking his supernatural intervention in their favor. An inscription from Smyrna illustrates this when it refers to the way "the whole world sacrifices and prays on behalf of the emperor's eternal duration and unconquered rule."[64] There are only a few known expressions of faith that the emperor *could* answer prayer, and *none* asserting a specific case in which he supposedly did so.[65]

Some have speculated that the credibility of the cult was enhanced by pseudo-miracles, such as talking statues and miraculously produced fire signs. Such phenomena were effective thrill-making devices for the then-contemporary theater and were well within first-century technical abilities. John's description of such pseudo-miracles as furthering worship of the emperor (Rv 13:13–15) has been introduced as evidence that the cult engaged in such unscrupulous conduct.[66]

(Not only echoes of the imperial *cult,* but also of imperial *practice* have been detected in the book as well. Both have been identified as present in Revelation 5 and other texts where one reads of a great multitude praising the divine ruler. The emperor had a group of up to five thousand young men whose function was to cheer, applaud, and celebrate each of his public appearances.[67])

The cult sponsored provincial imperial festivals in eight Asian cities on a regular basis—including six of the seven cities John wrote to—only Thyatira not being included.[68] These festivals consisted primarily of athletic contexts of various types;

such activities as acting contests provided a kind of "cultural" dignity to the festive occasions. In a typical year two of the eight cities were holding games in the emperor's honor.[69] Each city had its own schedule rather than the honor passing from one to the other.[70] Smaller communities, such as Sardis, Laodicea, and Philadelphia, likely followed an every-three-year schedule, while more substantial metropolises, such as Ephesus, Smyrna, and Pergamon, may have had them more frequently—perhaps every other year or even annually.[71] (If nothing else, local civic pride would have demanded that these more prestigious communities somehow exceed—either qualitatively, quantitatively, or both—the efforts of their less prestigious rivals.)

### Asian Persecution and the Legal Basis for John's Exile

Based upon the first three chapters of Revelation, Asian Christians faced varying degrees of pressure and danger, but the situation had not become a widespread, major persecution. There is a vague reference to those in Ephesus having "persevered" and having had "patience" (2:3), but there is nothing to suggest attempted suppression. In Thyatira the main problem was the temptation to compromise on moral issues. Faithfulness is to be rewarded with "power over the nations" (2:26–27), which would certainly suggest a perceived *hostility* being endured from the surrounding world. On the other hand, the vagueness gives no grounds for suspecting any specific major threat.

When we think of Sardis, we find yet another congregation faced with the danger of moral compromise, and it is the triumph over *that* danger that occupies John's mind. If a major difficulty with persecuting authorities exists, there is no hint of it. Laodicea's problem is not so much compromise as unconcern, and John weighs in vigorously against it. Again, there is a conspicuous silence as to persecution.

We read of "tribulation" in Smyrna, but it is attributed to neither paganism, the emperor cult, nor to official persecution but rather to the vehement opposition of the Jewish community

(2:9). There is the danger that "some" would be cast into jail in the near future (2:10). Although "some" is a translator's addition to complete the sentence, the reference to a highly limited period of "tribulation [for] ten days" *is* clearly in the text. "Be faithful until death, and I will give you the crown of life" *may* be a hint that martyrdom could occur as well. But in that case one would think that the "test[ing]" would be defined as facing death rather than facing imprisonment, since death is the far more frightening foe. John's point seems neither to rule in nor to rule out the danger of death but to implore faithfulness *regardless* of what the imprisonment might or might not lead to.

In Philadelphia we find the inference of substantial diffi-culty. They are praised for "hav[ing] not denied my name" (3:8); the opposition is again rooted in Jewish rather than pagan foes (3:9). Under the Roman system these foes could initiate proceedings against the Christians, but this would be dragging the government into the picture rather than the gov-ernment being the initiator of the opposition. This intense Jewish antagonism did not exist in all places. Archaeologi-cally, it is well known that Sardis had a major Jewish commu-nity and its large synagogue was located in the heart of the city. Yet the epistle to Sardis gives no hint of any problem with Jewish foes. The pivotal role of individual personalities in the various cities—rather than theological differences alone—must be introduced to explain the varying picture.

In Pergamon the Christians are praised for not denying their faith (2:13); and if the reference to dwelling "where Satan's throne is" refers to the city as the site of the Roman provincial capital, then one finds here and only here an (almost) explicit reference to official persecution. The praise for not denying the faith *does* indicate that there had been a great deal of pressure upon the believing community. On the other hand, it is conspicuous that there had been one and only one martyr, Antipas (2:13). If *anywhere* in Asia there had been widespread casualties from government suppression, that place would have been Pergamon. As capital, as resi-dence of the proconsul,[72] and as a proud center of the impe-rial cult, the probability of blood persecution—if it were to occur anywhere—is highest here. The *minimal* nature of what had happened (and note that John puts the martyrdom at some undefined period in the *past*) argues that whether Christianity was as yet officially illegal, the government was still exercising a general hands-off policy.

Hence in Ephesus, Sardis, Thyatira, and Laodicea we find congregations with varying internal problems that needed to be resolved. Only in Smyrna, Philadelphia, and Pergamon is there real danger. In Smyrna and Philadelphia the foes are Jewish rather than pagan. In Philadelphia the problem appears ongoing; in Smyrna it is about to explode in a way that will affect some with imprisonment and perhaps death. In regal Pergamon the death threat is not placed in the future but in the past, and then it happened to only one person, Antipas.

We find nothing in this picture to suggest a major *province-wide* persecution. The evidence indicates an ongoing problem due to Jewish-Christian tensions in two cities, and a danger from Roman opposition (in Pergamon) that is presented as past rather than current. From this picture we can find no evidence that the imperial cult (or paganism in general) played a major role in persecuting the Asian churches[73] or that the death penalty was a serious danger for believers. Whatever the future might hold, for the present the situation is, overall, calm and manageable. Whatever persecution *John* is now enduring, it has not embroiled the entire believing community.[74]

Just as there were Jewish-Christian tensions that could be exploited by rabble-rousers, there were Gentile/pagan-Christian tensions that could be exploited as well. In the mini-epistles John does not allude to them, but Peter does in his first epistle, which had a destination of both Roman Asia and nearby provinces. On the one hand, the Christian refusal to engage in socially sanctioned forms of evil seemed incomprehensible to many, and therefore they assumed the worst: "For we have spent enough of our past lifetime in doing the will of the Gentiles—when we walked in licentiousness, lusts, drunkenness, revelries, drinking parties, and abominable idolatries. In regard to these, they think it strange that you do not run with them in the same flood of dissipation, speaking evil of you" (1 Pt 4:3–4). Many of the guild socio-religious gatherings are concisely summarized in these few words, as are many of the popular civic-religious festivals of the various gods.

This monotheistically produced restraint had the Christians censured from both extremes: condemned for not participating in polytheistic licentiousness, and condemned for doing just as bad (or even worse) while hidden away from public sight. Peter urged Christians to live a life so exemplary that it would refute the libels of misconduct (1 Pt 2:12, 15–16; 3:16), but human nature being what it is, there are always those who refuse to believe anything good about those they dislike.

Perhaps such tensions had resulted in Antipas's death—being in a stronghold of the Roman government and of polytheism and emperor worship it is a quite reasonable scenario. Be that as it may, John is conspicuously silent in the mini-epistles of cultic, governmental, or pagan adversity.[75] We might call such dangers the ongoing "background noise" that was ever present, never absent. The fact that it had not yet risen to the level of explicit mention is remarkable when one considers the future danger from the Roman government that John sees in the remainder of the book.

*Something* is about to occur that is going to change the entire equation. John hints at it in the mini-epistles. Persecuted Philadelphia is assured that because of past faithfulness "I also will keep you from the hour of trail which shall come upon *the whole world,* to test those who dwell on the earth" (3:10). If one assumes an early date for the book, the turmoil of Nero's fall and the disputed succession could have pushed social anxieties beyond the breaking point, with Christians as easy scapegoats. Anti-Jewish anger over the Jewish Revolt could easily have reinforced this rage and "rationalized" it due to the Christian ties with Judaism. Such upheavals could have resulted in both official government persecution and the explicit launching of it by individual pagans in defense of their traditional religion when the political props of paganism appeared to be falling apart.

But all this is yet in the future when John writes the epistles. The policy of governmental restraint is still in place. We do not know how John came to be singled out for persecution, but the significant fact is that he was. If he was on Patmos in flight from persecution, the legality of his exile is irrelevant; it wasn't a matter of law at all but of personal security, if not literal survival.

Usually, however, it is assumed that John was placed on the island due to the direct action of the Roman government. If so, one of two legal processes would have been involved: *relegation* or *deportation*. An individual subjected to deportation lost both his citizenship and all property except for that specifically exempted by the individual decreeing the sentence.[76] In contrast, the individual subjected to relegation was permitted to retain his citizenship.[77]

Deportation was to a specific site. According to the terms of the decision, the individual might have freedom of the place or be subjected to imprisonment.[78] Relegation could be as limited as simple exclusion from the province where one resided.[79] It could also, however, involve confinement to a specific location, "normally an island," as Peter Garnsey notes.[80]

Deportation was intended to be permanent.[81] Relegation was more flexible; it could last from a stated period of time to the remainder of one's life, depending upon the wording of the punishment decree.[82] Typically, it was for ten years or less.[83]

The deported individual typically had free and open contact with the local inhabitants and had the right to earn a livelihood.[84] On the other hand, anything he earned went to the state when he died, and any bequest that came his way was also diverted to the government.[85] In contrast, one suffering relegation could inherit from others, write a legally acceptable will of his own, and continue to own property that came his way in the future.[86] It is possible (though here the specialists hedge more) that he was also permitted to retain the property he already possessed.[87]

The terms for both deportation and relegation could be prematurely ended. When an emperor died or was killed, his acts might be revoked en masse by his successor (though many would ultimately be reinstated in the name of the new monarch). This revocation was especially likely to happen when the predecessor was in disrepute. Hence it is not surprising that Domitian's decisions quickly suffered this indignity at the hands of his successor.[88] If the Revelation was written at this time, the change of administrations would conveniently explain both John's initial exile (due to Domitian inspired hostility to Christianity) and the occasion of his release. On the other hand, if the volume dates from the last days of Nero, for example, then the upheavals of the Year of the Four Emperors might well explain both a short exile and a rather quick bestowal of freedom.

Furthermore, at least as early as the reign of Antonius Pius (A.D. 138–161), it was established that deportation could be revoked after a minimum term of ten years. This was conditional, however, upon the existence of special factors such as old age, broken health, or the intervention of relatives willing to care for the person.[89]

For John to have been the victim of deportation would mean that his case had come to the direct attention of the emperor in Rome. Only he could order deportation,[90] though he also had the option of relegation available as well.[91] In contrast, the provincial governor had the power to order relegation, provided there was a place within his jurisdiction to send the individual.[92]

Relegation could easily come to an end in a short period of time as well. This could happen in one of two ways: It appears to have been not uncommon for procurators and proconsuls to have either terminated all existing proceedings at the end of their term of office (officially one year, though sometimes prolonged for one or more additional years). Likewise, a new officeholder was quite capable of beginning his administration with a clean sheet, canceling actions such as relegations ordered by his predecessor.[93] Because of the brief term of office of a governor, any sentence of relegation would almost inevitably carry with it an opportunity for reversal every year when a new governor took office.

An individual might petition for release—and be granted it. Furthermore, sloppy record keeping existed in the first century and might easily have resulted in a prisoner being released either prematurely or because someone in authority was under the misapprehension that he was *supposed* to be released. This danger was increased by the rapid turnover in top personnel and the natural reliance of a new governor on the evaluation of his predecessor's intentions in regard to a particular prisoner. When Pliny went into nearby Bithynia, this problem of undocumented releases was one that very clearly disturbed him.[94]

Both relegation and deportation were forms of punishment normally reserved for the prestigious and well-to-do rather than the lower classes.[95] John, whatever his virtues as a Christian, could hardly have been regarded as being in a higher social class. Implicitly, this would rule out John being on the receiving end of *either* type of punishment.

Just what *was* John's perceived status? Being a Christian and a leader of a fringe group does not necessarily reduce him to insignificance or poverty. We know that he came from at least a moderately well-to-do family, one well enough off to have "hired servants" (Mk 1:19–20). Hence it is quite possible for him to have received financial support from his kinsmen at home, which would have raised him above whatever additional sources of income he personally earned. For that matter, we don't know how widespread a social spectrum existed within Ephesian Christianity (assuming John's residence there, which seems likely). If he was apostle to one or more significant locales, John's own status would have been enhanced. Furthermore, there is the intangible of personal friendship. If the apostle Paul could count Asiarchs as his personal friends (Acts 19:31), it is quite possible that John also enjoyed close friendships with key players in the local power structure. All of these factors would play a role in the governor's evaluation of John's social status; the higher he ranked it, the more likely that he would not be as harsh as he would be toward someone lower on the societal totem pole.[96]

Furthermore, both deportation and relegation were utilized, upon occasion, on other less prestigious elements in the social structure. Religious nonconformity brought down the wrath of Tiberius upon some four thousand individuals; he deported them because of the Egyptian and Jewish "superstitions" these freedmen were advocating.[97]

Peter Garnsey, in his detailed examination of the use of

deportation and relegation, notes that relegation was also not quite the class-specific penalty sometimes attributed to it:

> Reference is made in both literary and legal sources to the magisterial use of *relegatio* or *leve exilium* as a coercive measure against troublemakers. The former tell of actors, Jews, philosophers, the latter of soothsayers *(vaticinatores)*, astrologers and simply gangs of youths *(iuvenes)* expelled in this way. Most of these enemies of order would have been low in rank.[98]

Lower-class impact was inevitable when mass relegations were invoked, as they were upon a number of occasions. For example, all Jews were expelled from Rome in A.D. 19 and again in A.D. 48.[99]

In A.D. 19 a sex scandal produced the banishment of all Isis worshipers from Rome.[100]

Astrologers—with their potentially dangerous ability to "predict" the death of political leaders—were repeatedly banished. Such relegations occurred, among other occasions, in 139 and 33 B.C. and in A.D. 16 and 52 and during the reign of Vespasian as well.[101]

Actors were mass relegated under both Tiberius (A.D. 23) and Nero (A.D. 56).[102]

These are all cases of relegation as *expulsion from* rather than *expulsion to.* These measures were only short-term expedients, as indicated by the "need" to impose relegation upon multiple occasions upon the same groups of people.

In choosing between relegation and deportation, relegation seems more likely to have been John's punishment. Although it would have required at least the passive acceptance of the emperor, it was primarily a decision the local governor could implement on his own initiative. It may make for a less dramatic story, but, if anything, that argues for its greater likelihood. It should also be noted that the ancient church writer Tertullian, who was a trained lawyer, actually uses the term in describing John's exile. A layman might use the expression in a broader, generic sense, but with Tertullian's specialized background one would naturally anticipate his using it in its correct legal sense.[103]

# Epilogue:
## The Seven Churches as
## Reflections of Romanized Culture

No one can write even a modest-length piece of literature without reflecting the culture in which he or she lives.
The allusions may come in terms of conduct taken for
granted at the time, but which does not enjoy exact parallels
at a later date. The references may be specific linguistic
expressions typical of the era or mention of practices later
abandoned or institutions then thriving but later merged or
bankrupt. These injections of immediacy are not always inten-
tional or even conscious. Without them, then-contemporary
readers would not realize that their own age is under discussion rather than some past one. Indeed, so commonplace may
the references be that they are virtually indistinguishable to
the contemporary reader—they are part of the *given,* part of
the underlying *reality* of the age. Yet to those of a future date
they clearly exhibit the period of their origin.

Although in the sequel volume we will be examining in
minute detail the local societal background of the seven cities to
whose churches John wrote, in this brief epilogue to the broad
current of Roman influence it is appropriate to provide an overall indication of some of the impact of the broader culture. This
will consist of an application of the broader currents we have
examined in the previous chapters to the situations stated or
implied in John's seven mini-epistles of Revelation 2 and 3.
Hence, for the documentation of those cultural references, the
text (and notes) of the earlier chapters should be examined.
Brief allusion will be made to matters examined in detail in the
city-specific volume that follows.

## Jesus as Caesar

At the heart of the political system was Caesar: ruler, general-in-chief, sometimes a benevolent dictator, sometimes a despot in the worst sense of the word. Although he ruled *for* Rome and *on behalf* of the senate, the balance of power lay in his hands. Although actual practice often fell short of it, the ideal was that of a ruler whose wisdom, restraint, and judicious use of power would win the respect of his own people and the submission of his foes. Internally, he carried out justice and punished evildoers; externally, he kept the empire's enemies at bay and, when desirable or feasible, secured their defeat. He kept his people's hungry stomachs filled, the nation at peace, and dealt with those who endangered it. If war seemed essential, he crushed his foes.

We see Jesus pictured in terms of such an idealized king in the first chapters of the book of Revelation.

To Ephesus Jesus is the one who has power over "the seven stars in his right hand" (2:1)—even the powers of the universe he controls. The same image of control is used in writing to Sardis (3:1). He can even give "power over the nations" (2:26) to those he selects. He rules from strength not weakness, as if "with a rod of iron"; those who rebel he can smash as a potter does a rejected vessel (2:27).

To Smyrna he is the one who conquered even death (2:8) and could give that blessing to others as well (2:10). The Pergamonese are reminded that he possesses the power and authority of the armed warrior, one with a "sharp two-edged sword" (2:12). This image is repeated in the following verses. The believing fellowship is reminded that he "will fight against them [the local sectarians] with the sword of my mouth" (2:16). Likewise, he warns the internal schismatics in Thyatira that he can bring both "tribulation" (2:22) and death upon them (2:24).

A Jewish frame of reference is provided when Jesus is described as having "the key of David" and, due to having this key, can open and close any door he wants. And no power on earth can reverse him when he has done that (3:7).

The image of power is presented to the Laodiceans in the

regal term of sitting "down with my Father on his throne" (3:21). It is also pictured in the form of the ability to "chasten," but this would be inflicted out of love and the desire to produce reform rather than out of vengefulness (3:19).

Throughout the seven letters, it is *Jesus* who decides whether and when and how to act. His power to act in whatever way he wishes cannot be prevented or postponed. All that can be changed is whether one will be reconciled with him by the time he decides that action must be taken. He is the spiritual Caesar over a spiritual kingdom.

### The Imperfection of Human Relationships

The ideal king and the ideal citizen were goals, seldom reached. Residents of first-century Asia recognized this all too well from events that had occurred in their own lifetimes and from those that were part of the oral and written history passed on from past generations. The scandals were too many; the rebellions too numerous. This did not cause the ideal to be abandoned, but it caused it to be tempered by a realistic appraisal of human weaknesses and human imperfection.

The picture of the ruler Jesus is not limited in such a way by the book of Revelation. He is the *holy* Lord, without imperfection. The very human nature and failures of his *subjects* are clearly portrayed, however. Smyrna escapes censure, as does Philadelphia. But not the other church locations.

Even the most outstanding church had its problems. Ephesus—so exemplary in so many ways (2:2–3, 6)—had lost the passion of its first love (2:4) and needed to return to the zeal of its initial attitudes and conduct (2:5) in order to be acceptable to its spiritual Caesar.

In some cases the nature of the problem is left unspecified. Philadelphia had remained steadfast (3:10) even though it was weak (3:8), but the *practical manifestation* of its weakness—numerical? financial? emotionally?—is not specified.

In other cases the source of the problem can be identified. Pergamon had faced the death of its members yet had remained steadfast (2:13). But moral rot was being encouraged by Christian sectarians in its midst (2:15–16). Thyatira faced a particularly grievous series of tests from a self-proclaimed prophetess who advocated compromise with pagan religious practices (2:20)

The degree of internal departure from the ideal naturally varied. In Pergamon we read of the vague "those" who held to Balaamite doctrine (2:14) and that of the Nicolaitans (2:15). The implication in Thyatira seems to be that the proportion following a different path was substantial. In Sardis the picture is even darker; only "a few" had not "defiled" themselves with compromise (3:4). In both Ephesus and Laodicea the rhetoric leaves one with the impression that the *entire congregation* had drifted from its roots—in the first case into a lack of "love" (2:4), and in the latter into a lackadaisical lack of commitment (3:15). Actually, these are two different ways of expressing much the same idea.

## Jesus as Patron

If on the political level, the ultimate authority lay in Caesar, on a personal level, the most important interpersonal relationship (outside one's immediate family) lay in one's patron. One counted on the patron to further one's interests and to provide necessary assistance. As Jesus' power is symbolized in the Caesar/ruler imagery, Jesus' humanity and friendship are exhibited in patron rhetoric.

To the Ephesians he promises to fulfill that role by granting them access to the "tree of life, which is in the midst of the paradise of God" (2:7), if they maintain their loyalty to him. The rewards promised the Smyrnians are the limitation of adversity to a short term and a "crown of life" at death (2:10). They will also escape the danger of "the second death" (2:11). Any adversity they face will come from "the devil" and not from their patron (2:10).

The Christians in Pergamon are promised several future rewards if they reject the temptation to compromise with those who would dilute proper morality (2:17). The imagery is changed in the description of the rewards promised to Thyatira

(2:26–28), though it also expresses the idea of being singled out for special honor and recognition. The rewards are pictured as both positive *and* negative in writing to Sardis: the faithful will be "clothed in white garments" and "I will not blot out" their names from "the book of life" (3:5)

As a good patron would, Jesus kept in mind the limitations of those who were his clients. The Philadelphians had only "a little strength," so he set before them "an open door" of opportunity that no one would have the power to close (3:8). Likewise, he would keep them from "the hour of trial" that was coming upon the entire world (3:10). Their rewards are pictured in terms of receiving a crown (3:11) and being a pillar in God's eternal temple (3:12).

The reverse side of the patron-client relationship was loyalty. There were fewer more basic violations of the fundamental relationship than to ignore or repudiate one's commitment. Some of the Christians John wrote to were in danger of doing just that.

The Ephesians had manifested their loyalty by "test[ing] those who say they are apostles" and finding that they had been attempting to deceive them (2:2). They had been faithful not only in opposing evil but in the positive cultivation of the good: they had "persevered" and had "patience" and had "labored for my name's sake and have not become weary" (2:3). They hated the evil lifestyle of the Nicolaitans as well (2:6). In spite of these words of praise, something had vanished in their love (2:4), and this posed a potential danger for the future of the relationship (2:5).

The client relationship is summed up in the words "be faithful until death," used when addressing the Smyrnians (2:10). In Thyatira it is described as "hold[ing] fast what you have till I come" (2:25). Loyalty to their spiritual patron is depicted to Sardis in terms of being "worthy" (3:4). In writing to Philadelphia the terminology shifts to the earlier one of "hold[ing] fast" (3:11). Their loyalty is pictured as fulfillment of "my command to persevere" (3:10).

This was not idle moralizing. Jesus recognized that real effort and real commitment were needed as well as the rejection of obstacles both inside and outside the Christian fellowship. The external was easier to reject because it *was* external. The internal was harder to reject out of hand because it came from those one accepted as spiritual equals and those one would normally have confidence in. Yet human weakness had compromised the Christian commitment of some, and those compromised were quite willing to draw others into their version of Christianity. For example, the Pergamonese were tempted to accept at least token sacrifice to idols and to have sexual relationships with whomever they pleased (2:14). In Thyatira a similar theology of amorality was proclaimed (2:20).

A client forgot his patron at his own risk. Not only would he lose his active friendship, but he would risk his active displeasure. Throughout these mini-epistles there is a combination of reward for maintaining the relationship and the threat of retribution if it is abandoned. There is a constant assumption throughout that *enough* cared and that their caring was *sufficiently deep* that the local imperfections might yet be reversed. The situation in Laodicea was, in some ways, the most dangerous. No mention is made of the danger of subversion through compromise with paganism or immorality. No mention is made of the danger of doctrinal eccentricities that could lead them in strange and dangerous directions. *They simply didn't care any more.* They were "lukewarm," "neither cold nor hot" (3:16). They were "wealthy" and "needed nothing" (3:17). But their patron reminds them that he is quite capable of acting against them (3:19), just as he previously had acted for them—and was quite willing to act for them yet again (3:21).

## Varied Religious Life

The empire included a wide variety of religions. The exact number is incalculable because the same god or goddess might be worshiped under a number of different names, even though a citizen of one city would immediately recognize the deity when introduced to the cult in a different community. In the other direction, the *same* name might be applied to a cult, but substantial local variations required them to be considered distinct. To what extent should we consider them the *same* religion and to what extent a *different* one? Quite possibly the answer was not always clear, even to those of the first century.

In our specific seven-cities studies we will see that there are some possible/probable allusions to these cults. The picture of Jesus as one "with eyes like a flame of fire and his feet like fine brass" (2:18) may well reflect the popular imagery of one ancient cult. The reference to "Satan's throne" in Pergamon could well include at least a passing allusion to the emperor cult at that provincial capital (2:13). The only *explicit* polytheistic allusion is to the cult of Balaam (2:14), and it is made not in reference to an actual contemporary cult but to a contemporary movement with similar ideas—apparently one inside the Christian community itself.

The death of Antipas in the provincial capital (2:13) was probably the result of pagan hostility to Christianity. Jewish opponents are not mentioned in the epistle, and the city of Pergamon was the official capital of the province, as well as the center of emperor worship.

The inroads of a potential polytheist-monotheist compromise may have existed in Thyatira. There we read of a prophetess who did not reject Christianity yet saw no difficulty in "eat[ing] things sacrificed to idols" (2:20).

The Jewish community formed an important element in Asia. The references to that religion are explicit. Whatever long-term danger polytheism in general and emperor worship in particular might pose to Christianity, the immediate, short-term danger lay in persecution stirred up by the Christians' monotheistic rival. This existed in Smyrna, where the intensity of the Jewish opposition is described by the word "blasphemy" (2:9), or "slander" (NRSV). In Philadelphia they are branded as "the synagogue of Satan" and as mere imitation Jews (3:9). Since the "little strength" of the Christian group had just been mentioned in the previous verse (3:8), that weakness was presumably produced by the intensity of the Jewish opposition.

## The Regional Connection

However centralized the empire was, actual administration had to be carried out primarily on a regional and local basis. The Romans were extremely flexible in adapting to local customs. So long as the final *result* was that which they desired, they were quite willing to adopt local practices to secure that result. Only defiance that made them unable to accomplish their policy goals incurred their wrath; short of that, they were willing to accommodate local preferences and prejudices. Hence they were always alert to regional peculiarities that affected their power to govern effectively.

Likewise, the mini-epistles of John are alert to the peculiarities of the individual cities whose churches are addressed. Ephesus liked to think of itself as the first city of Asia. To these proud urbanites Jesus pictures himself as one even richer, as one who walked "in the midst of the seven golden lampstands" (2:1). Pergamon could boast of its status as capital of Asia, but this Jesus himself bore a "sharp two-edged sword" (2:12) and was quite capable of successfully "fight[ing]" against all opponents (2:16).

Philadelphia had been founded to be a door through which civilization could flow into the surrounding region. Hence Jesus speaks in terms of providing the Christians there "an open door" that "no one can shut" (3:7).

Laodicea *was* a wealthy city. When it had been destroyed by earthquake it did not need imperial assistance to rebuild; it was quite capable of doing so with its own resources. This admirable self-reliance could easily degenerate into spiritual arrogance when applied to one's need for religious commitment (3:17–18).

Each community was distinct, and locally significant allusions are made when most appropriate. (These are discussed in detail in the sequel volume.)

## The Social Realities

However prosperous a city or region might be, there was never a certainty that collectively or individually such prosperity could be guaranteed in the long term. Even prosperous communities faced the danger of short-term hunger and economic hardship. In these epistles John refers to the evils that might come upon the Christian element in those communities.

## Poverty and Wealth

In a society dominated by agriculture, poverty will not be as conspicuous as in an urban setting. Since most of those one lives around will be functioning on the same level of temporal success, everyone blends in in the countryside. In the cities (and all John's epistles were written to urban congregations) the varying levels of well-being would be painfully obvious.

Smyrna was a city whose Christian community was characterized by poverty (2:9). It has been reasonably speculated that this was produced by the "tribulation" (persecution) that they had endured (2:9), and that may well be the case. Indeed, their poverty was emotionally worsened because of the "blasphemy" of their monotheist Jewish opponents (2:9). Although this is often interpreted as a reference to their encouraging persecution of the followers of Jesus, it may also have a reference to the relative ease and prosperity of the Jewish community within the city. Indeed, since the Jewish society of the province is known to have been well established in most cities (and *that* status is almost invariably accompanied by economic well-being) it is a great probability. If there is anything worse than being poor, it is to see one's theological opponents enjoying all the blessings of prosperity.

If there is only modest evidence for Christian poverty in Asia, there is only one case of documented wealth. That is in the case of Laodicea, which could boast, "I am rich, have become wealthy, and have need of nothing" (3:17). The first two assertions are not questioned by John, only the dangerous conclusion they had drawn from their financial well-being.

## Hunger

The agricultural capacity of Asia was such that shortages could easily occur and these quickly develop into famine. Famines were normally short term and affected all of society. Those who were financially troubled were likely to encounter repeated bouts of at least temporary hunger, even in a period of societal prosperity. Alternately, their poverty would permit them only the cheaper and poorer quality foodstuffs.

Hence, when we read of poor Christians, we can reasonably infer their difficulties on this score. This situation is only explicitly referred to in Smyrna. Since it is referred to in connection with the persecution the Christians had endured (2:9), it is possible that these were *new* poor, poor caused by destruction or confiscation of goods due to their Christianity. If so, they at least had the prospect of—perhaps—recouping their losses if the local situation improved. The fact that the imprisonment some of them faced would last only ten days (2:10) would hold out that possibility. It could also mean that they would be imprisoned only a short period before facing the death penalty. But Smyrna enjoyed a reputation for civic moderation, and that argues for the first possibility as the more likely.

### Disease and Death

When Jesus promises the Ephesians access to the "tree of life" (2:7), not only the spiritual implications were likely to have come to their mind but also the fact that disease and death could strike with little warning and deny them their very existence. Jesus "was dead and came to life" (2:8); to the Smyrnians this was not only an assertion of Jesus' resurrection, but also a reminder of their own coming death. *That* was certain. Only the *timing* was an issue. Through Jesus they might escape that which was inevitable, even though enduring the pangs of it before being liberated from its hurt and pain. Afterward they would gain "the crown of life," the Smyrnians were assured (2:10).

Jesus held within his hands the power to "kill...with death" (2:23), and the implication of the text seems to be that this includes in the *present* world as well as in the future one.

### Divisiveness

Society will always have internal conflicts as it attempts to determine which set of policies is best. Differences can become self-perpetuating and excuses for never-ending conflict. In addition, there are misguided and futile policies—though seldom recognized as such by their advocates. When one is certain that the victory of a contrary approach is fundamentally antithetical to the interests of truth, it becomes a matter of the spiritual survival of one's own convictions.

Asia was wracked by controversies both small and great. Ephesus and Smyrna constantly warred for the position of economic pivot of Asia. Ephesus and Pergamon warred over the site of the Roman capital. Pergamon had been the initial capital, but over decades functions were gradually transferred to Ephesus until it became the de facto capital and, ultimately, the de jure one. The war with Smyrna was also won—more or less—but it remained such a vigorous competitor that things could (and eventually did) move the other way.

Although we do not read of conflicts between the Asian churches John addresses, we certainly read of vivid conflicts *within* them. As presented by the author of Revelation, these represented fundamental issues on which compromise could only be reached at the cost of selling out the moral foundation of Christianity. In Ephesus the pseudo-apostles were readily detected (2:2) and they had no problem rejecting the lifestyle advocated by the Nicolaitans (2:6).

Consistency did not always exist: one internal challenge might be rejected while another would be successful. In Pergamon, the believers had successfully resisted the temptation to apostatize in the face of severe persecution (2:13). Their danger came internally, from the moral subversion of the Nicolaitans (2:15) and the Balaamites (2:14).

The Thyatirans had exhibited great "love, service, faith" and "patience" (2:19) yet they were being controverted by those accepting compromise with idolatry (2:20). This was a particularly strong challenge because they claimed a kind of mystical insight into the "depths of Satan" (2:24) and used this to justify their practices.

## Men and Women

Although men dominated the public culture of the day (but to what extent public culture represented the real world in which most of life was lived is a totally different question), women played periodically important public roles as well. The gender proportion among the internal Nicolaitan (2:6; 2:15) and Balaamite (2:14) sectarians is unknown. At least one prominent local troublemaker was female and presented to the readers as a contemporary "Jezebel" (2:20). The lack of any other specific allusion to women would suggest that Asian heresies were, by and large, driven by male excesses rather than female ones.

These are some of the ways that John, probably without conscious effort, reflects the prevailing realities of the Romanized world to which he wrote. In the following volume we will go beyond this and document in detail how he reflected the *local* realities as well.

# Notes

## 1. OVERVIEW: FIRST-CENTURY ROMAN GOVERNMENT AND SOCIETY

1. Raymond W. Goldsmith, "An Estimate of the Size and Structure of the National Product in the Early Roman Empire," *Review of Income and Wealth* 30 (1984): 27.

2. Robert M. Grant, *Augustus to Constantine: The Thrust of the Christian Movement into the Roman World* (New York: Harper & Row, 1970), 11, prefers the larger figure. In his economic calculations Keith Hopkins assumes fifty-four million empire residents ("Taxes and Trade in the Roman Empire (200 B.C.–A.D. 400)," *Journal of Roman Studies* 70 [1980]: 119). Raymond W. Goldsmith works from only a slightly larger million (see "An Estimate," 270).

3. Stephen Mitchell estimates a population of 8,190,000 (*Anatolia: Land, Men, and Gods in Asia Minor,* vol. 1: *The Celts in Anatolia and the Impact of Roman Rule* [Oxford: Clarendon Press, 1993], 244).

4. J. C. Russell, *Late Ancient and Medieval Population* (Philadelphia: American Philosophical Society, 1958), 81, opts for a figure of 8,800,000. Although Russell argues for a total population roughly one-quarter less than that of Broughton (note 5), his estimates of the population of individual cities are typically far, far in excess of a 25 percent reduction. Hence he mainly "purchases" a lower urban population by assuming a larger rural one.

5. T. R. S. Broughton, "Roman Asia," in *An Economic Survey of Ancient Rome*, ed. Tenney Frank (Baltimore: Johns Hopkins Press, 1938), 4:815 (full page chart). He believes this may actually *under*estimate the population of the region by several million (816).

6. Working on the basis of his figure of 8,190,000 residents, Stephen Mitchell estimates that there were 910,000 city dwellers in the province and 7,280,000 rural ones. (*Anatolia,* 1:244).

7. Russell, *Population*. 81.

8. Broughton, "Roman Asia," 815, gives the figure of 4,600,000.

143

9. Goldsmith, "An Estimate," 270.

10. Edwin Yamauchi, *Harper's World of the New Testament* (San Francisco: Harper & Row, 1981), 100.

11. Ibid., 85.

12. Ibid., 86.

13. Ibid., 88. Although marriage by the lower ranks was not formally banned until A.D. 197 (88), the economics of military life would strongly argue that such enlistment-period marriages were unlikely to have been common, much less dominant.

14. William V. Harris, *Ancient Literacy* (Cambridge, Mass.: Harvard University Press, 1989), 274.

15. J. P. V. D. Balsdon, *Romans and Aliens* (Chapel Hill, N. C.: University of North Carolina Press, 1979), 135–36, discusses intra-Asian linguistic differences.

16. Mitchell, *Anatolia*, 1:174.

17. J. Nelson Kraybill, "Cult and Commerce in Revelation 18," Ph.D. diss., Union Theological Seminary, Richmond, Virginia, 1992, 63.

18. Ibid.

19. Steven M. Baugh, "Paul and Ephesus: The Apostle Among His Contemporaries," Ph.D. diss., University of California (Irvine), 1990, 54.

20. Kraybill, "Cult and Commerce," 63. Balsdon, *Romans and Aliens*, 52–53, cites various examples of the honor being bestowed upon Asians and those in adjoining provinces of Asia Minor.

21. Ibid.

22. Mary Gordon, "The Freedman's Son in Municipal Life," *Journal of Roman Studies* 21 (1931): 71.

23. Kraybill, "Cult and Commerce," 63.

24. A. N. Sherwin-White, "The Roman Citizenship: A Survey of Its Development into a World Franchise," in *Aufstieg und Niedergang der Romischen Welt* (Berlin: Walter de Gruyter, 1972), I, 2, 22.

25. Stephen Mitchell, in *The Cambridge Encyclopedia of Archaeology*, ed. Andrew Sheratt (New York: Crown Publishers/Cambridge University Press, 1980), 244.

26. Sherwin-White, "The Roman Citizenship," 51.

27. Ibid.

28. Ibid.

29. P. J. J. Botha, "The Historical Domitian—Illustrating Some Problems of Historiography," *Neotestamentica: Journal of the New Testament Society of South Africa* 23 (1989): 52.

30. For a discussion of the provincial power structure, see Kraybill, "Cult and Commerce," 63–66.

31. Steven Mitchell, "The Plancii in Asia Minor," *Journal of Roman Studies* 64 (1974): 27.

32. For a discussion of the system see Kraybill, "Cult and Commerce," 67–73. For the theoretical assumptions underlying it, also see Halvor Maxnes, "Patron-Client Relations and the New Community in Luke-Acts," in *The Social World of Luke-Acts: Models for Interpretation*, ed. Jerome H. Neyrey (Peabody, Mass.: Hendrickson Publishers, 1991), 241–52. For the use of the patron-client model as an interpretive tool for the understanding of the book of Hebrews, see David A. deSilva, "Exchanging Favor for Wrath," *Journal of Biblical Literature* 115 (Spring 1996): 91–116.

33. Ibid.

34. Ibid., 70.

35. Ibid.

36. Hopkins, "Taxes and Trade," 119.

37. Ibid.

38. Goldsmith, "An Estimate," 263.

39. Ibid.

40. Ibid.

41. Hopkins, "Taxes and Trade," 119.

42. Goldsmith, "An Estimate," 263.

43. John J. O'Rourke, "Roman Law and the Early Church," in *The Catacombs and the Colosseum: The Roman Empire as the Setting of Primitive Christianity*, ed. Stephen Benko and John J. O'Rourke (Valley Forge, Pa.: Judson Press, 1971).

44. Ibid.

45. Kraybill, "Cult and Commerce," 99: A. H. M. Jones, *The Roman Economy: Studies in Ancient Economic and Administrative History*, ed. P. A. Brunt (Oxford: Basil Blackwell, 1974), 141; A. H. M. Jones, *A History of Rome Through the Fifth Century*, vol. 2: *The Empire* (London: Macmillan, 1970), 261. Cf. A. H. M. Jones, *The Greek City: From Alexander to Justinian* (Oxford: Clarendon Press, 1940; 1971 reprint), 244. Ephesus is one specific port city where this percentage is documented. See Mitchell, *Anatolia*, 1:256–57.

46. Jones, *Roman Economy*, 141; Jones, *History of Rome*, 261.

47. O'Rourke, "Roman Law and the Early Church," 183. For a copy of the (translated) text of the customs law in effect for Ephesus, as revised in the first century A.D., see Fik Meijer and Onno van Nijf, *Trade, Transport and Society in the Ancient World: A Sourcebook* (London: Routledge, 1992), 80–81.

48. Jones, *History of Rome*, 261, cf. 262; Yamauchi, *World*, 84.

49. Paul-Louis, *Ancient Rome at Work: An Economic History of Rome from the Origins to the Empire*, trans. E. B. F. Wareing (1927; reprint New York: Barnes & Noble, 1965), 295.

50. William H. Stephens, *The New Testament World in Pictures* (Nashville, Tenn.: Broadman Press, 1987), 122. This volume includes both useful text and a multitude of photographs of ancient cities, idols, tools, and other items, many of which one does not usually find discussed or depicted.

51. Ibid., 45.

52. Claude Mosse, "The Economist," in *The Greeks*, ed. Jean-Pierre Vernant, trans. Charles Lambert and Teresa Lavender Fagan (Chicago: University of Chicago Press, 1995), 44–45. The March 1995 issue of *Biblical Archaeologist: Perspectives on the Ancient World from Mesopotamia to the Mediterranean* provides a useful discussion of ancient sailing vessels—their building, cargoes, harbors, and other ascertainable data. Of special interest are three articles: Steve Vinson, "Ships in the Ancient Mediterranean" (13–18), Nicolle Hirschfeld, "The Ship of Saint Paul, Part 1: Historical Background" (25–30), and Michael Fitzgerald, "The Ship of Saint Paul, Part 2: Comparative Archaeology" (31–39).

53. Ibid., 45.

54. Kraybill, "Cult and Commerce," 79.

55. Ibid., 91–92. Kraybill, however, interprets Revelation 18:17 as censure of Christians who in an earlier decade had followed the same trade. If so, it is odd that Marcion's fervent critics did not explicitly use against him the "evil" of his trade. Verses 12 and 13 of the same chapter list a number of products that Rome imported from the provinces. For an interesting rebuttal of the common assumption that John is here rebuking Rome's use ("prostitution") of the resources of the rest of the world for her own economic advancement, see Iaian Provan, "Foul Spirits, Fornication, and Finance: Revelation 18 from an Old Testament Perspective," *Journal for the Study of the New Testament* 64 (December 1996): 81–100.

56. Kraybill, "Cult and Commerce," 99.

57. John Ferguson presents the evidence that this trade went so far as the establishment of an actual Roman colony in China starting at about the beginning of the first century A.D. ("China and Rome," *Aufstieg und Niedergang der Römischen Welt* [Berlin: Walter de Gruyter, 1978], II, 9.2, 581–603). Manfred G. Rasschke has vigorously challenged the claim of a community of expatriate Romans in China ("New Studies in Roman Commerce with the East," *Aufstieg*

*und Niedergang der Romischen Welt* [Berlin: Walter de Gruyter, 1978], II, 9.2, 679–81).

58. Kraybill, "Cult and Commerce," 98.

59. Aelius Aristides, "Roman Oration," 12, in James H. Oliver, *The Ruling Power: A Study of the Roman Empire in the Second Century After Christ Through the Oration of Aelius Aristides* (Philadelphia: American Philosophical Society, 1953).

60. Kraybill, "Cult and Commerce," 98.

61. Ibid., 99.

62. Esther V. Hanse, *The Attalids of Pergamon*, 2d ed., rev. and exp. (Ithaca, N.Y.: Cornell University Press, 1971), 152. Cf. Paul-Louis, *Ancient Rome at Work*, 295.

63. Peter Garnsey, "Grain for Rome," in *Trade in the Ancient Economy*, ed. Peter Garnsey, Keith Hopkins, and C. R. Whittaker (Berkeley: University of California Press, 1983), 122.

64. Ibid.

65. Jones, *Roman Economy*, 163–64.

66. For a discussion of tax farming in Asia in particular, see W. T. Arnold, *The Roman System of Provincial Administration*, 3d ed., rev. E. S. Bouchier (Oxford: Oxford University Press, 1914; reprint Chicago: Ares Publishers, 1974), 88–89.

67. Ibid., 89–90.

68. Ramsay MacMullen, *Roman Social Relations: 508 B.C. to A.D. 284* (New Haven: Yale University Press, 1974), 34.

69. Ibid.

70. Ibid., 34–35.

71. Cato provided his slaves three *modii* of wheat per month when engaged in light labor, 4–4 1/2 when engaged in moderate labor, and 4.8–6 *modii* of the grain when involved in strenuous labor (Richard Duncan-Jones, *The Economy of the Roman Empire: Quantitative Studies*, 2d ed. [Cambridge: Cambridge University Press, 1982], 146). At the point when the Republic was coming to an end, the free wheat ration in Rome itself was set at 5 *modii* per individual (ibid.). In the days of Seneca an urban slave was given the same amount (ibid.).

72. Ibid.

73. Ibid.

74. On the extent of first-century food shortages and outright famine, see Bruce W. Winter, "Acts and Food Shortages," in *The Book of Acts in Its Graeco-Roman Setting*, vol. 2: *The Book of Acts in Its First-Century Setting*, ed. David W. J. Gill and Conrad Gempf (Grand Rapids, Mich.: William B. Eerdmans Publishing Company, 1994),

62–69. On the difficulty of determining grain yields in the Roman Empire (and hence the actual amount of grain available at any given time), see Philip Mayerson, "Wheat in the Roman World: An Addendum," *Classical Quarterly* 34 (1984), 243–45, reprinted in Philip Mayerson, *Monks, Martyrs, Soldiers, and Saracens: Papers on the Near East in Late Antiquity (1962–1993)* (Jerusalem: Israel Exploration Society in association with New York University, 1994), 222–23.

75.  Winter, "Acts and Food Shortages," 252 (note).

76.  Ibid., 252 (text).

77.  Ibid., 346.

78.  Kevin Greene, *The Archaeology of the Roman Economy* (Berkeley and Los Angeles: University of California Press, 1986), 59.

79.  Allan C. Johnson, *Egypt and the Roman Empire,* Jerome lectures, second series (Ann Arbor, Mich.: University of Michigan Press, 1951), 45.

80.  Greene, *Archaeology,* 69; Duncan-Jones, *Economy,* 10.

81.  Duncan-Jones, *Economy,* 10.

82.  Stephens, *Pictures,* 122. For photographs of different types of wagons used for travel, see 126–27.

83.  Ibid., 122–23.

84.  Ibid., 123.

85.  Mitchell, *Anatolia,* 1:134.

86.  Ibid.

87.  Ibid., 245–46.

88.  Ibid., 122.

89.  On the economic costs of sea shipment versus land shipment see Mitchell, *Anatolia,* 1:246–47.

90.  Ibid., 123.

91.  Ibid.

92.  Ibid.

93.  Ibid.

94.  Ibid., 122.

95.  Ibid., 123.

96.  Ibid.

97.  Ibid.

98.  Ibid.

99.  Diana Delia, *Alexandrian Citizenship During the Roman Principate* (Atlanta, Ga.: Scholars Press, 1991), 39–40.

100.  Ibid., 40.

101.  The term of service was set at this length under Augustus (13 B.C.). It was expanded to twenty-five years total service in A.D. 6. It was shortened to the previous twenty-year term as part of the offi-

cial reaction to the military revolt of A.D. 14 and then returned to twenty-five years the following year (H. M. D. Parker, *The Roman Legions* [1928; reprinted with minor corrections of factual errors, Chicago, Ill.: Ares Publishers, 1954, 1980], 212–13). This was later changed to the shorter period once again. Although land-based forces faced a career service of varying lengths, it remained shorter than that for the Navy. Under Vespasian anyone in the naval forces had to serve twenty-six years before being mustered out (Yvon Garlan, *War in the Ancient World–A Social History*, trans. Janet Lloyd [New York: W. W. Norton, 1975], 112).

102. Parker, *Legions*, 212–13.

103. Ibid., 214.

104. Sjef van Tilborg, *Reading John in Ephesus* (Leiden: E. J. Brill, 1996), 98–99.

105. Kraybill, "Cult and Commerce," 81. On recruitment of military forces from throughout the entire Asia Minor region (a substantially more restricted region), see Mitchell, *Anatolia*, 1:136–42. Michael P. Speidel ("Legionnaires from Asia Minor," *Aufstieg und Niedergang der Romischen Welt*, II, 7.2, 744) speaks vaguely of the "large numbers" provided by Asia Minor. The statistics he presents (731, 732) actually point in the opposite direction.

106. Steven J. Friesen, *Twice Neokoros: Ephesus, Asia and the Cult of the Flavian Imperial Family* (Leiden: E. J. Brill, 1993), 165, speaks in terms of one *cohort* (600 men) being stationed in Asia, a remarkably small number when one considers that even a single *legion* (6,000 men) would have been a modest commitment considering the size and total population of the province.

107. For the *non*-application of this generalization to Jerusalem, see Roy W. Davies, "Daily Life of the Roman Soldier Under the Principate," *Aufstieg und Niedergang der Romischen Welt* (Berlin: Walter de Gruyter, 1974), II, 1, 323. For Alexandria, see James M. Alexander's note in Aristides, *The Ruling Power*, 932.

108. Aristides, "Roman Oration," *Ruling Power*, 67a (Greek text of entire work, 982–91; English translation, 895–907). Graham Webster, *The Roman Imperial Army of the First and Second Centuries A.D.*, 3d ed. (Totowa, N.J.: Barnes & Noble Books, 1985), 35, dissents from the rural-basing assertion, dating urban basing as early as the first and second centuries.

109. Ramsay MacMullen, *Corruption and the Decline of Rome* (New Haven: Yale University Press, 1988), 215.

110. Ibid.

111. Ibid., 216.

112. Zosimus, 2.31ff., quoted in ibid., 210.

113. For quotations see ibid., 215.

114. Davies, "Daily Life," 321.

115. Tertullian, in Jones, *Greek City*, 212.

116. Jones, *Greek City*, 212.

117. Ibid.

118. Ibid. The specific case in which this occurred appears to be one related to the frontier guards based in Hierapolis.

119. Ibid., 212–13.

120. Ibid., 213. For civilian police auxiliaries in Pergamon, see van Tilborg, *Ephesus*, 98.

121. Davies, "Daily Life," 313.

122. Ibid., 323–24.

123. Ibid., 328–29.

124. Ibid., 330.

125. Ibid., 312–13.

126. Howard C. Kee, *Medicine, Miracle, and Magic in New Testament Times* (Cambridge: Cambridge University Press, 1986), 34–35.

127. For the Latin text and English translation of the calendar as of c. 225, see John Helgeland, "Roman Army Religion," in *Aufstieg und Niedergang der Romischen Welt* (Berlin: Walter de Gruyter, 1978), 16.2, 1481–86.

128. Ibid., 1479.

129. Tertullian, *Apologeticum* 16.8, trans. and quoted in ibid., 1476.

130. Tertullian, *Ad nationes* i.12, trans. and quoted in ibid.

131. Ibid., 1497–98. By this time the cult was also widespread in the civilian community. For a map of known third-century cities where Mithras was worshiped, see David Ulansey, "Solving the Mithraic Mysteries," *Biblical Archaeology Review* 20 (September/October, 1994), 42.

132. Samuel Laeuchi, "Urban Mithraism," *Biblical Archaeologist* 31 (1968), 74.

133. Ibid., 85.

134. Helgeland, "Roman Army Religion," 1498.

135. For a discussion of the similarities, see Gary Lease, "Mithraism and Christianity: Borrowings and Transformations, *Aufstieg und Niedergang der Romischen Welt* (Berlin: Walter de Gruyter, 1980), II, 23.2, 1318–26. Cf. Richard M. Krill, "Roman Paganism Under the Antonines and Severans," *Aufstieg und Niedergang der Romischen Welt* (Berlin: Walter de Gruyter, 1978), 16.1, 37.

136. Mithras was born in a cave, and in the early second cen-

tury Jesus' birthplace began to be attributed to a similar location. The celebration of Mithras's birth on December 25 is an even more obvious parallel, but the dating of Jesus' birth at that date is also a result of non-biblical theological speculation. Indeed, although scholars have placed Jesus' birth in every month of the year, December is one of the least likely ones: shepherds were rarely in the fields that late in the year, as they are presented as being in the New Testament narrative.

137. The broader ideals of redemption, a mediator between humankind and the Divine, and a resurrection are examples. The New Testament cites various Old Testament texts as at least *consistent* with such deductions and even as *explicit* proofs of them. In other words, the New Testament writers were reaching back to the Hebraic roots of their faith to establish their premises rather than grounding them in the convictions of the pagan world.

138. Some type of repeated ceremonial washings in Mithraism has been paralleled with baptism. However, baptism is presented in the New Testament as a one-time (rather than repeated) act. The chronology also differs: for Christianity baptism was the entrance act *into* the group rather than an act, as in Mithraism's washings, for those *already* in the group. Some type of cultic meal also appears to have been practiced, and that has been paralleled with the Lord's Supper. In Mithraism the meal seems centered on the triumph over death, while communion was centered on remembering the death of the group's originator and leader (Jesus), with only an implicit rather than explicit reference to his triumph over death.

139. Helgeland, "Roman Army Religion," 1498.

140. For the societal roots of this cult's popularity, see Gaston H. Halsberghe, *The Cult of Sol Invictus* (Leiden: E. J. Brill, 1972), 38–40.

141. For a discussion of this subject see H. Mary Smallwood, *The Jews Under Roman Rule: From Pompey to Diocletian*, vol. 20 of *Studies in Judaism in Late Antiquity*, ed. Jacob Neusner (Leiden: E. J. Brill, 1978), 127–28. Oddly, the matter of religious conflict—monotheism versus polytheism—is not mentioned.

142. Ibid.

143. For a consideration of the evidence for exceptions to the generalization of noncombat on the Sabbath, see Robert Goldenberg, "The Jewish Sabbath in the Roman World up to the Time of Constantine the Great," *Aufstieg und Niedergang der Romischen Welt* (Berlin: Walter de Gruyter, 1979), II, 19.1, 430–34.

144. Smallwood, *Jews Under Roman Rule*, 127–28.

145. Kraybill, "Cult and Commerce," 82–83 (notes).

146. Ibid., 82 (text).

147. Cf. ibid., 82–84.

148. J. P. V. D. Balsdon, *Rome: The Story of an Empire* (New York: McGraw-Hill Book Company, 1970), 170.

149. Thomas Wiedemann, *Emperors and Gladiators* (London: Routledge, 1992), 44.

150. Michael Grant, *Gladiators* (New York: Delacorte Press, 1967), 88.

151. Ibid.

152. Irene R. Arnold, "Festivals of Ephesus," *American Journal of Archaeology* 76 (1972): 22.

153. Ibid.

154. Ibid.

155. Friesen, *Twice Neokoros*, 98.

156. Ibid.

157. Grant, *Gladiators*, 56–57.

158. Ibid., 56.

159. Ibid.

160. Ibid., 88.

161. Arnold, "Festivals of Ephesus," 22.

162. John H. Humphrey, "Roman Games," *Civilization of the Ancient Mediterranean*, ed. Michael Grant and Rachel Kitzinger (New York: Charles Scribner's, 1988), 2:1162.

163. Ibid.

164. Ibid., 2:1163.

165. For interpretations of the nature of the banquet, see Marc Z. Brettler and Michael B. Poliakoff, "Rabbi Simeon ben Lakish at the Gladiator's Banquet: Rabbinic Observations on the Roman Arena," *Harvard Theological Review* 83 (January 1990): 93–97.

166. On the diet of gladiators, including that recommended by the physician Galen, see ibid., 97–98.

167. Grant, *Gladiators*, 49.

168. Ibid., 56.

169. Wiedermann, *Emperors and Gladiators*, 43.

170. Grant, *Gladiators,* 57.

171. Ibid.

172. John Scarborough, "Roman Medicine to Galen," *Aufstieg und Niedergang der Romischen Welt* (Berlin: Walter de Gruyter, 1993), II, 37.1, 44–46. Also see Kee, *Medicine, Miracle, and Magic*, 47–55.

173. Rufus of Ephesus, quoted in Kee, *Medicine, Miracle, and Magic*, 49.

174. For Soranus's thought, see Scarborough, "Roman Medicine to Galen," 46–47, and Yamauchi, *World*, 108. For an interesting lengthy quote from Soranus defining the qualities of a good midwife, see Scarborough, "Roman Medicine to Galen," 47. For a much longer extract from his writings on female medical problems, see Mary R. Lefkowitz and Maureen B. Fant, *Women's Life in Greece and Rome: A Sourcebook in Translation*, 2d ed. (Baltimore: Johns Hopkins University Press, 1992), 256–258.

175. For a concise summary of Galen's early years, see Stephen Benko, *Pagan Rome and the Early Christians* (Bloomington, Ind.: Indiana University Press, 1984), 140–42.

176. See the discussion in Kee, *Medicine, Miracle, and Magic*, 62.

177. Ibid., 60–61.

178. Ibid., 60.

179. Howard C. Kee presents a different though very similar psychological approach: the dreams were "confirmation of insights" he had *already* "gained through his combination of reason and experience" (*Medicine, Miracle, and Magic*, 61). To me, it seems more likely that they did *not* become full conclusions or "insights" *until* he had projected them into the mouth of the god, thereby gaining both assurance and authority for what he was about to do.

180. Yamauchi, *World*, 108. For a concise summary of Galen's medical views, see Kee, *Medicine, Miracle, and Magic*, 55–57.

181. Yamauchi, *World*, 108.

182. Kee, *Medicine, Miracle, and Magic*, 57.

183. F. F. Peters, *The Harvest of Hellenism: A History of the Near East from Alexander the Great to the Triumph of Christianity* (New York: Simon and Schuster, 1970), 401–2.

184. Felix Marti-Ibanez, *A Prelude to Medical History* (New York: Bloch Publishing Company, 1959), 202.

185. Ibid.

186. For an overview of ancient medicine, see the collection of studies in Irene and Walter Jacob, *The Healing Past: Pharmaceuticals in the Biblical and Rabbinic World* (Leiden: E. J. Brill, 1993), especially the articles by Samuel Kottek, "Medicinal Drugs in the Works of Flavius Josephus," 95–105, and Stephen Newmyer, "Asaph the Jew and Greco-Roman Pharmaceutics," 107–20. For archeological data related to medical knowledge of the Roman world in particular (derived from coins, statuettes, and other sources), see Robert North, "Medical Discoveries of Biblical Times" in *Scripture and Other Artifacts: Essays on the Bible and Archaeology in Honor of Philip J. King*,

ed. Michael D. Coogan, J. Cheryl Exum, and Lawrence E. Stager (Louisville, Ky.: Westminster/John Knox Press, 1994), 311–32.

187. Although it is impossible for modern people to put much faith in many of the ancient remedies for disease, occasionally contemporary self-confidence is challenged by one that seems to work in spite of its apparent unlikelihood. For an example, see Pinchas Amitai, "Scorpion Ash Saves Woman's Eyesight," *Bible Review* 11 (April 1995): 36–37.

188. Galen, quoted in Immanuel Jakobovits, *Jewish Medical Ethics: A Comparative and Historical Study of the Jewish Religious Attitude to Medicine and Its Practice* (New York: Bloch Publishing Company, 1959), 202.

189. Scarborough, "Roman Medicine to Galen," 34.

190. Epiketios, quoted in Harold Nielsen, *Ancient Ophthamological Agents: A Pharmacohistorical Study of the Collyria and Seals for Collyria Used During Roman Antiquity, as Well as of the Most Frequent Components of the Collyria*, trans. Lars McBridge (Odense, Denmark: Odense University Press, 1974), 9.

191. Plutarch, *Moralia*, 71A, quoted in Scarborough, "Roman Medicine to Galen," 33.

192. Cf. citations in ibid.

193. For quotations, see ibid., 35.

194. Claudius, quoted in ibid., 36.

195. Jones, *Greek City*, 219.

196. Ibid.

197. G. H. Horsley, "Doctors in the Graeco-Roman World," *New Documents Illustrating Early Christianity*, vol. 2 (Marrickville, Australia: Macquarie University, Ancient History Documentary Research Centre, 1982), 12.

198. Ibid.

199. Ibid.

200. Ibid., 13.

201. Ibid.

202. Plutarch, *Moralia*, 267A, quoted in Ramsay MacMullen, "Women in Public in the Roman Empire," *Historia* 29 (1980): 208.

203. Tertullian, *De virgin veland* 2.1, quoted in ibid., 209

204. Ibid.

205. Ibid., 217.

206. Ibid.

207. Cornelius Nepos, Preface to *Lives*, quoted in Waldo Sweet, *Sport and Recreation in Ancient Greece: A Sourcebook with Trans-*

*lations* (New York: Oxford University Press, 1987), 205, 207 (pictures are on the intervening page).

208. For a discussion of shifting customs concerning use of the baths, see the Roy B. Ward, "Women in Roman Baths," *Harvard Theological Review* 85 (April 1992): 125–47. On Christian use of the public baths in Asia Minor and other regions in the middle and late second century A.D., see ibid., 125–26.

209. E. R. Hardy, "The Priestess in the Greco-Roman World," *Churchman: A Quarterly Journal of Anglican Theology* 84 (1970): 266.

210. For an extract from Eunapius's *Lives of the Philosophers*, describing her life, see Lefkowitz and Fant, *Women's Life*, 333–34.

211. Horsley, "Doctors in the Graeco-Roman World," 16. For a survey of the inscriptional evidence, see 16–17.

212. Quoted in Lefkowitz and Fant, *Women's Life*, 265.

213. Ramsay MacMullen, "Late Roman Slavery," *Historia* 36 (1987): 255. He cites Egypt as an example of the maximum figure.

214. Goldsmith, "An Estimate," 270.

215. William V. Harris, "Towards a Study of the Roman Slave Trade," in *The Seaborne Commerce of Ancient Rome: Studies in Archaeology and History*, volume. 36 of *Memoirs of the American Academy in Rome*, ed. J. H. D'Arms and E. C. Kopff (Rome: American Academy in Rome, 1980), 117–18. He regards slavery in Egypt as representing only a little above 10 percent but implicitly regards this as an example of the *minimum* percentage rather than the maximum (as Ramsay MacMullen, note 213, above).

216. Goldsmith, "An Estimate," 270.

217. MacMullen, "Late Roman Slavery," 362 (of Pergamon, in particular, based upon Galen's contemporary population estimate), 375 (of "middle-sized or larger cities," in general). Working from the same source William V. Harris estimates 25 percent or just a little below ("Roman Slave Trade," 117, 133). William L. Westermann, *The Slave Systems of Greek and Roman Antiquity* (Philadelphia: American Philosophical Society, 1955), 127, works from Galen's figures also and arrives at a slave population of 33 percent in both Pergamon and other urban centers.

218. Westermann, *Slave Systems*, 127.

219. Broughton, "Roman Asia," 840.

220. Ibid., 840–41.

221. MacMullen, "Late Roman Slavery," 375; Westermann, *Slave Systems*, 127 (implied).

222. Varro, *Agriculture*, 1.17.2–3, quoted in Thomas Wiedemann, *Greek and Roman Slavery* (London: Routledge, 1981), 139–40.

223. MacMullen, "Peasants During the Principate," *Aufstieg und Niedergang der Romischen Welt* (Berlin: Walter de Gruyter, 1974), II, 1 256.

224. M. I. Finley, *The Ancient Economy* (Berkley and Los Angeles: University of California Press, 1973), 71.

225. Harris, "Roman Slave Trade," 122.

226. Westermann, *Slave Systems*, 30.

227. A. M. Duff, *Freedmen in the Early Roman Empire* (Oxford: Oxford University Press, 1928; reprint Cambridge: W. Heffer & Sons, 1958), 3.

228. Ibid., 3.

229. Ibid., 5.

230. Ibid., 6–7.

231. Harris, "Roman Slave Trade," 122–23. Stephen Mitchell, in *Anatolia*, 1:257, speaks of those provinces to the east of Roman Asia as being a major source of new slaves. William L. Westermann adds Syria to Asia Minor as an additional major supplier (*Slave Systems*, 97).

232. Varro, *De lingua latina* 8.21, quoted in M. I. Finley, *Economy and Society in Ancient Greece*, ed. Brent D. Shaw and Richard P. Satler (London: Chatto & Winus, 1981), 171.

233. Ibid.

234. Ibid.

235. Seneca, quoted in Yamauchi, *World*, 95.

236. S. Scott Bartchy surveys the evidence in *First-Century Slavery and the Interpretation of 1 Corinthians 7:21*, Dissertation Series, 11 (Missoula, Mont.: Society of Biblical Literature, 1973), 67–71.

237. Varro, *De Agricultura* I, xvii, 4, quoted in B. K. Workman, *They Saw It Happen in Classical Times: An Anthology of Eyewitnesses' Accounts of Events in the History of Greece and Rome, 1400 B.C.–A.D. 540* (Oxford: Basil Blackwell, 1964), 115.

238. Cicero, quoted in Yamauchi, *World*, 94.

239. This piece of data suggests that "slaves were free in their religious life as long as it did not interfere with their official duties" (John G. Gager, "Religion and Social Class in the Early Roman Empire," in Benko and O'Rourke, *The Catacombs and the Colosseum*, 111. Gager repeats this verbatim in his later *Kingdom and Community: The Social World of Early Christianity* (Englewood Cliffs, N.J.: Prentice-Hall, 1975), 105.

240. Gager, *Kingdom and Community*, 105.

241. Ibid.

242. For the Roman government, see T. M. Finn, "Social

Mobility, Imperial Civil Service, and the Spread of Early Christianity," *Studia Patristica* 17, 1 (Oxford: Pergamon Press, 1982), 31–37. Although training for future slave-bureaucrats began as early as the middle of the first century A.D., it was not formalized in the *Caput Africae* until the reign of Trajan (A.D. 98–117). It had a curriculum that was practical rather than theoretical and stressed math, Latin, and Greek. Completion often marked the beginning of a successful career. "Such was the prestige of the [Imperial bureaucratic] service that he could confidently expect to marry a freeborn woman even prior to manumission (normally out of the question for the slaveborn), to acquire important economic advantages (and so, wealth), and to exercise sometimes considerable power" (32).

243. Bartchy, *First-Century Slavery*, 63–64.

244. Juvenal, quoted in Yamauchi, *World*, 91.

245. Helmut Koester, *History, Culture, and Religion of the Hellenistic Age*, vol. 1 (Philadelphia: Fortress Press, 1982), 331.

246. Bartchy, *First-Century Slavery*, 80–81.

247. Ibid.

248. Ibid.

249. Ibid., 80.

250. Gager, "Religion and Social Class," 168.

251. Varro, *Agriculture*, 1.17.2–3, quoted in Wiedemann, *Greek and Roman Slavery*, 139–40.

252. Peter Garnsey and Richard Saller describe the phenomena as "dependent non-slave labour systems of one kind or another" rather than lumping them together under one conceptual catchphrase (*The Roman Empire: Economy, Society and Culture* [Berkeley and Los Angeles: University of California Press, 1987], 111). Fritz M. Heichelhem sees the first century A.D. as a period in which Asia saw "the principle of temporary feudal service evolve into one of 'inherited feudal service'" (*An Ancient Economic History*, vol. 3, trans. Mrs. Joyce Stevens [Leyden, Netherlands: A. W. Sijthoff, 1970], 155). G. E. M. de Ste. Croix sees the Roman presence as, on balance, a constructive one: it tended to raise the status of most serfs toward a free status while repressing to slave rank only a lesser number (*The Class Struggle in the Ancient Greek World–From the Archaic Age to the Arab Conquests* [Ithaca, N.Y.: Cornell University Press, 1981], especially 151–58, where he discusses the ambiguity of the evidence). He alludes to the fact that the situation had not become rigid by referring to "serfs and quasi-serfs" (172). Finley speaks in terms of serflike conditions but rejects the term "serfdom" itself because of the

danger of reading into it a medieval European meaning (*Ancient Economy*, 184–85).

253. Even the terminology used to describe the free and non-free tended to merge (MacMullen, "Late Roman Slavery," 378). A good example of the curbing of freedmen's rights can be seen in the treatment of the *coloni*. In A.D. 332 a proclamation was issued that any such individuals who abandoned their original estate to move to another place "must be bound with chains and reduced to a servile condition, so that they shall be compelled to fulfill the duties that befit a free man" (quoted in MacMullen [above], 378). When slavery is justified as teaching us freedom's obligations, the conceptual categories become whatever the speaker wants them to mean.

## 2. ROME AND ITS ASIAN PROVINCE

1. Enrich S. Gruen, *The Hellenistic World and the Coming of Rome*, vol. 2 (Berkeley and Los Angeles: University of California Press, 1984), 539.

2. For use of the term *eccentric* as his description and a discussion of the characteristics of his reign see ibid., 592–93.

3. Ibid., 593.

4. Ibid.

5. Esther V. Hansen, *The Attalids of Pergamon*, 2d ed., rev. and exp. (Ithaca, N.Y.: Cornell University Press, 1971), 148.

6. Cf. Gruen, *Hellenistic World*, which summarized various views, including this one (594–99).

7. See ibid., 593–94. Gruen sees the bequest as a power play against the danger that Aristonicus would take his place.

8. On the expansion as proof that Rome had gained the decisive balance of power in the region see Hansen, *Attalids*, 148–49; and Martin Robertson, *A History of Greek Art*, vol. 1 (Cambridge: Cambridge University Press, 1975), 537–38.

9. T. R. S. Broughton, "Roman Asia," in *An Economic Survey of Ancient Rome*, vol. 4, ed. Tenney Frank (Baltimore, Md.: Johns Hopkins Press, 1938), 505–6.

10. Anthony D. Marco, "The Cities of Asia Minor Under the Roman Imperium," *Aufstieg und Niedergang der Romischen Welt* (Berlin: Walter de Gruyter, 1980), II, 7.2, 663.

11. A. H. M. Jones, *The Decline of the Ancient World* (London: Longman, 1966), 10.

12. Morton S. Enslin, "Rome in the East," in *Religions in*

*Antiquity: Essays in Memory of Erwin Ramsdell Goodenough*, ed. Jacob Neusner (Leiden: E. J. Brill, 1968), 128.

13. Cicero, *Manilian Law*, 7, quoted in Neusner (above), 128.

14. W. T. Arnold, *The Roman System of Provincial Administration*, 3d ed., rev. E. S. Bouchier (Oxford: Oxford University Press, 1914; reprint Chicago: Ares Publishers, 1974), 94.

15. Ibid., 95.

16. Geoffrey Rickmann, *The Corn Supply of Ancient Rome* (Oxford: Clarendon Press, 1980), 60; E. Badian, *Publicans and Sinners: Private Enterprise in the Service of the Roman Republic* (Oxford: Basil Blackwell, 1972), 116, 157; Peter Garnsey, "Grain for Rome," in *Trade in the Ancient Economy*, ed. Peter Garnsey, Keith Hopkins, and C. R. Whittaker (Berkeley and Los Angeles: University of California Press, 1983), 122.

17. Rickmann, *Corn Supply*, 60.

18. Broughton, "Roman Asia," 542.

19. The publican percentage in Sicily was "probably...more than 10%" (Broughton [above], 542), and though that for Asia is unknown, one would naturally expect it to be similar. Broughton thinks it might well have been as high as a third because "the crops in the Asiatic provinces were more variegated and the yield less certain" (Broughton, 542). Since prosperity was, in that day and age, built on an agricultural foundation, and because Asia was renowned for its prosperity, such a downgrading of that province's agriculture seems improbable. On the other hand, the agricultural success of Asia was an example of willpower overcoming nature (William Ramsay, "A Sketch of the History of Asia Minor," *National Geographic* 42 [November 1922], 557), and these uncertainties might have been used to rationalize an increase in the usual percentage of profit. Regardless, the problem was not so much the margin of profit as the inflated publican demands.

20. Arnold, *Provincial Administration*, 95.

21. Cicero, *ad Qu. Fr.*, i. I, 11, quoted in ibid.

22. Jones, *Decline of the Ancient World*, 12.

23. Clive Foss, *Ephesus After Antiquity: A Late Antique, Byzantine, and Turkish City* (Cambridge: Cambridge University Press, 1979), 4–5, 181.

24. Among others are Cady H. Allen, *The Message of the Book of Revelation* (Nashville, Tenn.: Cokesbury Press, 1939), 63; Hermann Bengston, *History of Greece–From the Beginnings to the Byzantine Era*, trans. Edmund F. Bloedow (Ottawa, Canada: University of Ottawa Press, 1988), 326; James J. Draper, *The Unveiling* (Nashville,

Tenn.: Broadman Press, 1984), 54; Wilfried J. Harrington, *Revelation (Sacra Pagina*, vol. 16) (Collegeville, Minn.: Liturgical Press/A Michael Glazier Book, 1993), 62; Richard J. Jeske, *Revelation for Today: Images of Hope* (Philadelphia: Fortress Press, 1983), 46; Marcus L. Loane, *They Overcame: An Exposition of the First Three Chapters of Revelation* (n.p.; Angus and Robertson, 1971; reprint Grand Rapids, Mich.: Baker Book House, 1981), 56; Robert H. Mounce, *New International Commentary on Revelation* (Grand Rapids, Mich.: William B. Eerdmans Publishing Company, 1977), 9; Randall C. Webber, "Group Solidarity in the Revelation of John," in *Society of Biblical Literature 1988 Seminar Papers*, ed. Davis L. Lull (Atlanta, Ga.: Scholars Press, 1988), 134; Michael Wilcock, *I Saw Heaven Opened: The Message of Revelation* (London: Inter-Varsity Press, 1975), 47.

25. Among others are George E. Bean, *Aegean Turkey: An Archaeological Guide* (New York: Frederick A. Praeger, Publishers, 1966), 163; John A. Calkin, *Historical Geography of Bible Lands* (Philadelphia: Westminster Press, 1904), 105; Dan P. Cole, "Corinth and Ephesus: Why Did Paul Spend Half His Journeys in These Cities?" *Bible Review* 4 (December 1988), 27; Harry T. Frank, *An Archaeological Companion to the Bible* (Abingdon Press, 1971; London: SCM Press Ltd., 1972), 311; David French, "Acts and the Roman Roads of Asia Minor" in *The Book of Acts in Its Graeco-Roman Setting*, vol. 2 of *The Book of Acts in Its First-Century Setting*, ed. David W. J. Gill and Conrad Gempf (Grand Rapids, Mich.: William B. Eerdmans Publishing Company, 1994), 57; A. A. M. van der Heyden and H. H. Scullard, *Atlas of the Classical World* (London: Thomas Nelson & Sons, Ltd., 1959), 203; Alan F. Johnson, *Revelation* (Grand Rapids, Mich.: Zondervan Publishing House, 1983), 40; Helmut Koester, "Ephesos in Early Christian Literature," in *Ephesos: Metropolis of Asia–An Interdisciplinary Approach to Its Archaeology, Religion, and Culture*, ed. Helmut Koester, Harvard Theological Studies 41 (Valley Forge, Pa.: Trinity Press International, 1995), 265; Paul MacKendrick, *The Greek Stones Speak: The Story of Archaeology in Greek Lands*, 2d ed. (New York: W. W. Norton & Company, 1981), 466; Otto A. Meinardus, "The Christian Remains of the Seven Churches of Asia," in *Biblical Archaeologist Reader, IV*, ed. Edward F. Campbell Jr. and David Noel Freedman (Sheffield, England: Almond Press, 1983), 347; Ulrich B. Miller, "Apocalyptic Currents," trans. Annemarie S. Kidder, in *Christian Beginnings: Word and Community from Jesus to Post-Apostolic Times*, ed. Jurgen Becker (Louisville, Ky.: Westminster/John Knox Press, 1993), 311; Martin P. Nilsson, *Imperial Rome* (London: G. Bell & Sons Ltd., 1962; reprint New York: Schocken Books, 1967), 184; Richard E. Oster, "Numis-

matic Windows in the World of Early Christianity: A Methodological Inquiry," *Journal of Biblical Literature* 101 (1982), 216; Paul Petit, *Pax Romana*, trans. James Willis (London: B. T. Batsford, 1976), 102; W. M. Ramsay, *St. Paul the Traveller and the Roman Citizen* (New York: G. P. Putnam's Sons, 1896; reprint 1905), 274; C. Anderson Scott, *The Book of the Revelation* (New York: George H. Doran Company, [n.d.]), 53; Andrew Tait, *The Messages to the Seven Churches of Asia* (London: Hodder and Stoughton, 1884), 119.

26. It is presented as an unsettled issue by Steve Moyise, *The Old Testament in the Book of Revelation* (Sheffield, England: Sheffield Academic Press, 1995), 29, n.15. Paul W. Barnett merely refers to the question as one that "scholars debate" in his "Revelation in Its Roman Setting," *Reformed Theological Review* 50 (May-August 1991): 59.

27. J. P. W. Sweet, *Revelation* (Philadelphia: Westminster Press, 1979), 87. C. J. Hemer speaks vaguely of the eventual change of capital but does not provide an estimated date (C. J. Hemer, "Seven Cities of Asia Minor," in *Major Cities of the Biblical World*, ed. R. K. Harrison [Nashville, Tenn.: Thomas Nelson Publishers, 1985], 236). Edwin M. Yamauchi cautions that "there is some doubt as to how long Peramum remained the capital of the province before it yielded this title to Ephesus" (*The Archaeology of New Testament Cities in Western Asia Minor* [Grand Rapids, Mich.: Baker Book House, 1980], 41).

28. Francis Lyall, *Slaves, Citizens, Sons: Legal Metaphors in the Epistles* (Grand Rapids, Mich.: Academie Books/Zondervan Publishing House, 1984), 230.

29. Alan Johnson uses the phase, while later noting that the official capital remained at Pergamon ("Revelation," in *The Expositor's Bible Commentary*, vol. 12, ed. Frank E. Gaebelin [Grand Rapids, Mich.: Zondervan Publishing House, 1981], 439-40). Theodor Mommsen does as well in his *The Provinces of the Roman Empire*, vol. 1, trans. William P. Dickson (London: 1909; reprint Chicago: Ares Publishers, 1974), 329-30. Cf. the similar distinction of W. W. Tarn, *Hellenistic Civilization*, 3d ed., rev. W. W. Tarn and G. T. Griffith (London: Edward Arnold & Company, 1952), 173. Although she does not use the terms, Wendy Cotter clearly presents Pergamon as the de jure capital and Ephesus as the de facto one in her study "Women's Authority Roles in Paul's Churches: Countercultural or Conventional?" *Novum Testamentum: An International Quarterly for New Testament and Related Studies* 36 (October 1994): 357-58.

30. Cecil J. Cadoux, *Ancient Smyrna: A History from the Earliest Times to 324 A.D.* (Oxford: Basil Blackwell, 1938), refers to Ephesus

twice as the capital (147, 149); a third time he expresses the more modest claim of it being "the virtual capital" (228).

31. Cuthbert H. Turner, *Studies in Early Church History* (Oxford: Clarendon Press, 1912), 206.

32. Guy Pentreath, "Early Christianity in 'Asia,'" in *Geology and History of Turkey*, ed. Angus S. Campbell (Tripoli, Libya: Petroleum Exploration Society of Libya, 1971), 42.

33. Stewart Perowne, *Archaeology of Greece and the Aegean* (New York: A Studio Book/Viking Press, 1974), 122.

34. Stewart Perowne, *The Journeys of St. Paul* (London: Hamlyn, 1973), 75.

35. 30 B.C.: Alan W. Johnston and Malcolm A. R. Colledge, "The Classical World," in *Atlas of Archaeology*, ed. K. Branigan (New York: St. Martin's Press, 1982), 73.

29 B.C.: Steven J. Friesen, *Twice Neokoros: Ephesus, Asia and the Cult of the Flavian Imperial Family* (Leiden: E. J. Brill, 1993), 158.

Clive Foss hedges: "Ephesus had *apparently* been the capital of Roman Asia since Augustus" (*Ephesus After Antiquity*, 4, emphasis added). Rivka Gonen provides no specific dating beyond Augustus's reign (*Biblical Holy Places–An Illustrated Guide* [Jerusalem: Palphot Ltd., 1987], 264; cf. 272). Paul Trebilco uses the term "probably" to describe Ephesus becoming capital under this ruler in his essay "Asia," in Gill and Gempf, *The Book of Acts in Its Graeco-Roman Setting*, 304.

S. M. Baugh speaks of the city as being "confirmed" as capital during a visit by Augustus in his study "A Foreign World: Ephesus in the First Century," in *Women in the Church: A Fresh Analysis of 1 Timothy 2:9–15*, ed. Andreas J. Kostenberger, Thomas R. Schreiner, and H. Scott Baldwin (Grand Rapids, Mich.: Baker Book House, 1995), 17. Properly speaking, "confirmed" implies that the change had already been made; Augustus, therefore, was confirming rather than initiating the shift from Pergamon. On the other hand, the author may simply be claiming that Augustus had made the decision prior to his visit and that he "confirmed" it during his stay.

36. Cemil Toksoz, *Ephesus: Legends and Facts*, trans. Amhmet E. Uysal (Akara, Turkey: Ayyildiz Matbaasi As, 1969), 15.

37. Michael Avi-Yonah, "End of the First Century," *Views of the Biblical World*, vol. 5 of *The New Testament* (Jerusalem: International Publishing Company Ltd., 1961), 271.

38. William M. Ramsay, "Ephesus," *Biblical World* 17 (1901), 168–69. Christine Trevett dates it as "c. 125 C.E." in *The Study of*

*Ignatius of Antioch in Syria and Asia* (Lewiston, N.Y.: Edwin Mellen Press, 1992), 78.

39. Friesen, *Twice Neokoros*, 158.

40. Ibid.

41. Ramsay dates the establishment of the official residence of the governor in Ephesus as "soon after 100 A.D." ("Ephesus," 168). T. R. S. Broughton believed that Ephesus was the capital ("Roman Asia," 538). Yet, 170 pages later he implicitly concedes that this is an assumption rather than a certainty: He mentions that the centralization of the proconsul and tax offices at Ephesus "was probably an old custom" but was only "stereotyped in law when a rescript of Antoninius Pius commanded all governors of Asia to touch there first" (708).

42. Charles C. Whiting, *The Revelation of John* (Boston: Gorham Press, 1918), 77, sees Pergamon losing the battle for popular recognition "as the capital" in the second century A.D.

43. For a discussion of some of these points see Richard J. Cassidy, *Society and Politics in the Acts of the Apostles* (Maryknoll, N.Y.: Orbis Books, 1987), 84.

44. David Magie, *Roman Rule in Asia Minor to the End of the Third Century After Christ* (Princeton, N.J.: Princeton University Press, 1950; reprint Salem, N.H.: Ayer Company, Publishers, 1988), 506–7. Although issued in two volumes (the first consisting exclusively of text and the second of footnotes and related material) the page numbers are consecutive and continue uninterrupted in the second volume. Hence volume number references are omitted.

45. K. M. T. Atkinson, "The Governors of the Province of Asia in the Reign of Augustus," *Historia* 7 (1958), 308–9.

46. Magie, *Asia Minor*, 506.

47. Ibid.

48. Ibid., 1363, which refers to one scholar's suggestion of this as a motive to turn down the post.

49. Charles E. Smith, *Tiberius and the Roman Empire* (Baton Rouge, La.: Louisiana State University Press, 1942), 203–5, argues that Tacitus slanted his reporting of the case in behalf of the accused.

50. M. H. Sitwell, *Roman Roads of Europe* (New York: St. Martin's Press, 1981), 192.

51. Atkinson, "Governors of the Province of Asia," 300.

52. For some of the reasons see ibid., 303. For a list of known governors in Asia from 131 B.C. to A.D. 276, see Magie, *Asia Minor*, 1581–83.

53. Friesen, *Twice Neokoros*, 44.

54. Steven M. Baugh, "Paul and Ephesus: The Apostle Among His Contemporaries," Ph.D. diss., University of California (Irvine), 1990, 47.

55. Ibid., 27

56. R. A. G. Carson, *Coins of the Roman Empire* (London: Routledge, 1990), 273.

57. For a discussion, see Ramsay MacMullen, "Imperial Bureaucrats in the Roman Provinces," *Harvard Studies in Classical Philology*, 68 (1964), 305–16. For their direct reporting authority, see 307.

58. Ibid., 306–7.

59. Ibid., 311.

60. Petit, *Pax Romana*, 83–84; Badian, *Publicans and Sinners*, 60. We find a similar pattern of assuming the property of local royalty when Rome took over Cappadocia and Phrygia (Petit, *Pax Romana*, 83–84).

61. T. R. S. Broughton argues that the confiscation-of-profits approach rests on a major *mis*reading of the evidence ("New Evidence on Temple-Estates in Asia Minor," in *Studies in Roman Economic and Social History–in Honor of Allen Chester Johnson*, ed. P. R. Coleman-Norton with the assistance of F. C. Bourne and J. B. A. Find [Princeton: Princeton University Press, 1951], 236–50). Barbara Levick vigorously criticizes the temple-land-seizure theory and the assumption that ancient governments believed that all land within their borders was automatically government owned (*Roman Colonies in Southern Asia Minor* [Oxford: Clarendon Press, 1967], 215–23). She argues that when ancient Asian governments seized property it was simply the exercise of naked power rather than the expression of some *theoretical* expression of complete control (217–18).

62. Badian, *Publicans and Sinners*, 132.

63. Barbara Levick cautions against exaggerating the admittedly large amount of imperial land ownership in the province (*Roman Colonies*, 224–26). For a discussion of the amount of land owned and when individual properties became imperially owned, see Broughton, "Roman Asia," 648–63.

64. G. P. Burton, "Proconsuls, Assizes, and the Administration of Justice Under the Empire," *Journal of Roman Studies* 65 (1975), 92. Cf. Jones, *Greek City: From Alexander to Justinian* (Oxford: Clarendon Press, 1940; reprint 1971), 123.

65. G. P. Burton, "Proconsuls, Assizes, and the Administration of Justice," 92–93. Of an unspecified period earlier than this,

A. H. M. Jones indicates there were twelve judicial districts in Asia. He specifically lists five of the seven church/cities of John's Revelation: Ephesus, Pergamon, Laodicea, Smyrna, and Sardis (*Greek City*, 123).

66. In Burton, "Proconsuls, Assizes, and the Administration of Justice," 93.

67. Ibid.

68. Ibid.

69. Ibid. For a discussion emphasizing the importance of this inscription, see Christian Habicht, "New Evidence on the Province of Asia," *Journal of Roman Studies* 65 (1975), 64–91.

70. Burton, "Proconsuls, Assizes, and the Administration of Justice," 94.

71. Ibid.

72. The evidence is very skimpy and rests primarily upon the grounds of efficiency. See Marco, "Cities of Asia Minor," 670–71.

73. Ibid., 671.

74. Robert K. Skerk, *Roman Documents from the Greek East: "Senatus Consulta" and "Epistulae" to the Age of Augustus* (Baltimore: Johns Hopkins Press, 1969), 336.

75. Ibid., 334; Lily Ross Taylor, *The Divinity of the Roman Emperor* (Middletown: American Philological Association, 1931; reprint Philadelphia, Pa.: Porcupine Press, 1975), 205.

76. Taylor, *Divinity*, 273. The longest surviving version of the assembly's calendar-changing decree (eighty-four lines), and the accompanying correspondence of the Roman governor, comes from Priene; fragments have survived from four other cities (Robert K. Sherk, *Roman Documents from the Greek East: "Senatus Consulta" and "Epistulae" to the Age of Augustus* [Baltimore: Johns Hopkins Press, 1969], 328). For original language texts of these documents see Sherk, *Roman Documents*, 329–33.

### 3. CHARACTERISTICS OF LIFE IN ROMAN ASIA

1. W. M. Ramsay, *The Historical Geography of Asia Minor*, vol. 4 of Royal Geographical Society: Supplementary Papers (London: John Murray, 1890), 23.

2. Ibid.

3. J. Mckee Adams, *Biblical Backgrounds* (Nashville, Tenn.: Broadman Press, 1965), 181–82.

4. T. R. S. Broughton, "Roman Asia," in *An Economic Survey*

*of Ancient Rome*, ed. Tenney Frank (Baltimore: Johns Hopkins Press, 1938), 603.

   5. Ibid.
   6. Ibid.
   7. Ibid.
   8. Ibid.
   9. Ibid.
  10. Ibid.
  11. Emil Ilhan, "Earthquakes in Turkey," in *Geology and History of Turkey*, ed. Angus S. Campbell (Tripoli, Libya: Petroleum Exploration Society of Libya, 1971), 431.
  12. Ibid.
  13. Ibid.
  14. Ibid., 433.
  15. Ibid.
  16. Broughton, "Roman Asia," 601.
  17. Shimon Applebaum, *Jews and Greeks in Ancient Cyrene* (Leiden: E. J. Brill, 1979), 268.
  18. Broughton, "Roman Asia," 601.
  19. Ibid.
  20. M. Rostovtzeff, *The Social and Economic History of the Roman Empire*, 2d ed., rev. P. M. Fraser (Oxford: Clarendon Press, 1957), 563. (Two volumes with consecutive page numbering throughout.).
  21. Edward T. Salmon, *A History of the Roman World–From 30 B.C. to A.D. 138*, 5th ed. (London: Methuen & Company, 1966), 143.
  22. Robert S. Rogers, *Studies in the Reign of Tiberius* (Baltimore, Md.: Johns Hopkins Press, 1943), 16. Cf. T. R. S. Broughton's reference to such a quake "before 30 A.D." (601). On the basis of Tiberius's earlier earthquake relief, Rogers believes that some type of special imperial bequest likely occurred in this instance as well.
  23. Salmon, *Roman World*, 143.
  24. Rostovtzeff, *Roman Empire*, 563.
  25. Broughton, "Roman Asia," 601.
  26. K. M. T. Atkinson, "The Governors of the Province of Asia in the Reign of Augustus," *Historia* 7 (1958), 308–9.
  27. Charles E. Smith, *Tiberius and the Roman Empire* (Baton Rouge, La.: Louisiana State University Press, 1942), 209.
  28. Clarence A. Wendel, "Land-tilting or Silting? Which Ruined Ancient Harbors?" *Archaeology* 22 (1969), 323.
  29. Tacitus, *The Annals* II.47 (Bohn's Classical Library Translation).

30. Ibid.

31. Frank B. Marsh, *The Reign of Tiberius* (Oxford: Oxford University Press, 1931), 156.

32. Ibid. Tacitus refers to Tiberius's promise of "a hundred thousand great sesterces" to underwriting the rebuilding (*Annals*, II.47). Dio's *Roman History* (LVII.17) cites both Tiberius's acts of omission (tax relief) and commission (financial aid) as working together to encourage the rebuilding of the devastated area: "The cities in Asia which had been damaged by the earthquakes were assigned to an ex-praetor with five lictors; and large sums of money were remitted from their taxes and large sums were also given them by Tiberius."

33. "Nor did he ever relieve the provinces by any act of generosity, excepting Asia, where some cities had been destroyed by an earthquake" (*Tiberius*, 48; see the entire section for Suetonius's censure of the emperor).

34. G. W. Bowersock, *Augustus and the Greek World* (Oxford: Clarendon Press, 1965), 99.

35. Marsh, *Tiberius*, 156.

36. Ibid.

37. Donald Strong, *Roman Art*, prepared for press by J. M. C. Toynbee, rev. and annotated by Roger Ling (Middlesex, England: Penguin Books, 1988), 165.

38. Ibid.

39. George M. A. Hanfmann, *From Croessus to Constantine: The Cities of Western Asia Minor and Their Arts in the Greek and Roman Times*, Jerome lectures, tenth series (Ann Arbor, Mich.: University of Michigan Press, 1975), 51. For a detailed discussion of Roman architecture in Asia, also see J. B. Ward-Perkins, *Roman Imperial Architecture* (London: Penguin Books, 1981), 273–306.

40. Hanfmann, *From Croessus to Constantine*, 51. For a photograph illustrating the thickness of many Asian walls, see that of the early-third-century Serapaeum at Pergamon, where Egyptian deities were worshiped (Ward-Perkins, *Roman Imperial Architecture*, 285).

41. Ross S. Kraemer, "Hellenistic Jewish Women: The Epigraphical Evidence," in *Society of Biblical Literature Seminar Papers Series: 1986*, ed. Kent H. Richards (Atlanta, Ga.: Scholars Press, 1986), 193.

42. For a discussion of surviving inscribed curses upon grave disturbers that have been found in both Asia and surrounding provinces, see J. H. M. Strubbe, "Cursed Be He That Moves My Bones," in *Magika Hiera: Ancient Greek Magic and Religion*, ed.

Christopher A. Faraone and Dirk Obbink (New York: Oxford University Press, 1991), 33–59.

43. William Ramsay, "Ephesus," *Biblical World* 17 (1901): 167.

44. Martin P. Nilsson, *Imperial Rome* (London: G. Bell & Sons, 1962; reprint New York: Schocken Books, 1967), 185.

45. Aelius Aristides, from his eulogy "To Rome," quoted by Anthony D. Marco, "The Cities of Asia Minor Under the Roman Imperium," *Aufstieg und Niedergang der Romischen Welt* (Berlin: Walter de Gruyter, 1980), 673.

46. Ibid., 676.

47. Ibid.

48. Broughton, "Roman Asia," 800. This is so different from the practice in other regions that it *could* be explained as the result of a lack of relevant data having survived.

49. A. H. M. Jones, *The Greek City: From Alexander to Justinian* (Oxford: Clarendon Press, 1940; reprint 1971), 245.

50. Ibid.

51. Broughton, "Roman Asia," 800; Jones, *Greek City*, 245.

52. Jones, *Greek City*, 245.

53. Broughton, "Roman Asia," 798.

54. Ibid.

55. Jones, *Greek City*, 247.

56. Broughton, "Roman Asia," 798; Jones, *Greek City*, 246–47.

57. Jones, *Greek City*, 246.

58. Ibid.

59. Ibid.

60. Broughton, "Roman Asia," 802.

61. Marco, "Cities of Asia Minor," 684. Cf. L. William Countryman, "Welfare in the Churches of Asia Minor Under the Early Roman Empire," *Society of Biblical Literature 1979 Seminar Papers*, vol. 1, ed. Paul J. Achtemeier (Atlanta, Ga.: Scholars Press, 1979), 141.

62. Jones, *Greek City*, 247.

63. Broughton, "Roman Asia," 804.

64. Jones, *Greek City*, 247.

65. Broughton, "Roman Asia," 804.

66. Ibid., 802.

67. Jones, *Greek City*, 248–49.

68. Cf. ibid., 249.

69. Broughton, "Roman Asia," 804. Here, of course, the key was the *nature* of the expenditure: an aqueduct would remain of great value for many decades regardless of maintenance expenditures;

ornamental statues might flatter the giver but only be a maintenance expense for the next generation.

70. Ibid.

71. Ibid., citing nearby Bithynia in the days of Pliny as an example.

72. Ibid., 805.

73. Ibid., 805–6.

74. Ibid., 804–5.

75. Implied in Ibid., 805.

76. Ibid., 806.

77. Ibid., 808.

78. Ibid., 806.

79. Ibid.

80. Ibid., 807.

81. Ibid.

82. Ibid.

83. Ibid., 807–8. The emperors, however, were suspicious of voluntary associations that might become the focus of opposition to the regime. Hence one emperor refused to grant permission to form a volunteer firefighting group in a nearby province (ibid., 808).

84. William M. Ramsay, *The Social Basis of Roman Power in Asia Minor* (Aberdeen, Scotland: Aberdeen University Press, 1941; reprint Amsterdam: Adolf M. Hakkert, Publisher, 1967), 251.

85. Marco, "Cities of Asia Minor," 668–69.

86. Ramsay, *Social Basis*, 251–52.

87. Pliny, quoted in Marco, "Cities of Asia Minor," 669.

88. Ibid.

89. Raymond W. Goldsmith, "An Estimate of the Size and Structure of the National Product in the Early Roman Empire," *Review of Income and Wealth* 30 (1984): 276.

90. Keith Hopkins, "Taxes and Trade in the Roman Empire (200 B.C.–A.D. 400)," *Journal of Roman Studies* 70 (1980): 104.

91. Ibid.

92. Ramsay MacMullen, "Peasants During the Principate," *Aufstieg und Niedergang der Romischen Welt* (Berlin: Walter de Gruyter, 1974), II, 1, 259–60. On theories of the nature of cities in the ancient world, see Richard L. Rohrbaugh, "The Pre-industrial City in Luke-Acts: Urban Social Relations," in *The Social World of Luke-Acts: Models for Interpretation*, ed. Jerome H. Neyrey (Peabody, Mass.: Hendrickson Publishers, 1991), 125–36. For an analysis of rural society in the first century, see Douglas E. Oakman, "The Countryside in Luke-Acts," in Neyrey, *The Social World of Luke-Acts,*

151–64. On rural living conditions throughout the entire Asia Minor region in particular, see Stephen Mitchell, *Anatolia: Land, Men, and Gods in Asia Minor*, vol. 1: *The Celts in Anatolia and the Impact of Roman Rule* (Oxford: Clarendon Press, 1993), 196–97.

93. Ramsay MacMullen, *Roman Social Relations: 508 B.C. to A.D. 284* (New Haven: Yale University Press, 1974), 24–25.

94. Stephen Mitchell, *Anatolia: Land, Men, and Gods in Asia Minor*, vol. 2: *The Rise of the Church* (Oxford: Clarendon Press, 1993), 16.

95. Implied in ibid.

96. Ibid.

97. William Ramsay, "A Sketch of the History of Asia Minor," *National Geographic* 42 (November 1922), 557.

98. Peter Garnsey, *Famine and Food Supply in the Graeco-Roman World: Responses to Risk and Crisis* (Cambridge: Cambridge University Press, 1988), 55.

99. Ibid.

100. Ibid.

101. Colin J. Hemer, *The Letters to the Seven Churches of Asia in Their Local Setting*, Journal for the Study of the New Testament Supplement Series 11 (Sheffield, England: University of Sheffield, 1986), 158.

102. Garnsey, *Famine and Food Supply*, 256.

103. Ibid.

104. "Among the first after the fatherland," that is, Italy, was how the emperor worded it. This did not give Ephesus *absolute* priority but put it in that top level of *secondary* markets for surplus grain (as quoted in ibid., 257).

105. Ibid., 256–67.

106. Ibid.

107. For the probable double motivation of this policy, see Barbara Levick, "Domitian and the Provinces," *Latomus* 41 (1982), 67; cf. David Magie, *Roman Rule in Asia Minor to the End of the Third Century After Christ* (Princeton, N.J.: Princeton University Press, 1950; reprint Salem, N.H.: Ayer Company, Publishers, 1988), 580, 1443.

108. For a discussion of the famine and a possible reference to the high price of grain at the time being embodied in Revelation 6:6, see Magie, *Asia Minor*, 580–82, 1443–44. Sherman E. Johnson is among those who also see a reference to the famine in that passage ("The Apostle Paul and the Riot in Ephesus," *Lexington Theological Quarterly* 14 [October 1979], 87). The assumption among such inter-

preters, of course, is that Revelation is to be dated late in the first century rather than c. Nero's reign and immediately thereafter.

109. On Philadelphia's dependence and on economic injury as a prime cause for local outrage, see Hemer, *Local Setting*, 159.

110. Magie, *Asia Minor*, 580.

111. Levick, "Domitian and the Provinces," 57. Levick provides an effective rebuttal of the claim that this humanitarian gesture was produced by the direct order of Domitian (57–60). She reasons that by the time the two months had passed that would have been required to send a message to Rome and to receive a response back, the people "could have starved." Hence the legate would have been compelled to act on his own initiative if positive action were to be taken in time to salvage the situation.

112. Magie, *Asia Minor*, 580–82.

113. Marco, "Cities of Asia Minor," 659–60.

114. Cicero, quoted in Guy Pentreath, "Early Christianity in 'Asia,'" in *Geology and History of Turkey*, ed. Angus S. Campbell (Tripoli, Libya: Petroleum Exploration Society of Libya, 1971), 40.

115. Ramsay, "History of Asia Minor," 555.

116. Magie, *Asia Minor*, 582; cf. 1444.

117. George A. Barton, *Archaeology and the Bible*, 7th ed., rev. (Philadelphia: American Sunday-School Union, 1937), 264–65.

118. In contrast to the earlier view, which substantially overstated both the degree and pervasiveness of the decline. Cf. Mitchell, "Roman Empire in the East," in *The Cambridge Encyclopedia of Archaeology*, ed. Andrew Sherratt (New York: Crown Publishers/Cambridge University Press, 1980), 244.

119. Ibid.

120. Jones, *Greek City*, 216.

121. Ibid.

122. In ibid.

123. Ibid.

124. See ibid. for an example of this power being exercised in Greece proper.

125. The surviving text is incomplete and the exact nature of the cause of the delay is uncertain. For the Greek text and a discussion of the incident, see W. H. Buckler, "Labour Disputes in Asia Minor," in *Anatolian Studies–Presented to Sir William Mitchell Ramsay*, ed. W. H. Buckler and W. M. Calder (Manchester, England: Manchester University Press, 1923), 33–34.

126. For the full text in both Greek and English, see ibid., 30–31.

127. For full Greek and English texts, see ibid., 36–40.

128. Jules Toutain, *The Economic Life of the Ancient World*, trans. M. R. Dobie (London: Kegan Paul, Trench, Trubner & Co. Ltd., 1930), 306.

129. J. Nelson Kraybill, "Cult and Commerce in Revelation 18," Ph.D. diss., Union Theological Seminary, Richmond, Virginia, 1992, 55, for these specific cities; for Asia in general as a source, see Toutain, *Economic Life*, 307.

130. Kraybill, "Cult and Commerce," 55.

131. Ibid., for Smyrna; for the province as a source, see Smith, *Tiberius*, 209.

132. Smith, *Tiberius*, 209.

133. *The Geography of Strabo*, 14:1.15 (Greek text with English translation by Horace Leonard Jones [Loeb Classical Library]), bks. 10–12 (London: William Heinemann, 1928); bks. 13–14 (London: William Heinemann, 1929).

134. Toutain, *Economic Life*, 306; Smith, *Tiberius*, 209. On the varying techniques of Roman wine making, see E. Loeta Tyree and Evangelia Stefanoundaki, "The Olive Pit and Roman Oil Making," *Biblical Archaeologist: Perspectives on the Ancient World from Mesopotamia to the Mediterranean* 59 (September 1996): 171–78.

135. Smith, *Tiberius*, 209.

136. Ibid.

137. Edwin Yamauchi, *Harper's World of the New Testament* (San Francisco: Harper & Row, 1981), 103.

138. Toutain, *Economic Life*, 306.

139. Ibid.

140. Ibid., 307, from Pergamon in particular.

141. Smith, *Tiberius*, 209; Mitchell, "Roman Empire in the East," 244.

142. Smith, *Tiberius*, 209.

143. Ibid.; Yamauchi, *World*, 103; Mitchell, "Roman Empire in the East," 244.

144. Although not located in Asia itself, modern excavation has turned up an extraordinary amount of high-quality sculpture in local marble that was produced in Aphrodisias (Nancy M. Ramage and Andrew Ramage, *Roman Art–Romulus to Constantine* [New York: Harry N. Abrams, 1991], 107).

145. Toutain, *Economic Life*, 306; Mitchell, "Roman Empire in the East," 244.

146. Michael H. Balance and Olwen Brogan, "Roman Marble: A Link Between Asia Minor and Libya," in *Geology and History of*

*Turkey*, ed. Angus S. Campbell (Tripoli, Libya: Petroleum Exploration Society of Libya, 1971), 34.

147. For discussion of these techniques, see ibid.

148. Machteld J. Mellink, "Archaeology in Asia Minor," *American Journal of Archaeology*, 81 (1977), 308. For a map of Roman-era quarries located from Italy eastward to and including Asia Minor, see Keith Muckelroy, *Archaeology Under Water: An Atlas of the World's Submerged Sites* (New York: McGraw-Hill Book Company, 1980), 58, which shows that Asia Minor had a greater proportion than any other. For a slightly different map of the sites (but more effective because reproduced in color), see Peter Throckmorton and A. J. Parker, "A Million Tons of Marble," in *The Sea Remembers: Shipwrecks and Archaeology*, ed. Peter Throckmorton (New York: Weidenfeld & Nicolson, 1987), 75.

149. Peter Throckmorton, "Romans on the Sea," in *History of Seafaring–Based on Underwater Archaeology*, ed. George F. Bass (New York: Walker and Company, 1872), 75. For a picture of a diver investigating this ruin, see page 79, with accompanying description on the preceding page.

150. For a discussion of Greek inscriptions from Asia Minor and their possible implication as to whether *Jews* referred to the religion or ethnicity (the former a broader usage, since it would include converts), see Rose S. Kraemer, "On the Meaning of the Term 'Jew' in Greco-Roman Inscriptions," *Harvard Theological Review* 82 (January 1989): 43–48.

151. Josephus, *Antiquities*, XII:147–53 refers to this removal. Ellen S. Saltman, "The Jews of Asia Minor in the Greco-Roman Period: A Religious and Social Study," M. A. thesis, Smith College, 1971, 17, summarized the explicit and even more common implicit acceptance of this approach. Mitchell, *Anatolia*, 2:32, interprets the action of Antiochus as significant in that it provided a large impetus to the Jewish community's growth, rather than being its initial implantation into the region. Irina Levinskaya presents a similar view in *The Book of Acts in Its Diaspora Setting*, vol. 5 of *The Book of Acts in Its First-Century Setting* (Grand Rapids, Mich.: William B. Eerdmans Publishing Company, 1996), 138.

152. Saltman, "The Jews of Asia Minor," 17–29.

153. Ibid., 18.

154. Ibid., 19–20.

155. Ibid., 21.

156. E. Silberschlag, "The Earliest Record of Jews in Asia Minor," *Journal of Biblical Literature* 52 (1933): 75. Their presence in

fifty Asia Minor cities has been documented (Peter W. van der Horst, *Essays on the Jewish World of Early Christianity* [Cottingen, Germany: Vandehnoeck & Ruprecht, 1990], 167.

157. H. Mary Smallwood, *The Jews Under Roman Rule: From Pompey to Diocletion, Studies in Judaism in Late Antiquity*, vol. 20, ed. Jacob Reusner (Leiden: E. J. Brill, 1978), 121.

158. Robert A. Kraft sums up the approaches as three to four million minimal population, eight million at the most ("Judaism on the World Scene," in *The Catacombs and the Colosseum: The Roman Empire as the Setting of Primitive Christianity*, ed. Stephen Benko and John J. O'Rourke [Valley Forge, Pa.: Judson Press, 1971], 83). Peter W. van der Horst sums up the estimates as beginning at two million and peaking at over eight million (*Jewish World*, 146). He himself suggests about five million as a reasonable figure (146–47). Robert Goldenberg estimates five to seven million Jews within the Roman Empire and one to one-and a half million in Parthia (Persia), for a total of between eight and nine million ("The Jewish Sabbath in the Roman World up to the Time of Constantine the Great," in *Aufstieg und Niedergang der Romischen Welt* [Berlin: Walter de Gruyter, 1979], II, 19.1, 419).

159. By van der Horst, *Jewish World*, 167.

160. By Goldenberg, "Jewish Sabbath," 419.

161. Jerry L. Daniel, "Anti-Semitism in the Hellenistic-Roman Period," *Journal of Biblical Literature* 98 (1979): 46. Daniel notes that "the great majority of the comments" about Jews in ancient litera-ture "are negative," from "serious historians" to "lesser writers" (46). For an ample collection of lengthy extracts expressing these atti-tudes in detail (in both the original languages and English transla-tion), see Menahem Stern, *Greek and Latin Authors on Jews and Judaism*, vol. 1: *From Herodotus to Plutarch* (Jerusalem: Israel Acad-emy of Sciences and Humanities, 1974) and vol. 2: *From Tacitus to Simplicius* (Jerusalem: Israel Academy of Sciences and Humanities, 1980). For Galen's views, see 2:306–28.

A letter discovered in Egypt, dating from the early first century B.C., alludes to how pervasive and intense anti-Semitic feelings could become. Writing to an apparent friend in Memphis, Egypt, one Her-akles requests assistance for a Jewish priest: Please provide him both good advice and lodging in your residence "for you know that they are nauseated by Jews." For the full text of the letter, see Roger S. Bagnall and Peter Derow, *Greek Historical Documents: The Hellenistic Period*, SBL Sources for Biblical Study 16, (Chico, Calif.: Scholars Press for the Society of Biblical Literature, 1981), 236.

162. Applebaum, *Jews and Greeks*, 243.

163. Marcel Simon points to two actions of the Emperor Hadrian as precipitating the revolt: "The first was his decision to build a pagan temple in the reconstructed Jerusalem, the second was his prohibition of circumcision" (*Verus Israel: A Study of the Relations Between Christians and Jews in the Roman Empire (135–425)*, trans. H. McKeating [Oxford: Oxford University Press, 1986], 99). Short of outright extermination of the Jewish community, no more inflammatory policies could conceivably have been adopted.

164. On the absence of revolt in Asia and nearby provinces, see Applebaum, *Jews and Greeks*, 336. Martin Hengel argues that economic/social matters played the major role in producing the provincial revolts: in places like North Africa the Jewish situation was, overall, on the decline, while in Greece and Asia the community continued to do well (*Jews, Greeks, and Barbarians: Aspects of the Hellenization of Judaism in the Pre-Christian Period*, trans. John Bowden [Philadelphia: Fortress Press, 1980], 87).

165. For an analysis of the conflicts between the Jewish minority and the communities in which they resided in Asia Minor that led up to these decrees, see Christopher D. Stanley, "'Neither Jew nor Greek': Ethnic Conflict in Graeco-Roman Society," *Journal for the Study of the New Testament* 64 (December 1996): 101–24.

166. Josephus, *Antiquities*, 10.14.25. All quotations from Josephus in this section come from Josephus, *Josephus: Complete Works*, trans. William Whiston (1867; reprint Grand Rapids, Mich.: Kregel Publications, 1972).

167. Ibid., 10.14.22.

168. Ibid., 10.14.20.

169. Ibid., 10.14.24.

170. Peter Garnsey, "Religious Toleration in Classical Antiquity," in *Persecution and Toleration*, vol. 21 of *Studies in Church History*, ed. W. J. Sheils (Great Britain: Basil Blackwell, 1984), 10–11.

171. As Peter Garnsey notes, "The documents [asserting Jewish rights] regularly acknowledge that the Romans are extending privileged treatment to the Jews because of services rendered. And that is all. No further motivation or justification is offered. There is an absolute lack of any apologia for religious pluralism or religious freedom. The Jewish right to their ancestral customs is not built up into a general principle applicable to every *ethnos* (people) let alone every individual" (ibid., 11).

172. Hanfmann, *From Croessus to Constantine*, 55.

173. Smallwood, *Jews Under Roman Rule*, 124.

176 THE SEVEN CITIES OF THE APOCALYPSE

174. Ibid., 124–25.

175. Ibid., 125.

176. Cicero, *Pro Flacco*, 28.66–69. For the Latin text, see Stern, *Greek and Latin Authors on Jews and Judaism*, 1:196–97; for the English translation, see 1:197–98.

177. As suggested by Smallwood, *Jews Under Roman Rule*, 126.

178. Cf. the remarks in ibid., 126–27.

179. A. J. Marshall, "Flaccus and the Jews of Asia (Cicero, *Pro Flacco* 28.67–69)," *Phoenix* 29 (1975), 148.

180. Ibid. Caution must be taken on this point, though the geographic logic of compiling the funds in a major nearby city makes full sense. By arguing the importance or prominence of the seven churches of Asia, some have deduced a first-century regional bishopric system. Does anyone wish to argue for an equivalent strictly Jewish system in which the synagogue of each major city held control over all synagogues in the surrounding region?

181. Ibid., 149.

182. Smallwood, *Jews Under Roman Rule*, 127, 236–41.

183. The tax was actually imposed by Vespasian as soon as his son Titus completed the suppression of the Jewish revolt (Richard J. Cassidy, *John's Gospel in New Perspective: Christology and the Realities of Roman Power* [Maryknoll, N.Y.: Orbis Books, 1992], 8). From the practical standpoint, after the fall of Jerusalem all else were mopping-up operations.

184. A. Thompson, "Domitian and the Jewish Tax," *Historia* 31 (1982), 333.

185. For the *fiscus Asiaticus*, see Michael J. Ginsburg, "Fiscus Judaicus," *Jewish Quarterly Review*, 21 (1930–31), 286–87. The large Jewish community in Alexandria, Egypt, was similarly double-taxed due to the *fiscus Alexandrius* bound upon all citizens of that great metropolitan center (286).

186. Cassidy, *New Perspective*, 8–9.

187. It would also have been difficult to make the argument because Christians considered themselves the true Jews and those who continued in traditional Judaism as the imitation or fallen-away Jews. Paul touches on this theme (Rom 2:28–29), as does John in his reference to pseudo-Jews that Christians came in contact with (Rv 2:9; 3:9).

188. Thompson, "Domitian and the Jewish Tax," 334.

189. Ibid., 339.

190. Ibid. Thompson's article provides a useful study of the

persistent effort to maximize the number of individuals covered by the tax.

191. For the coin inscription, see Cassidy, *New Perspectives*, 10.

192. Tord Fornberg, *An Early Church in a Pluralistic Society: A Study of 2 Peter*, trans. Jean Gray (Sweden: CWK Gleerup, 1977), 122, argues that this misreads the evidence.

193. Edwin M. Yamauchi, *The Archaeology of New Testament Cities in Western Asia Minor* (Grand Rapids, Mich.: Baker Book House, 1980), mentions this approach and rejects it.

194. Cf. A. Thomas Kraabel, "The Synagogue at Sardis: Jews and Christians," in *Sardis: Twenty-seven Years of Discovery*, ed. Eleanor Gurainick (Chicago: [n.p.], 1987), 69, who uses this incident as an example of how difficult it is to be certain of the validity of the inferences we draw from the evidence. He notes that so far as literary evidence is concerned, the problem is complicated by inconsistency in use of the term *Asia* by the rabbis: sometimes it is used in the technical provincial sense, sometimes of the entire western Turkey area, and sometimes even of locations outside the region.

195. Adolph Schlatter cites this text as proof of the connection between the Diaspora and Palestine (*The Church in the New Testament Period*, trans. Paul P. Levertoff [London: S.P.C.K., 1961], 162).

196. Kraabel, "Synagogue at Sardis," 69, refers to such individuals.

197. Jacob Neusner, *A History of the Jews in Babylonia*, vol. 1: *The Parthian Period* (Leiden: E. J. Brill, 1965), 42, citing Philo, *De Spec Leg* 1.69, and Josephus, *Bell* 6.3.3.

198. Ibid., 42.

199. William Horbury, "The Jewish Dimension," in *Early Christianity: Origins and Evolution to A.D. 600*, ed. Ian Hazlett (Nashville, Tenn.: Abingdon Press, 1991), 44. Horbury writes that, for example, in the first centuries A.D., Jewish inscriptions in Rome itself are 75 percent in Greek, with nearly all the rest in Latin; there is only a smattering in other languages. (These come primarily from the third and fourth centuries.)

200. A. Thomas Kraabel, "Judaism in Western Asia Minor Under the Roman Empire, with a Preliminary Study of the Jewish Community at Sardis, Lydia," Ph.D. diss., Harvard University, 1968, 59. Kraabel notes that the synagogue in Sardis represents the major exception to this generalization and even in *that* context the "Jewish" finds are essentially limited to the synagogue area itself.

201. Ibid., 134.

202. Ibid.

203. Timothy Barnes, "Pagan Perceptions of Christianity," in Hazlett, *Early Christianity*, 232.

204. Ibid., 232–36.

205. Ibid., 238–39.

206. Ibid.

207. For full translated texts, see Stephen Benko, *Pagan Rome and the Early Christians* (Bloomington, Ind.: Indiana University Press, 1984), 142.

208. Fornberg, *Pluralistic Society*, 117, takes this a step further and argues that "most people were poverty-stricken," but there are major differences in the *degree* of poverty, from destitute to self-sufficient but hurting.

209. Ibid. Fornberg's textual references are transferred from his footnote into the text itself for current reader convenience.


### 4. JOHN, PATMOS, AND THE RECIPIENTS OF HIS "REVELATION"

1. For a discussion of the nature and significance of such differences see, for example, Alan Johnson, "Revelation," in *The Expositor's Bible Commentary*, vol. 12, ed. Frank E. Gaebelein (Grand Rapids, Mich.: Zondervan Publishing House, 1981), 400–2.

2. It is common to argue that authorial *backdating* of the time of the writer's life is found even in biblical apocalyptic, Daniel in particular. Even if this were true (and we reject it), John's narrative would still represent a dramatic break from the traditional point-in-history at which apocalyptic writers traditionally placed themselves.

3. Cf. R. H. Charles, *Revelation*, International Critical Commentary series (Edinburgh: T. & T. Clark, 1920; reprint 1979), xxxviii.

4. Cf. ibid., xxxix.

5. Morris Ashcroft, "Revelation," in *The Broadman Bible Commentary*, vol. 12: *Hebrews-Revelation* (Nashville, Tenn.: Broadman Press, 1972), 247.

6. Ibid.

7. Ibid.

8. Cf. William Barclay, *The Revelation of John*, vol. 1, rev. ed. (Philadelphia: Westminster Press, 1976), 13.

9. Charles Foster Kent, *Work and Teaching of Apostles* (New York: Charles Scribner's Sons, 1916), 273.

10. George Eldon Ladd seems inclined to one of these options as the best explanation (*A Commentary on the Revelation of*

*John* [Grand Rapids, Mich.: William B. Eerdmans Publishing Company, 1972], 7). Although commonly utilized by conservative Bible believers in regard to certain other Bible books as well, the approach raises a theological dilemma: *who* was the inspired party, the apostle or his amanuensis? Or both? And if the latter, shouldn't we really speak in terms of *joint* authorship rather than Johannine authorship? Actually, multi-authorship of a single work is not an outlandish principle, from a conservative standpoint, when a specific book, such as certain of the Pauline epistles, is *explicitly* presented in the text as coming from Paul *and* someone else. The problem arises when one effectively makes the amanuensis the coauthor and when one faces a book that, like Revelation, refers to only *one* human composer.

11. Cf. Leon Morris, "It is not that the writer does not know the rules of Greek grammar, but that he decides for himself which rules he will keep" (*The Revelation of St. John*, Tyndale New Testament Commentary series [Grand Rapids, Mich.: William B. Eerdmans Publishing Company, 1969], 39).

12. G. B. Caird speculates that John "may have adopted this style quite deliberately for *reasons of his own*," though he does not speculate as to what they may have been (*A Commentary on the Revelation of St. John the Divine*, Harper's New Testament Commentaries series [New York: Harper & Row, 1966], 5).

13. For a brilliant book-length defense of the early date approach, see Kenneth L. Gentry Jr., *Before Jerusalem Fell: Dating the Book of Revelation* (Tyler, Tx.: Institute for Christian Economics, 1989). For a shorter and more concise defense of a pre-70 writing of the book, see J. Christian Wilson, "The Problem of the Domitianic Date of Revelation," *New Testament Studies: An International Journal* 39 (October 1993): 587–605.

14. Alan J. Beagley pointed to Revelation 7:9–10 as evidence that the churches of Asia "already included Gentiles, perhaps in considerable numbers" (*The "Sitz Im Leben" of the Apocalypse with Particular Reference to the Role of the Church's Enemies* [Berlin: Walter de Gruyter, 1987], 32).

15. G. R. Beasley-Murray, *The Book of Revelation*, New Century Bible series (Greenwood, S.C.: Attic Press, 1974), 64; Hugh Martin, *The Seven Letters* (Philadelphia: Westminster Press, 1965), 31. The postponement theory is sometimes associated with a "low" concept of inspiration. As one writer argued, "Besides requiring 'inspiration,' masterpieces invariably need 'perspiration'" (William C. Tremmel, *The Twenty-Seven Books that Changed the World* [New York:

Holt, Rinehart and Winston, 1981], 219–20). This would certainly be true if inspiration consists merely of *self-generated* ideas; if, however, inspiration consists of a message coming from a superior, external Source, then one runs into profound difficulties. Is that Source to be considered so inadequate in revelatory ability that the *recipient* must somehow polish the message up and overcome its inadequacies?

16. Charles C. Whiting, *The Revelation of John* (Boston: Gorham Press, 1918), 60.

17. *1, 2 & 3 John, Revelation*, The Communicator's Commentary series (Waco, Tx.: Word Books, 1982), 120.

18. Stuart Moses, *A Commentary on the Apocalypse*, vol. 2 (Andover: Allen, Morrill, and Wardwell, 1845), 55.

19. For a study of how John is pictured on Patmos in modern versus ancient reconstruction, see the study of post-Renaissance painting on the theme in Kevin Lewis, "John on Patmos and the Painters," *ARTS: The Arts in Religious and Theological Studies* 5 (Summer 1993): 18–23.

20. Whiting, *Revelation*, 60.

21. Charles F. Pfeiffer and Howard F. Vos, *The Wycliffe Historical Geography of Bible Lands* (Chicago: Moody Press, 1967), 402.

22. Henry F. Tozer, *The Islands of the Aegean* (Oxford: Oxford University Press, 1889; reprint Chicago: Obol International, 1976), 179–81.

23. Ibid.; Harry R. Boer, *The Book of Revelation* (Grand Rapids, Mich.: William B. Eerdmans Publishing Company, 1979), 23; Emil G. Kraeling, *Rand McNally Bible Atlas* (New York: Rand McNally & Company, 1956), 466; Merrill F. Unger, *The New Unger's Bible Handbook*, rev. Gary N. Larson (Chicago: Moody Press, 1984), 649; and John F. Walvoord, *The Revelation of Jesus Christ* (Chicago: Moody Press, 1966), 41. William Barclay (*Revelation*, 41), Marcus L. Loane (*They Overcame: An Exposition of the First Three Chapters of Revelation* [n.p.; Angus and Robertson, 1971; reprint Grand Rapids, Mich.: Baker Book House, 1981], 19), and Colin J. Hemer (*The Letters to the Seven Churches of Asia in Their Local Setting, Journal for the Study of the New Testament* Supplement Series 11 [Sheffield, England: University of Sheffield, 1986], 26) describe it as five rather than six miles wide but with the same ten-mile length. Leon Morris speaks of its measurement as only four miles wide and eight miles long (*Revelation*, 51). Henry F. Tozer (*Islands*, 180) does not provide a width estimate but gives the length as eight miles.

24. Catherine B. Avery, *The New Century Classical Handbook* (New York: Appleton-Century, Crofts, 1962), 824, describes it as hav-

ing approximately twenty-two square miles; Alan F. Johnson (*Revelation*, 31) speaks of 25 square miles, as does Colin J. Hemer (*Local Setting*, 26.).

25. Kraeling, *Atlas*, 466.

26. Otto F. A. Meinardus, *St. John of Patmos and the Seven Churches of the Apocalypse* (New Rochelle, N.Y.: Caratzas Brothers, Publishers, 1979), 13.

27. Leonard Thompson, "A Sociological Analysis of Tribulation in the Apocalypse of John," *Semeia* no. 36 (1986), 150.

28. M. Eugene Boring, *Revelation*, in the Interpretation commentary series (Louisville, Ky.: John Knox Press, 1989), 81. Otto F. A. Meinardus refers to the existence of this cult but without a dating (*Patmos*, 13).

29. Thompson, "Sociological Analysis," 150; Boring, *Revelation*, 81.

30. Meinardus, *Patmos*, 13.

31. Ibid.

32. For a survey of the medieval and modern history of the island, see ibid., 13–18.

33. "This sounds like a preaching mission there," argues Paul Trudinger, "The Ephesus Milieu," *Downside Review* 105 (October 1988), 289.

34. "The Greek does not give a hint of a suggestion that John was banished, deported, relegated or imprisoned on Patmos" (Thompson, "Sociological Analysis," 150). Alan J. Beagley (*Sitz Im Leben*, 31) argues that the wording "could" be taken in a non-persecutionary way but that "the prevailing view" favors the traditional understanding.

35. Wilfrid J. Harrington, *Revelation (Sacra Pagina*, vol. 16) (Collegeville, Minn.: Liturgical Press/A Michael Glazier Book, 1993), 50.

36. Homer Hailey, *Revelation: An Introduction and Commentary* (Grand Rapids, Mich.: Baker Book House, 1979), 105.

37. Leonard Thompson considers this as "quite possibly" the explanation for John's presence ("Sociological Analysis," 150). Bernard Weiss also embraced this approach (*A Commentary on the New Testament*, vol. 4: *Thessalonians-Revelation*, trans. George H. Schodde and Epiphanius Wilson [New York: Funk & Wagnalls Company, 1906], 390).

38. Richard C. Trench argues against this reading by those introducing it in defense of a preaching mission to Patmos (*Commen-*

*tary on the Epistles to the Seven Churches in Asia* [New York: Charles Scribner & Co., 1872], 37).

39. Henry Alford argues against the revelation-giving interpretation put on the text in *The New Testament for English Readers,* vol. 2: *The Epistles to the Hebrews, the Catholic Epistles, and the Revelation,* new ed. (Boston: Lee and Shepard, Publishers, 1880), 946.

40. Trench, *Seven Churches,* 37.

41. Alford, *New Testament,* 946. He concedes that the Pauline usage of the expression could lead to a different conclusion, but that "St. John's own usage is a better guide" for interpreting John's writings "than that of St. Paul." Homer Hailey (*Revelation,* 106) introduces these two additional texts to refute both the missionary work and revelation receiving scenarios. Cf. Kalus Wengst on the Greek grammatical construction and its interpretation, *Pax Romana and the Peace of Jesus Christ,* trans. John Bowden (Philadelphia: Fortress Press, 1987), 231.

42. J. P. V. D. Balsdon (*Romans and Aliens,* Chapel Hill, N. C.: University of North Carolina Press, 1979, 113–15) provides a two-and-a-half page list of places where those relegated and deported were sent. Of thirteen specific islands listed in the Aegean, Patmos is conspicuously absent. Asia itself is listed as receiving three prominent exiles from the city of Rome, of whom two were resident in Smyrna in the century before Christ was born.

43. Suetonius, *Titus,* 8, specifically of those being marked for special judicial censure. In *The Lives of the Twelve Caesars,* trans. Alexander Thomson, rev. T. Forester (London: George Bell Sons, 1896 reprint).

44. Loane, *They Overcame,* 22.

45. C. Anderson Scott, *The Book of the Revelation* (New York: George H. Doran Company, [n.d.]), 87. Marcus L. Loane considers stone quarrying to have been John's likely method of punishment (*They Overcame,* 87).

46. For one expression of the theory that the author of Revelation had a far more hostile attitude toward surrounding society than Paul, see C. Rowland, "Moses and Patmos: Reflections on the Jewish Background of Early Christianity," in *Words Remembered, Texts Renewed: Essays in Honour of John F. A. Sawyer,* ed. Jon Davies, Graham Harvey, and Wilfred G. E. Watson, 280–99, *Journal for the Study of the Old Testament,* supplement 195 (Sheffield, England: Sheffield Academic Press, 1995), 291–92.

47. Kraeling, *Atlas,* 466.

48. William Barclay quotes Ramsay and appears to accept the view himself (*Revelation*, 41).

49. Barclay, *Revelation*, 51.

50. Ibid., 120.

51. M. Eugene Boring *(Revelation*, 81) uses the expression "penal colony" in rejecting the concept. Leonard Thompson ("Sociological Analysis," 150) uses the term "prison settlement" in rejecting the concept.

52. Thucydides, *The Peloponnesian War*, III.33, trans. Benjamin Jowett, in *The Greek Historians: The Complete and Unabridged Historical Works of Herodotus, Thucydides, Xenophon, Arrian*, ed. Francis R. B. Godolphin (New York: Random House, 1942).

53. Strabo, *Geography*, x.5.13.

54. Pliny, *Natural History* 4.12.69.

55. See Hemer, *Local Setting*, 221, note 1, for examples of those who make this error.

56. Otto A. Meinardus, "The Christian Remains of the Seven Churches of Asia," in *Biblical Archaeologist Reader IV*, ed. Edward F. Campbell Jr. and David Nobel Freedman (Sheffield, England: Almond Press, 1983), 346–47.

57. J. Theodore Bent, "What St. John Saw on Patmos," *Nineteenth Century* 24 (1888), 813–21. He cites various medieval and later writers who had seen such volcanic explosions and analyzes how they described what they had observed.

58. Martin, *Seven Letters*, 41–42.

59. These questions assume (we believe, legitimately) that addressing the seven churches is more than a mere literary technique—that the mini-epistles represent actual communications to seven distinct congregations, each with its unique set of problems. For a defense of the approach that sees these as seven real letters—rather than just a literary form utilized by John to effectively present his vision—see M. Eugene Boring, "The Voice of Jesus in the Apocalypse of John," *Novum Testamentum: An International Quarterly for New Testament and Related Studies* 34 (October 1992): 349–50.

60. William M. Ramsay, *The Letters to the Seven Churches of Asia* (New York: George H. Doran Company, 1905), 25.

61. For example, Boer, *Revelation*, 28; Cuthbert H. Turner, *Studies in Early Church History* (Oxford: Clarendon Press, 1912), 200; and Bruce M. Metzger, *Breaking the Code: Understanding the Book of Revelation* (Nashville, Tenn.: Abingdon Press, 1993), 29.

62. Steve Moyise, *The Old Testament in the Book of Revelation* (Sheffield, England: Sheffield Academic Press, 1995), 24, notes that

seven is used in other references in the book (i.e., to seals, trumpets, and bowls) as representative of the entire number of events necessary to accomplish the complete description.

63. See the brief discussion in Fuller B. Saunders, "The Seven Churches of the Apocalypse," Ph.D. diss., Southern Baptist Theological Seminary, 1949, 58–59.

64. These examples are provided in ibid., 60. Saunders adds that examination of a concordance will quickly reveal that this is only a modest sampling. He is pushing the evidence when he attempts to find a similar pattern of significant "sevens" in New Testament literature outside the Apocalypse (60). Mary Magdalene is described as being possessed by seven devils (Lk 8:2) and one Sceva had seven sons (Acts 19:14). Unless these descriptions were cut out of whole cloth, however, the number was chosen because it was *accurate* rather than because of any symbolism. Saunders may be on stronger ground when he refers to the seven deacons appointed in Acts 6:5 and how the Sadducees' test question about the resurrection involved seven brothers (Mk 12:20ff.).

65. Richard Bauckham, for example, ties in the theoretical importance of seven as "the number of completeness" with John's practical desire to say something of value to any and all readers, "The range of different situations in these seven churches is sufficient for any Christian church in the late first century to find analogies to its own situation in one or more of the messages and therefore to find the whole book relevant to itself. Churches in later periods have been able to do the same, allowing for a necessary degree of adjustment to changing historical contexts" (*The Theology of the Book of Revelation* [Cambridge: Cambridge University Press, 1993], 16–17).

66. William M. Ramsay, *The Letters to the Seven Churches of Asia* (New York: George H. Doran Company, 1905), 28.

67. Cf. Martin, *Seven Letters*, for examples.

68. Paul W. Barnett, "Revelation in Its Roman Setting," *Reformed Theological Review* 50 (May–August 1991), 61.

69. The maps are reprinted on pages 66–68.

70. David L. Barr, "Elephants and Holograms: From Metaphor to Methodology in the Study of John's Apocalypse," in *Society of Biblical Literature Seminar Papers Series: 1986*, ed. Kent H. Richards (Atlanta, Ga.: Scholars Press, 1986), 408, argues this not to establish the point we are currently concerned with but the related one of proving why the seven churches might be objects of special harassment.

71. Ibid., 407–8.

72. Arthur C. McGiffer (*A History of Christianity in the Apostolic Age* [Edinburgh: T. & T. Clark, 1897], 624–25) gives this as one of his two explanations. The second is the degree of spiritual need in the selected congregations.

73. Otto F. A. Meinardus, *Patmos*, 29, hedges by saying "it seems" that such a system had developed.

74. William M. Ramsay sees a hierarchy of prestige in existence at this time, which in the not distant future gave rise to a hierarchy of authority (*Seven Churches*, 178). "Before the end of the century," he argues, "the Province was divided into districts with representative cities, and Asia was advancing along a path that led to the institution of a regularly organized hierarchy with one supreme head of the Province" (182).

75. Ignatius's writings can be found translated in a number of places, among them, Edgar J. Goodspeed, *The Apostolic Fathers: An American Translation* (New York: Harper & Brothers, 1950), and Robert M. Grant, *The Apostolic Fathers: A New Translation and Commentary*, vol. 4: *Ignatius of Antioch* (New York: Thomas Nelson & Sons, 1966). For background on Ignatius, also see in Grant's series *The Apostolic Fathers: An Introduction* (New York: Thomas Nelson & Sons, 1964).

76. Walter Bauer, *Orthodoxy and Heresy in Earliest Christianity*, 2d German ed., trans. Robert A. Kraft, David Hay, et al., ed. Robert A. Kraft and Gerhard Kordel (Philadelphia: Fortress Press, 1971), 63. For a detailed elaboration of this scenario that Ignatius was attempting to create a new administrative orthodoxy, see pages 61–70.

77. M. F. Miles, "Ignatius and the Church," *Studia Patristica* 17, part 2 (Oxford: Pergamon Press, 1982), 754. For several arguments against Ignatius's system being the dominant one, see pages 752–55.

78. Ramsay, *Seven Churches*, 178.

79. Bauer, *Orthodoxy and Heresy*, 78. To take this line of reasoning a step further and suggest that "perhaps [these were] the only churches acknowledging John. . . ." goes too far (John M. Court, *Revelation* [in the *New Testament Guides* series] [Huddersfield (Great Britain): Scheffield Academic Press, 1994] 35). John points out the faults of even those he considers the very faithful by his standards (Ephesus is a fine example); why should we think he would have been any less willing to use those totally in apostasy as explicit negative role models, if they actually existed?

80. Boring, *Revelation*, 87.

81. Ramsay, *Seven Churches*, 186.

82. Ibid., 191–92. Ramsay then goes into detail about what communities may have been included in these specific subcircuits of communication and candidly discusses the degree of probability that can be attached to his various conjectures (192–96).

83. L. Selles, *The Book of Revelation,* vol. 1 (London, Ontario: Interleague Publication Board of Canadian Reformed Societies, 1965), 13.

84. Whiting, *Revelation*, 67.

85. Albertus Pieters, *The Lamb, the Woman and the Dragon: An Exposition of the Revelation of St. John* (Grand Rapids, Mich.: [n.p.], 1937), 94. Reprinted with different page number as *Studies in the Revelation of St. John* (Grand Rapids, Mich.: Wm. B. Eerdmans Publishing Company, 1943), 195.

86. Cf. Pieters, *Lamb*, 94. The parallel of Paul receiving visitors is not strong, especially if one believes that John was in exile as decreed judicial punishment (rather than fleeing prosecution). In Paul's case no final action had been taken. Furthermore, if Paul is to be introduced into the subject at all, his conduct would seem to be an argument *against* the angel as messenger correlation; when he received visitors he was quite candid that he had done so (Phil 4:10–18), while John is so vague that a "human visitor" interpretation has to be "reached" for, rather than coming unaided to the mind.

87. Bruce J. Malina implies that pagan mythology had triumphed over Judeo-Christian monotheism by arguing that the angels are intended to be "lesser astral deities" (*On the Genre and Message of Revelation: Star Visions and Sky Journeys* [Peabody, Mass.: Hendrickson Publishers, 1995], 28). If so, one wonders how John could have expected his material to be accepted by a strict monotheist community. For that matter, would not his denunciation of compromise with paganism have been regarded as ludicrous?

88. Margaret N. Ralph believes the text translates into a kind of "church guardian angel" (*Discovering the First-Century Church: The Acts of the Apostles, Letters of Paul and the Book of Revelation* [New York: Paulist Press, 1991], 231).

89. William Milligan, *The Book of Revelation (Expositor's Bible)* (New York: Funk & Wagnalls Company, 1900), 25–26.

90. Ibid., 25.

91. "God proclaims and executes His will by angels (7:2; 8:2; 14:6, 9; 15:1, 6). He addresses even the Son by an angel (14:15). The Son acts and reveals His truth by an angel (1:1; 20:1; 22:6). . . . On all

these occasions the 'angel' is interposed when the persons or things spoken of are represented as coming out of themselves and as taking their part in intercourse or in action" (ibid., 25–26.) Without the various proof texts, Albertus Pieters says much the same thing when he argues that the angels represent "the church itself, in its inward spiritual state and its active influence upon the world" (*Lamb*, 99).

    92. Whiting, *Revelation*, 68.

### 5. THE IMPERIAL CULT IN ROMAN ASIA AND THE NATURE OF OFFICIAL PERSECUTION

    1. J. H. W. G. Liebeschuetz, *Continuity and Change in Roman Religion* (Oxford: Clarendon Press, 1979), 66.

    2. Ibid.

    3. Ibid., 65–66.

    4. The interpretation of Arnaldo Momigliano, *On Pagans, Jews, and Christians* (Middletown, Conn.: Wesleyan University Press, 1987), 95. The question is further complicated by the fact that what was true among some worshipers might not be true of others, and what was true at the formation of the cult might dramatically differ from the attitude of most members a century later.

    5. Cecil J. Cadoux, *Ancient Smyrna: A History from the Earliest Times to 324 A.D.* (Oxford: Basil Blackwell, 1938), 224.

    6. For a discussion of the erection of these early temples, see Ibid., 136–37.

    7. Ibid., 224.

    8. William M. Ramsay, *The Social Basis of Roman Power in Asia Minor* (Aberdeen, Scotland: Aberdeen University Press, 1941; reprint Amsterdam: Adolf M. Hakkert, Publisher, 1967), 214.

    9. Bruce W. Winter, "Acts and Roman Religion: . . . B. The Imperial Cult," in *The Book of Acts in Its Graeco-Roman Setting*, ed. David W. J. Gill and Conrad Gempf, 93–103, vol. 2 of *The Book of Acts in Its First-Century Setting* (Grand Rapids, Mich.: William B. Eerdmans Publishing Company, 1994), 93.

    10. The naive elitism that often went with citizenship can be found in the words of praise Aelius Aristides wrote of Rome, "For you have divided all the people of the Empire . . . in two classes: the more cultured, better born, and more influential everywhere you have declared Roman citizens and even of the same stock; the rest vassels and subjects" (quoted in David W. J. Gill, "Acts and the Urban Elites," in Gill and Gempf, *The Book of Acts in Its Graeco-Roman Setting*, 107.

11. Alistair Kee describes the imperial cult as "ideology in the guise of religion" ("The Imperial Cult: The Unmasking of an Ideology," *Scottish Journal of Religious Studies* 8 [Autumn 1958]: 114; cf. 124). On the relative importance of religion and patriotism in the imperial cult, see J. Daryl Charles, "Imperial Pretensions and the Throne-Vision of the Lamb: Observations on the Function of Revelation 5," *Criswell Theological Review* 7 (Fall 1993): 86–87.

12. Jean-Pierre Vernant, "Introduction," in *The Greeks*, ed. Jean-Pierre Vernant, trans. Charles Lambert and Teresa Lavender Fagan (Chicago: University of Chicago Press, 1995), 9. On this point, Robert C. Gregg and Dan Urman, *Jews, Pagans, and Christians in the Golan Heights: Greek and Other Inscriptions of the Roman and Byzantine Eras*, South Florida Studies in the History of Judaism, vol. 140 (Atlanta, Ga.: Scholars Press, 1996), 290, note that the religious allusions were even found in boundary markers!

13. David A. deSilva, "The 'Image of the Beast' and the Christians in Asia Minor: Escalation of Sectarian Tension in Revelation 13," *Trinity Journal* 12 (Fall 1991), 190.

14. Paul Zanker, *The Power of Images in the Age of Augustus*, Jerome lectures: sixteenth series, trans. Alan Shapiro (Ann Arbor, Mich.: University of Michigan Press, 1988), 299.

15. On the importance of sacrifice in the state and stated approved cults, see Bruce J. Malina, "Mediterranean Sacrifice: Dimensions of Domestic and Political Religion," *Biblical Theology Bulletin* 26 (Spring 1996): 30–32. On the psychological significance of such sacrifice, see pages 36–42.

16. Quoted in Liebeschuetz, *Continuity and Change*, 89.

17. Quoted in ibid.

18. Keith Hopkins, *Conquerors and Slaves: Sociological Studies in Roman History*, vol. 1 (Cambridge: Cambridge University Press, 1978), 202–3.

19. Quoted in Edgar J. Goodspeed, *Introduction to the New Testament* (Chicago, Ill.: University of Chicago Press, 1937), 241.

20. Robert S. Rogers uses different terminology to make this central point (*Studies in the Reign of Tiberius* [Baltimore: Johns Hopkins Press, 1943], 67).

21. Hopkins, *Conquerors and Slaves*, 203–4.

22. David Magie, *Roman Rule in Asia Minor to the End of the Third Century After Christ* (Princeton, N.J.: Princeton University Press, 1950; reprint Salem, N.H.: Ayer Company, Publishers, 1988), 501. Although issued in two volumes (the first consisting exclusively of text and the second of footnotes and related material) the page

numbers are consecutive and continue uninterrupted in the second volume. Hence volume number references are omitted.

23. Ibid., 502.

24. Ibid.

25. Ibid., 511.

26. Ibid., 544.

27. Ibid., 512. An example of Caligula's well-known paranoia can be seen in Roman Asia. In light of his well-deserved reputation for brutality and suspiciousness, he quite naturally feared assassination. A supposed prophecy warned him that a man named Cassius was of great danger to him. One Gaius Cassius Longinus was then proconsul over Asia (in 40–41) and not only bore the right name but was also a descendent of a conspirator against the great Julius Caesar. Ignoring the legal authority of the senate over the post, Caligula unilaterally ordered him home—with an obvious death threat hanging over his head. In late January of 41 a repeatedly insulted tribune of the Praetorian Guard assassinated Caligula. Appropriately enough, the assassin's name was *Cassius* Chaerea. (For a discussion of the incident, see ibid., 515.)

28. Ibid., 577. Hedging the significance of Domitian's claim to be a god, Stephen D. Moore still concedes the extravagance of the titles that were given to him. See Moore, "The Beatific Vision as a Posing Exhibition: Revelation's Hypomasculine Deity," *Journal for the Study of the New Testament* 60 (December 1995): 43–52.

The popularity of the ongoing usage of *god* as a description of the emperor can be seen in the fact that ancient coins commonly represented the Roman emperors as such. For a discussion of ancient coins that carried such designations, see Larry Kreitzer, "Apotheosis of the Roman Emperor," *Biblical Archaeologist: Perspectives on the Ancient World from Mesopotamia to the Mediterranean* 53 (December 1990): 210–17. In a specifically Asian context, for examples of Ephesian inscriptions referring to Roman emperors as god, see Sjef van Tilborg, *Reading John in Ephesus* (Leiden: E. J. Brill, 1996), 39–47.

29. Magie, *Asia Minor*, 1440.

30. Anthony D. Marco, "The Cities of Asia Minor Under the Roman Imperium," *Aufstieg und Niedergang der Romischen Welt* (Berlin: Walter de Gruyter, 1980), 681–82. Since Augustus's birthday was the beginning of the new year in Asia, the double importance of that year (in both beginning a new year and in honoring the emperor) makes it the most likely date for the new high priest to assume his office. (Cf. Steven J. Friesen, *Twice Neokoros: Ephesus, Asia, and the Cult of the Flavian Imperial Family* [Leiden: E. J. Brill,

1993], 44.) In light of their longer official title (chief priest of Roma and Augustus), their position was not created as a unique function of the imperial cult but rather represented an expansion of their duties from an original function of serving the cult of Roma alone (Cf. Lily R. Taylor, "Asiarchs," in *The Beginnings of Christianity, Part I: The Acts of the Apostles,* vol. 5, ed. Kirsopp Lake and Henry J. Cadbury [London: Macmillan and Company, 1933], 261).

31. For a textual study of five of the ancient texts and coins that specifically mention the Asiarchs, see R. A. Kearsley, "The Asiarchs," in Gill and Gempf, *The Book of Acts in Its Graeco-Roman Setting,* 368–76.

32. Marco, "Cities of Asia Minor," 682. Nearly all scholarly discussions make this equation, states one scholar who rejects the approach (Friesen, *Twice Neokoros,* 99). For a discussion of inscriptions referring to high priests of the imperial cult in Ephesus and Pergamon, see van Tilborg, *Ephesus,* 101–7. For a chronological list of all known Asiarchs, see Steven M. Baugh, "Paul and Ephesus: The Apostle Among His Contemporaries," Ph.D. diss., University of California (Irvine), 1990, 214–21. For the period A.D. 1–114, see the list in Magie, *Asia Minor,* 1605–1607. The terminology was adapted to the name of the specific province involved. Hence, in other provinces of later-day Turkey, we read of *Galatarchs* and *Bithyniarchs* occupying the same type of position and exercising similar functions (R. Mello, "The Goddess Roman," in *Aufstieg und Niedergang der Romischen Welt* [Berlin: Walter de Gruyter, 1981], II, 17.2, 980.

33. For a discussion de-linking the two positions, see Kearsley, "Some Asiarchs," 49; this is also Kearsley's own view, 53–55. For a detailed presentation of the dissenting view, see Friesen, *Twice Neokoros,* 92–113.

34. G. H. Horsley, "Inscriptions of Ephesus and the New Testament," in *New Documents Illustrating Early Christianity,* ed. G. H. Horsley (Marrickville, Australia: Macquarie University: Ancient History Documentary Research Centre, 1985), 3:137.

35. Ramsay MacMullen, "Women in Public in the Roman Empire," *Historia* 29 (1980): 214, makes passing mention of this approach.

36. Robert F. Stoops Jr., "Riot and Assembly: The Social Context of Acts 19:23–41," *Journal of Biblical Literature* 108 (Spring 1989): 85.

37. Favorably argued by Friesen, *Twice Neokoros,* 77–79.

38. R. Mellor argues that the need to serve more than one imperial temple simultaneously required the existence of several

high priests/Asiarchs ("The Goddess Roma," *Aufstieg und Niedergang der Romischen Welt* [Berlin: Walter de Gruyter, 1981], II, 17.2, 980).

39. As also noted by Friesen, *Twice Neokoros*, 97. Hence delinking the two terms enhances, at least in this case, the power of the multi-chief priest position.

40. Ibid., 77-79. Of the term Asiarch, R. A. Kearsley refers to the names of over 100 being known ("Some Asiarchs," 48). He also distinguishes between the imperial priesthood and the position of Asiarch.

41. Marco, "Cities of Asia Minor," 682. Cf. Henry J. Cadbury, *The Book of Acts in History* (London: Adam and Charles Black, 1955), 43.

42. An example from one of the seven church-cities is Aristio. This late-first-century Asiarch served as the city's official secretary *(grammateus)*, gymnasiarch, and contributed to the cost of the Harbor Gymnasium complex. He also donated generously to the construction of an aqueduct that carried water to the city from the Kaystros River. The aqueduct was completed about A.D. 113 or 114. His ongoing public contributions did not protect him from damaging charges of misconduct from rival aristocratic families, however. These were resolved in Aristio's behalf after he appealed for imperial intervention. (For a discussion of Aristio, see R. A. Kearsley, "Some Asiarchs of Ephesus," in Horsley, *New Documents Illustrating Early Christianity*, 4:50.)

43. Mellor, "Goddess Roma," 981.

44. Ibid., 980-81.

45. This is "generally agreed," says Ramsay MacMullen ("Women in Public," 214). For a discussion of high priestesses, also see S. M. Baugh, "A Foreign World: Ephesus in the First Century," in *Women in the Church: A Fresh Analysis of 1 Timothy 2:9-15*, ed. Andreas J. Kostenberger, Thomas R. Schreiner, and H. Scott Baldwin (Grand Rapids, Mich.: Baker Book House, 1995), 42-44. For inscriptions referring to high priestesses in the imperial cult, see van Tilborg, *Ephesus*, 102-3.

46. The rationale for overt female activity of this nature probably began with the deification of Augustus's wife, Livia, to godhood in A.D. 41. An inscription from Magnesia on the Meander refers to one Juliane, who was "wife of Alkiphronos the highpriest of Asia, [who] was the first among women [to serve as] highpriestess of Asia" and who served as well Aphrodite, Demeter, and Agrippina, Nero's mother. Since Agrippina was being worshiped, Juliane's role in the cult had to be between Nero becoming emperor in A.D. 54 and his

murder of his mother five years later. The wording of the inscription indicates that she served as a precedent for other women who later played an active leadership role in the worship of imperial goddesses. For a discussion of the question and the reading of the inscription concerning Juliane, see Friesen, *Twice Neokoros*, 81–89.

47. Ibid., 57.

48. S. R. F. Price, *Rituals and Power: The Roman Imperial Cult in Asia Minor* (Cambridge: Cambridge University Press, 1984), 156. Price's maps are designed to illustrate the pervasiveness of imperial temples, but in his introductory remarks he makes it plain that much broader categories of facilities are also included: "I include both temples and shrines which are dedicated to the emperor or are very closely associated with him and also other sanctuaries where there was a significant imperial presence" (xvii). To lump these together certainly illustrates how widespread the cult was, but to label them all imperial temples (as they are called on the maps) is as misleading as lumping together cathedrals, normal church facilities, storefront places of worship, and homes where worship services are held—and identifying them all on a map as cathedrals.

49. This was located in the "middle" gymnasium of the complex. The evidence points in the direction of a cultic purpose but is not conclusive. See P. J. Bitha, "God, Emperor Worship and Society: Contemporary Experiences and the Book of Revelation," *Neotestamentica: Journal of the New Testament Society of South Africa* 22 (1988): 92.

50. Ibid., 91.

51. Ibid., 91–92.

52. Philip K. Smith, "The Apocalypse of St. John and the Earl Church," *Journal of Bible and Religion* 25 (1957): 189.

53. Royston Lambert, *Beloved and God: The Story of Hadrian and Antinous* (New York: Viking, 1984), 110.

54. For a discussion of the term *father* in the imperial cult, see Mary Rose D'Angelo, "'Abba and Father': Imperial Theology and the Jesus Traditions," *Journal of Biblical Literature* 111 (Winter 1992): 623–26.

55. For a discussion of such terms, see Helmut Koester, "A Political Christmas Story," *Bible Review* 10 (October 1994): 23, 58.

56. P. J. J. Botha, "God, Emperor Worship, and Society: Contemporary Experiences and the Book of Revelation," *Neotestamentica: Journal of the New Testament Society of South Africa* 22 (1988): 96; S. R. F. Price, "Between Man and God: Sacrifice in the Roman Imperial Cult," *Journal of Roman Studies* 70 (1980): 29.

57. Botha, "God, Emperor Worship, and Society," 96; Price, "Between Man and God," 29.

58. Botha, "God, Emperor Worship, and Society," 96; Price, "Between Man and God," 29.

59. Botha, "God, Emperor Worship, and Society," 96; Price, "Between Man and God," 29.

60. Botha, "God, Emperor Worship, and Society," 96.

61. For a discussion of hymn singing in both the imperial and other polytheistic cults, see David E. Aune, "The Influence of the Roman Imperial Court Ceremonial on the Apocalypse of John," *Biblical Research* 28 (1983): 12–20.

62. Philo stressed this before the hostile emperor Gaius. See Philo, *The Embassy to Gaius*, trans. F. H. Colsonson, *Philo*, vol. 10, Loeb Classical Library (Cambridge, Mass.: Harvard University Press, 1962; reprint 1971), 349–57, esp. 356.

63. The most exhaustive study of the system in Asia Minor goes so far as to conclude that, "In only one instance is a sacrifice to the emperor known to have been performed by an imperial priest. In all the other cases their sacrifices were on behalf of the emperor" (*Rituals and Power*, 211; cf. 221). A few pages later (216–217) he seems to imply that "sacrifices to the *living* emperor alone" (our emphasis) were more frequent than this.

64. Quoted in J. Nelson Kraybill, "Cult and Commerce in Revelation 18." Ph.D. diss., Union Theological Seminary (Richmond, Va.), 1992, 50.

65. G. W. Bowersock, "The Imperial Cult: Perceptions and Persistence," in *Jewish and Christian Self-Definition*, vol. 3: *Self-Definition in the Greco-Roman World*, ed. Ben F. Meyer and E. P. Sanders (Philadelphia: Fortress Press, 1982), 172.

66. The case still seems a bit too conjectural, however. For evidence that such phenomena were within the power of would-be miracleworkers of that age, see Steven J. Scherer, "Signs and Wonders in the Imperial Cult—Revelation 13:13–15," *Journal of Biblical Literature* 103 (1984): 599–610. Richard Baucham also accepts the validity of interpreting this text as evidence of imperial cult behavior in *The Theology of the Book of Revelation* (Cambridge: Cambridge University Press, 1993), 17.

67. Moore, "The Beatific Vision," 35–40. On chapter 5 in particular, see Charles, "Imperial Pretensions," 87, 95. Peder Borgen argues that Revelation 5 is intended as a Christian parallel to the religio-political practice of the Roman court ("Moses, Jesus, and the Roman Emperor: Observations in Philo's Writings and the

Revelation of John," *Novum Testamentum: An International Quarterly for New Testament and Related Studies*, 38 [April 1996]: 156–58. In addition, however, he seeks an Old Testament root, contending that John also desires to erect a parallel with a conception of the day as to Moses' relationship to God (158–59).

68.    Friesen, *Twice Neokoros*, 114. The two cities not mentioned in Revelation were Tralles and Kyzikos. We are assuming that the identification of these games with the regal cult is correct. Friesen, who challenges the linkage, concedes that "nearly all scholars who deal with the topic" accept the connection. Even if the linkage were severed, an appreciation of the importance of the contests would remain useful in understanding the culture of the day. In 1922 Laodicea's participation was still unknown (B. J. Kidd, *A History of the Church to A.D. 461*, vol. 1 [Oxford: Clarendon Press, 1922; reprint AMS, 1976], 75).

69.    Friesen, *Twice Neokoros*, 115.

70.    Irene R. Arnold, "Festivals of Ephesus," *American Journal of Archaeology* 76 (1972): 20.

71.    Irene R. Arnold asserts that they all held to a three-year local cycle, though noting that a minority believe that the competitions were annual or every other year. Steven J. Friesen believes that Pergamon provided the festivals at least every other year (for a discussion of the evidence, see his *Twice Neokoros*, 115–16).

72.    Albert A. Bell Jr., "The Date of John's Apocalypse: Evidence of Some Roman Historians Reconsidered," *New Testament Studies* 25 (1978–79): 101, mentions both of these factors as necessary to take into consideration when judging the degree of persecution Christians were undergoing.

73.    Paul Keresytes, "The Imperial Government and the Christian Church. I. From Nero to the Severi," *Aufstieg und Niedergang der Romischen Welt* (Berlin: Walter de Gruyter, 1979), II, 23.1, is typical in asserting that due to the popularity of emperor worship "not unnaturally Asia became a leading center of the persecution of Christians" (272). Logical, yes, but not at the stage the mini-epistles were written. The difficulty of reconciling the theory of massive persecution with the actual data from the mini-epistles is reduced—but far from eliminated—by speaking in terms of the Asian churches being on the *verge* of major persecution. Cf. Lucien Cerfaux, "The Church in the Book of Revelation," in *The Birth of the Church: A Biblical Study*, trans. Charles Underhill Quinn (Staten Island, N.Y.: Alba House, 1969), who writes: "The Church of Revelation is essentially a Church on the alert because of persecution" (141), and "The truce

between the Empire and Christianity was broken. Christians are gnawed by anxiety" (143).

74. Revelation is a hard book to fit into traditional explanations of the origin and popularity of apocalyptic. It is common to attribute the appeal of such literature to the fact that a group is "oppressed" and "persecuted." The evidence we have examined provides evidence for only modest persecution in Asia and only one case of martyrdom. Nor does the *economically* oppressed label work well. Poverty was clearly a problem in Pergamon (2:9), but the Laodiceans were endangered by their very prosperity. Hence the Asian Christians appear to have represented a typical cross-section of the provincial population.

Faced with such difficulties, some shift to a theory of "relative deprivation," that the Christians *perceived* themselves as more oppressed than the actual circumstances justified. Yet Revelation 1–3 provides no evidence of exaggeration. Indeed, compared to what is often assumed to have been the case, it is a model of restraint. Only when one enters into the actual apocalyptic (beginning in chapter 4) does one encounter "exaggeration," and here it is the "exaggeration" that is inherent in the apocalyptic style.

Adela Y. Collins retreats to deprivation in the sense of "frustration of new expectations" (*Crisis and Catharsis: The Power of the Apocalypse* [Philadelphia: Westminster Press, 1984], 106). John writes not because the community is in the depths of depression but out of annoyance at the failure of the surrounding world to respond positively to the gospel. Yet were not similar circumstances present in other places as well, such as Palestine? Yet the Revelation was born (of all places!) in Romanized Asia. Furthermore, the *fact* of nonacceptance is never singled out either in the "present" parts of the book (chapters 1–3) or in the "future" sections (chapters 4–22). What *is* stressed is active, antagonistic unbelief—something quite different.

75. For a discussion of the social pagan-Christian relationship as pictured in Peter, see Peter Lampe and Ulrich Luz, "Post-Pauline Christianity and Pagan Society," chap. trans. Annemarie S. Kidder, in *Christian Beginnings: Word and Community from Jesus to Post-Apostolic Times*, ed. Jurgen Becker (Louisville, Ky.: Westminster/John Knox Press, 1993), 258–61. Lampe and Luz insist that in Revelation the situation is different, with official government persecution occurring (259).

76. Peter Garnsey, *Social Status and Legal Privilege in the Roman Empire* (Oxford: Clarendon Press, 1970), 116; H. J. Jolowicz

and Barry Nicholas, *Historical Introduction to the Study of Roman Law*, 3d ed. (Cambridge: Cambridge University Press, 1972), 403.

77. Garnsey, *Legal Privilege*, 116; Jolowicz and Nicholas, *Roman Law*, 403.

78. William M. Ramsay, *The Letters to the Seven Churches of Asia* (New York: George H. Doran Company, 1905), 83.

79. Wolfgang Kunke, *An Introduction to Roman Legal and Constitutional History*, 2d ed. (based on the sixth German edition), trans. J. M. Kelly (Oxford: Clarendon Press, 1973), 73; J. P. V. D. Balsdon, *Romans and Aliens* (Chapel Hill, N.C.: University of North Carolina Press, 1979), 105.

80. Garnsey, *Legal Privilege*, 116.

81. Ramsay, *Seven Churches*, 83.

82. Garnsey, *Legal Privilege*, 116.

83. Balsdon, *Romans*, 104–5.

84. Ramsay, *Seven Churches*, 83.

85. Ibid.

86. Garnsey, *Legal Practice*, 116.

87. On the uncertainty on this matter, see Jolowicz and Nicholas, *Roman Law*, 403. Garnsey, *Legal Practice*, 116–17, provides citations of actual cases to show how the practice varied from case to case.

88. Ramsay, *Seven Churches*, 90.

89. William M. Ramsay (ibid., 90–91) refers to this but doubts that, even if the procedure were in existence in John's day, that "an obscure Christian" such as the apostle would have been regarded as worthy of being benefited by it. The question of John's social status will be touched upon shortly in the text.

90. G. B. Caird, *A Commentary on the Revelation of St. John the Divine*, Harper's New Testament Commentaries series (New York: Harper & Row, 1966), 22; Colin J. Hemer, *The Letters to the Seven Churches of Asia in Their Local Setting*, Journal for the Study of the New Testament Supplement Series 11 (Sheffield, England: University of Sheffield, 1986), 222.

91. Implied by Emil G. Kraeling, *Rand McNally Bible Atlas* (New York: Rand McNally & Company, 1956), 463.

92. Implied by Kraeling, *Atlas*, 466. Directly asserted by Caird, *Revelation*, 22; Balsdon, *Romans*, 104; and A. N. Sherwin-White, *Roman Society and Roman Law in the New Testament*, the Sarum Lectures, 1960–1961 (Oxford: Clarendon Press, 1963), 77.

Colin J. Hemer, *Local Setting*, 222, notes that though the governor could *initiate* the relegation, it still required the approval of the emperor. The fact that the governor could banish only *within* his province raises the question of whether Patmos lay within the jurisdiction of the governor of Asia. Hemer (*Local Setting*, 28–29) surveys the scanty evidence and concludes that most likely it was, though the data are not as decisive as one would prefer. From our standpoint, of course, we would "expect" more information to have survived because of the island's role in New Testament history. From the standpoint of those in the first-century Roman world, however, Patmos was a rather obscure island and the limited ancient references should not be surprising.

93. Sherwin-White, *Roman Law*, 119. He also notes that the early-second-century emperor Trajan "tried to stop" such practices, which carries the implication that they had become commonplace.

94. Pliny wrote to the emperor: "It was asserted, however, that these people were pardoned upon their petition to the proconsuls, or their legates, which seems likely enough to be the truth, as it is improbable any person should have cared to set them at liberty without authority" (Letter X, quoted in A. H. M. Jones, *A History of Rome Through the Fifth Century* [London: Macmillan, 1970], 243–44). William V. Harris cites this case as evidence that provincial governors were not surprised that record keeping was "somewhat haphazard: and that as a result decisions as to specific prisoners might come up missing" (*Ancient Literacy* [Cambridge, Mass.: Harvard University Press, 1989], 210).

95. Garnsey, *Legal Privilege*, 120–21; Kunke, *Constitutional History*, 73.

96. Robert M. Grand, "The Social Setting of Second Century Christianity," in *Jewish and Christian Self-Definition*, vol. 1: *The Shaping of Christianity in the Second and Third Centuries*, ed. E. P. Sanders (Philadelphia: Fortress Press, 1980), 23.

97. Kraeling, *Atlas*, 463.

98. Garnsey, *Legal Privilege*, 119.

99. Balsdon, *Romans*, 106.

100. Ibid., 107.

101. Ibid.

102. Ibid.

103. As argued by Caird, in *Revelation*, 22, concerning Tertullian's reference in *De Praescript. Haer*, 36.

# Bibliography

In order to facilitate the use of this bibliography, the subject matter has been divided into several major sections. It should be noted, however, that a number of works might be listed just as appropriately under a different section.

A dash as part of the date of a publication indicates that the publication date can only be determined to the degree of specificity indicated (century or decade).

Authors' names are as in the original books cited. Hence, the same individual may be listed under his or her initials *and* the full name because of a variance in procedure from one published work to another.

## Primary Sources: Ancient (Including Compendiums of Extracts from Ancient Sources)

*Apocalypse of Baruch.* Translated from the Syriac by R. H. Charles. London: Adam and Charles Black, 1896.

Aristides, Aelius. "Roman Oration." In James H. Oliver, *The Ruling Power: A Study of the Roman Empire in the Second Century after Christ through the Oration of Aelius Aristides*, 895–907 (English translation); 982–91. (Greek text). Philadelphia: American Philosophical Society, 1953.

Austin, M. M. *The Hellenistic World from Alexander to the Roman Conquest: A Selection of Ancient Sources in Translation.* Cambridge: Cambridge University Press, 1981.

Bagnall, Roger S., and Peter Derow. *Greek Historical Documents: The Hellenistic Period.* SBL Sources for Biblical Study 16. Chico, Calif.: Scholars Press for the Society of Biblical Literature, 1981.

Bets, Hans Dieter. "Introduction to the Greek Magical Papyri." In *The Greek Magical Papyri in Translation*, edited by Hans Dieter Beta, xli–liii. Chicago: University of Chicago Press, 1986.

*Book of Enoch or I Enoch.* Translated from the Ethiopian by R. H. Charles. Oxford: Clarendon Press, 1912.

Cicero. *Philippics.* Loeb Classical Library. Translated by Walter C. A. Ker. Cambridge, Mass.: Harvard University Press, 1926. Reprint, 1969.

"Dialogue with Trypho." In *The Ante-Nicene Fathers.* Volume 1: *The Apostolic Fathers: Justin Martyr, Irenaeus.* New York: Charles Scribner's Sons, 1899.

Dio. *Roman History* (Books LV–LX). Loeb Classical Library. London: William Heinemann, 19– .

Edelstein, Emma J., and Ludwig Edelstein. *Asclepius: A Collection and Interpretation of the Testimonies.* Volume 1. Baltimore: Johns Hopkins Press, 1945.

Eusebius. *Ecclesiastical History of Eusebius Pamphilus.* 1833. Reprint, London: G. Bell and Sons, 1917.

Ferguson, John. *Greek and Roman Religion–A Source Book.* Park Ridge, N.J.: Noyes Press, 1980.

"First and Second Esdras" (New English Bible translation). In *The Cambridge Bible Commentary: First and Second Book of Esdras,* with commentary by R. J. Coggins and M. A. Knibb. Cambridge: Cambridge University Press, 1979.

Goodspeed, Edgar J. *The Apostolic Fathers: An American Translation.* New York: Harper & Brothers, 1950.

Grant, Frederick C. *Ancient Roman Religion.* New York: Liberal Arts Press, 1957.

———. *Hellenistic Religions: The Age of Syncretism.* Indianapolis, Ind.: Bobbs-Merrill Company, 1953.

Grant, Robert M. *The Apostolic Fathers: A New Translation and Commentary.* Volume 1: *An Introduction.* New York: Thomas Nelson & Sons, 1964. Volume 4: *Ignatius of Antioch.* New York: Thomas Nelson & Sons, 1966.

Gregg, Robert C., and Dan Urman. *Jews, Pagans, and Christians in the Golan Heights: Greek and Other Inscriptions of the Roman and Byzantine Eras.* South Florida Studies in the History of Judaism, Volume 140. Atlanta, Ga.: Scholars Press, 1996.

Herodotus. *The History of Herodotus.* Translated by George Rawlinson. Four volumes. London: John Murray, 1858–60.

Ignatius. "Epistles of Ignatius." In *The Ante-Nicene Fathers.* Volume 1: *The Apostolic Fathers, Justin Martyr, Irenaeus,* edited by Alexander Roberts and James Donaldson, 45–96. New York: Charles Scribner's Sons, 1899.

Josephus. *Josephus: Complete Works.* Translated by William Whiston

(1867). Reprint, Grand Rapids, Mich.: Kregel Publications, 1972.

Lefkowitz, Mary R., and Maureen B. Fant. *Women's Life in Greece and Rome: A Sourcebook in Translation*. Second edition. Baltimore: Johns Hopkins University Press, 1992.

Lewis, Naphtali. *Greek Historical Documents–The Roman Principate: 27 B.C.–285 A.D.* Toronto (Canada): A. M. Hakkert, 1974.

LiDonnici, Lynn R. *The Epidaurian Miracle Inscriptions: Text, Translation, and Commentary*. Atlanta, Ga.: Scholars Press, 1995.

Livy (Titus Livius). *The History of Rome (Books XXI–XXX)*. Translated by D. Spillan and Cyrus Edmonds. New York: Harper & Brothers, Publishers, 1892.

MacMullen, Ramsay, and Eugene N. Lane. *Paganism and Christianity, 100–425 C.E.–A Sourcebook*. Minneapolis, Minn.: Fortress Press, 1992.

"Martyrdom of Polycarp." ["The Encyclical Epistle of the Church at Smyrna Concerning the Martyrdom of the Holy Polycarp."] In *The Ante-Nicene Fathers*, Volume 1: *The Apostolic Fathers: Justin Martyr, Irenaeus*, edited by Alexander Roberts and James Donaldson, 39–44. New York: Charles Scribner's Sons, 1899.

Meijer, Fik, and Onno van Nijf. *Trade, Transport, and Society in the Ancient World: A Sourcebook*. London: Routledge, 1992.

Pausanias. *Description of Greece*. Translated by Thomas Taylor. Three volumes. London: Richard Priestly, High Holborn, 1824.

———. *Pausanias' Guide to Greece*. Volume 1. Translated by Peter Levi. [Great Britain]: Penguin Books, 1979.

Pedley, John Griffiths. *Ancient Literary Sources on Sardis*. Archaeological Exploration of Sardis, monograph 2. Cambridge, Mass.: Harvard University Press, 1972.

Philo. *The Embassy to Gaius*. Loeb Classical Library. *Philo*, Volume 10. Translated by F. H. Colson. Cambridge, Mass.: Harvard University Press, 1962. Reprint, 1971.

Philostratus. *The Life of Apollonius of Tyana*. Translated by F. C. Conybeare. Volume 1. Loeb Classical Library. London: William Heinemann, 1912.

———. *Lives of the Sophists*. In *Philostratus and Eunapius: The Lives of the Sophists*. Revised edition. Translated by Wilmer C. Wright. Loeb Classical Library. London: William Heinemann, 1952.

Pliny. *Natural History* (Books III–VI). Loeb Classical Library. Translated by H. Rackhan. Cambridge, Mass.: Harvard University Press, 1942.

Pollitt, J. J. *The Art of Ancient Greece: Sources and Documents*. Cambridge: Cambridge University Press, 1990.

Polybius. *The Histories of Polybius*. Volume 1. Translated by Evelyn S. Shuckburgh. 1889. Reprinted with a new introduction by F. W. Wilbank. Bloomington [Ind.]: Indiana University Press, 1962.

Polycarp. "Epistle to the Philippians." In *The Ante-Nicene Fathers*. Volume 1: *The Apostolic Fathers: Justin Martyr, Irenaeus*, edited by Alexander Roberts and James Donaldson, 31–36. New York: Charles Scribner's Sons, 1899.

Rice, David G., and John E. Stambaugh. *Sources for the Study of Greek Religion*. Missoula, Mont.: Scholars Press, 1979.

Schneemelcher, Wilhelm. "The Epistle to the Laodiceans." In *New Testament Apocrypha*, edited by Wilhelm Schneemelcher, 42–46. Revised edition. Translated from the German by R. McL. Wilson. Louisville, Ky.: Westminster/John Knox Press, 1992.

Sherk, Robert K. *Roman Documents from the Greek East: "Senatus Consulta" and "Epistulae" to the Age of Augustus*. Baltimore, Md.: Johns Hopkins Press, 1969.

Stern, Menaham. *Greek and Latin Authors on Jews and Judaism*. Volume 1: *From Herodotus to Plutarch*. Jerusalem: Israel Academy of Sciences and Humanities, 1974. Volume 2: *From Tacitus to Simplicius*. Jerusalem: Israel Academy of Sciences and Humanities, 1980.

Strabo. *The Geography of Strabo*. Greek text with English translation by Horace Leonard Jones. Loeb Classical Library. Books 10–12: London: William Heinemann, 1928. Books 13–14: London: William Heinemann, 1929.

Suetonius. *The Lives of the Twelve Caesars*. Translated by Alexander Thomson. Revised by T. Forester. London: George Bell & Sons. 1896 reprint.

Sweet, Waldo. *Sport and Recreation in Ancient Greece: A Sourcebook with Translations*. New York: Oxford University Press, 1987.

"Syriac Apocalypse of Baruch," translated by R. H. Charles, revised by L. H. Brockington. In *The Apocryphal Old Testament*, edited by H. F. D. Sparks. Oxford: Clarendon Press, 1984.

Tacitus. *The Works of Tacitus*. Volume 1: *The Annals*. Bohn's Classical Library. The Oxford Translation, revised. London: Henry G. Bohn, 1854.

[Tatius, Achilles.] *Achilles Tatius [Clitophon and Leucippe]*. Loeb Classical Library. Translated by S. Gaselee. London: William Heinemann, 1917.

"Testament of Dan" and "Testament of Levi" in "The Testaments of the Twelve Patriarchs," translated by M. de Jonge. In *The Apocryphal Old Testament*, edited by H. F. D. Sparks. Oxford: Clarendon Press, 1984.

Thucydides. "The Peloponnesian War," translated by Benjamin Jowett. In *The Greek Historians: The Complete and Unabridged Historical Works of Herodotus, Thucydides, Xenophon, Arrian*, edited by Francis R. B. Godolphin. New York: Random House, 1942.

Varro, M. Terentius. *On Agriculture*. Loeb Classical Library. Translated by William D. Hooper. Revised by Harrison B. Ash. Cambridge, Mass.: Harvard University Press, 1935; 1967 reprint.

Vermaseren, M. J. *Corpus Cultus Cybelae Attidisque (CCCA) I. Asia Minor*. Leiden: E. J. Brill, 1987.

Victronius. "Commentary on the Apocalypse of the Blessed John." Translated by Robert E. Wallis. In *The Ante-Nicene Fathers*. Volume 7: *Lactantius, Venantius, Asterius, Victroninus, Dionysius, Apostolic Teaching and Constitutions, Homily, and Liturgies*, edited by Alexander Roberts and James Donaldson. Buffalo, N.Y.: Christian Literature Company, 1886.

Whittaker, Molly. *Jews and Christians: Graeco-Roman Views*. Cambridge [England]: Cambridge University Press, 1984.

Workman, B. K. *They Saw It Happen in Classical Times: An Anthology of Eyewitnesses' Accounts of Events in the Histories of Greece and Rome, 1400 B.C.–A.D. 540*. Oxford: Basil Blackwell, 1964.

Xenophon. *Cyropaedia*. Greek text with English translation by Walter Miller. Loeb Classical Library. London: William Heinemann, 1914.

## Primary Sources: Modern

Curtis, William E. *Today in Syria and Palestine*. Chicago: Fleming H. Revell Company, 1903.

Durbin, John P. *Observations in the East: Chiefly in Egypt, Palestine, Syria, and Asia Minor*. Volume 2. New York: Harper & Brothers, Publishers, 1845.

Fellows, [Sir] Charles. *Travels and Researches in Asia Minor*. London: John Murray, 1852.

Hamilton, William J. *Researches in Asia Minor*. Volume 1. London: John Murray, 1842. Reprint: Hildesheim [Germany]: Georg Olms Verlag, 1984.

Hawley, Walter A. *Asia Minor*. London: John Lane/Bodley Head, 1918.

McGarvey, J. W. *Lands of the Bible*. Philadelphia: J. B. Lippincott & Company, 1881.

Miller, Ellen Clare. *Eastern Sketches: Notes of Scenery, Schools, and Tent Life in Syria and Palestine*. Edinburgh [Scotland]: W. Oliphant, 1871. Reprint, New York: Arno Press, 1977.

Oliphant, Laurence. *Haifa or Life in Modern Palestine*. Edited by Charles A. Dane. New York: Harper & Brothers, 1886; 1887 printing.

Pentreath, Guy. *Hellenic Traveller: A Guide to the Ancient Sites of Greece*. New York: Crowell Company, 1964.

Stark, Freya. *Ionia: A Quest*. New York: Harcourt, Brace and Company, 1954.

Tozer, Henry F. *The Islands of the Aegean*. Oxford: Oxford University Press, 1889. Reprint, Chicago: Obol International, 1976.

Van Lennep, Henry J. *Travels in Little-Known Parts of Asia Minor*. Volume 2. London: John Murray, 1870.

Walsh, Robert. *Constantinople and the Scenery of the Seven Churches of Asia*. London: Fisher, Son, & Co., 1838.

Wilson, Charles Major-General Sir. *Handbook for Travellers in Asia Minor, Trans-caucasia, Persia, etc.* London: John Murray, 1895; 1911 reprint.

Wood, J. T. *Modern Discoveries on the Site of Ancient Ephesus*. Oxford: The Religious Tract Society, 1890.

Ximinez, Saturnio. *Asia Minor in Ruins*. Translated from the Spanish by Arthur Chambers. London: Hutchinson & Co., 1925.

### Commentaries and Related Literature: Revelation

Alford, Henry. *The New Testament for English Readers*. Volume 2: *The Epistle to the Hebrews, the Catholic Epistles, and the Revelation*. New edition. Boston: Lee and Shepard, Publishers, 1880.

Allen, Cady H. *The Message of the Book of Revelation*. Nashville, Tenn.: Cokesbury Press, 1939.

Ashcroft, Morris. "Revelation." In *The Broadman Bible Commentary*. Volume 12: *Hebrews-Revelation*. Nashville, Tenn.: Broadman Press, 1972.

Barclay, William. *The Revelation of John*. Volume 1: chapters 1 to 5. Revised edition. Philadelphia: Westminster Press, 1976.

Baucham, Richard. *The Theology of the Book of Revelation*. Cambridge: Cambridge University Press, 1993.

Beagley, Alan J. *The "Sitz Im Leben" of the Apocalypse with Particular Reference to the Role of the Church's Enemies*. Berlin: Walter de Gruyter, 1987.

Beasley-Murray, G. R. *The Book of Revelation*. The New Century Bible series. Greenwood, S.C.: Attic Press, 1974.

Beckwith, Isbon T. *The Apocalypse of John*. New York: Macmillan Company, 1919.

Best, W. E. *Diminishing Spirituality in Local Churches: Studies in Revelation 2 & 3*. Houston, Tx.: South Belt Grace Church, 1986.

Blaiklock, E. M. *The Seven Churches: An Exposition of Revelation Chapters Two and Three*. London: Marshall, Morgan & Scott, 19– .

Boer, Harry R. *The Book of Revelation*. Grand Rapids, Mich.: William B. Eerdmans Publishing Company, 1979.

Boring, M. Eugene. *Revelation*. The Interpretation Commentary series. Louisville, Ky.: John Knox Press, 1989.

Brown, Charles. *Heavenly Visions: An Exposition of the Book of Revelation*. Boston: Pilgrim Press, 1910.

Bruce, F. F. "Revelation." In *A New Testament Commentary*, general editor G. C. D. Howley. Grand Rapids, Mich.: Zondervan Publishing House, 1969.

Caird, G. B. *A Commentary on the Revelation of St. John the Divine*. The Harper's New Testament Commentaries series. New York: Harper & Row, Publishers, 1966.

Calkins, Raymond. *The Social Message of the Book of Revelation*. New York City: Women's Press, 1920.

Carpenter, W. Boyd. *The Revelation of St. John the Divine*. The Ellicott Bible Commentary series. London: Cassell and Company, 1877. 1903 printing.

Case, Shirley J. *The Revelation of John: A Historical Interpretation*. Chicago: University of Chicago Press, 1919.

Charles, R. H. *Revelation*. Volume 1 in the International Critical Commentary series. Edinburgh [Scotland]: T. & T. Clark, 1920; 1979 reprint.

Chilton, David. *The Days of Vengeance: An Exposition of the Book of Revelation*. Fort Worth, Tx.: Dominion Press, 1987.

Collins, Adela Yarbro. *Apocalypse*. The New Testament Message: A Biblical-Theological Commentary series. Wilmington, Del.: Michael Glazier, 1979.

———. *Crisis and Catharsis: The Power of the Apocalypse*. Philadelphia: Westminster Press, 1984.

Corsini, Eugenio. *The Apocalypse: The Perennial Revelation of Jesus Christ*. Translated and edited by Francis J. Moloney. Wilmington, Del.: Michael Glazier, 1983.

Court, John W. *Myth and History in the Book of Revelation*. Atlanta, Ga.: John Knox Press, 1979.

———. *Revelation*. The New Testament Guides series. Huddersfield [Great Britain]: Scheffield Academic Press, 1994.

Draper, James T., Jr. *The Unveiling*. Nashville, Tenn.: Broadman Press, 1984.

Efird, James M. *Revelation for Today*. Nashville, Tenn.: Abingdon Press, 1989.

Farrer, Austin. *The Revelation of St. John the Divine*. Oxford: Clarendon Press, 1964.

Fiorenza, Elisabeth Schüssler. *Revelation: Vision of a Just World*. Minneapolis, Minn.: Fortress Press, 1991.

Ford, J. Massyngberde. *Revelation*. The Anchor Bible series. Garden City, N.Y.: Doubleday & Company, 1975.

Franzmann, Martin F. *The Revelation to John*. St. Louis, Mo.: Concordia, 1976.

Gentry, Kenneth L., Jr. *Before Jerusalem Fell: Dating the Book of Revelation*. Tyler, Tx.: Institute for Christian Economics, 1989.

Giblin, Charles H. *The Book of Revelation: The Open Book of Prophecy*. Collegeville, Minn.: A Michael Glazier Book/The Liturgical Press, 1991.

Glasson, T. F. *The Revelation of John*. The Cambridge Bible Commentary. Cambridge [England]: Cambridge University Press, 1965.

Grant, Frederick C. *Nelson's Bible Commentary*. Volume 7: *New Testament: Romans-Revelation*. New York: Thomas Nelson & Sons, 1962.

Guimond, John. *The Silencing of Babylon: A Spiritual Commentary on the Revelation of John*. New York: Paulist Press, 1991.

Guthrie, Donald. *The Revelance of John's Apocalypse*. Exeter, Devon [England]: Paternoster Press, 1987.

Hailey, Homer. *Revelation: An Introduction and Commentary*. Grand Rapids, Mich.: Baker Book House, 1979.

Harrington, Wilfried J. *Revelation (Sacra Pagina, volume 16)*. Collegeville, Minn.: Luturgical Press/A Michael Glazier Book, 1993.

———. *Understanding the Apocalypse*. Washington, D.C.: Corpus Books, 1969.

Hengstenberg, E. W. *The Revelation of St. John*. Translated from the

German by Patrick Fairbairn. New York: Robert Carter & Brothers, 1852.

Hinds, John T. *A Commentary on the Book of Revelation*. Nashville, Tenn.: Gospel Advocate Company, 1937; 1974 reprint.

Hoeksema, Herman. *Behold, He Cometh! An Exposition of the Book of Revelation*. Grand Rapids, Mich.: Reformed Free Publishing Association, 1969.

Howard, Fred D. *1, 2, and 3 John, Jude and Revelation*. Volume 24 in the Layman's Bible Book Commentary. Nashville, Tenn.: Broadman Press, 1982.

Hughes, Philip E. *The Book of the Revelation: A Commentary*. Grand Rapids, Mich.: William B. Eerdmans Publishing Company, 1990.

Jeske, Richard L. *Revelation for Today: Images of Hope*. Philadelphia: Fortress Press, 1983.

Johnson, Alan. "Revelation." In volume 12 of The Expositor's Bible Commentary, edited by Frank E. Gaebelein. Grand Rapids, Mich.: Zondervan Publishing House, 1981.

———. *Revelation*. Grand Rapids, Mich.: Zondervan Publishing House, 1983.

Kee, Howard C. *Understanding the New Testament*. Fourth edition. Englewood Cliffs, N.J.: Prentice-Hall, 1983.

Kelshaw, Terence. *Send This Message to My Church: Christ's Words to the Seven Churches of Revelation*. Nashville, Tenn.: Thomas Nelson Publishers, 1984.

Kent, Charles Foster. *The Work and Teachings of the Apostles* ("The Historical Bible"). New York: Charles Scribner's Sons, 1916.

Kiddle, Martin. *The Revelation of St. John*. Moffatt New Testament Commentary series. New York: Harper and Brothers, Publishers, 1940.

Krodel, Gerhard A. *Augsburg Commentary on the New Testament: Revelation*. Minneapolis, Minn.: Augsburg Publishing House, 1989.

Ladd, George Eldon. *A Commentary on the Revelation of John*. Grand Rapids, Mich.: William B. Eerdmans Publishing Company, 1972.

Lang, G. H. *The Revelation of Jesus Christ: Select Studies*. Self-published. Distributed by: London: Oliphants Ltd., 1945.

Lenski, R. C. H. *The Interpretation of St. John's Revelation*. Columbus, Ohio: Warburg Press, 1943.

Lilje, Hans. *The Last Book of the Bible: The Meaning of the Revelation of St. John*. Translated from the fourth German edition by Olive Wyon. Philadelphia: Muhlenberg Press, 1957.

Loane, Marcus L. *They Overcame: An Exposition of the First Three Chapters of Revelation*. [n.p.]: Angus and Robertson, 1971. Reprint, Grand Rapids, Mich.: Baker Book House, 1981.

McDaniel, George W. *The Churches of the New Testament*. New York: Richard R. Smith, 1921; 1930 printing.

Martin, Hugh. *The Seven Letters*. Philadelphia: Westminster Press, 1956.

Meinardus, Otto F. A. *St. John of Patmos and the Seven Churches of the Apocalypse*. New Rochelle, N.Y.: Caratzas Brothers, Publishers, 1979.

————. *St. Paul in Ephesus–and the Cities of Galatia and Cyprus*. New Rochelle, N.Y.: Caratzas Brothers, Publishers, 1979.

Milligan, William. *The Book of Revelation (Expositor's Bible)*. New York: Funk & Wagnalls Company, 1900.

Morgan, G. Campbell. *The Letters of our Lord–A First Century Message to Twentieth Century Christians: Addresses Based upon the Letters to the Seven Churches of Asia*. New York: Fleming H. Revell Company, 1902.

Morris, Leon. *The Revelation of St. John*. Tyndale New Testament Commentary series. Grand Rapids, Mich.: William B. Eerdmans Publishing Company, 1969.

Mounce, Robert H. *New International Commentary on Revelation*. Grand Rapids, Mich.: William B. Eerdmans Publishing Company, 1977.

————. *What Are We Waiting For? A Commentary on Revelation*. Grand Rapids, Mich.: William. B. Eerdmans Publishing Company, 1992.

Moyise, Steve. *The Old Testament in the Book of Revelation*. Journal for the Study of the New Testament, Supplement 115. Sheffield, England: Sheffield Academic Press, 1995.

Onstad, Esther. *Courage for Today–Hope for Tomorrow: A Study of the Revelation*. Minneapolis, Minn.: Augsburg Publishing House, 1973, 1974.

Palmer, Earl F. *1, 2, and 3 John, Revelation*. The Communicator's Commentary series. Waco, Tx.: Word Books, Publishers, 1982.

Pieters, Albertus. *The Lamb, the Woman, and the Dragon: An Exposition of the Revelation of St. John*. Grand Rapids, Mich., 1937. Reprinted as *Studies in the Revelation of St. John*. Grand Rapids, Mich.: William B. Eerdmans Publishing Company, 1943, 1950.

Prevost, Jean-Pierre. *How to Read the Apocalypse*. Translated from the French by John Bowden and Margaret Lydamore. New York: Crossroad, 1993.

Ramsay, William M. *The Letters to the Seven Churches of Asia*. New York: George H. Doran Company, 1905.

Robbins, Ray F. *The Revelation of Jesus Christ*. Nashville, Tenn.: Broadman Press, 1975.

Scott, C. Anderson. *The Book of the Revelation*. New York: George H. Doran Company, (n.d.)

Seiss, Joseph A. *Letters to the Seven Churches*. Grand Rapids, Mich.: Baker Book House, 1956. Reprint of *Letters of Jesus*, 1889.

Selles, L. *The Book of Revelation*. Volume 1. London, Ontario: Inter-league Publication Board of Canadian Reformed Societies, 1965.

Sheppard, W. J. Limmer. *The Revelation of St. John the Divine: I–XI*. London: Religious Tract Society, 1923.

Sinclair, Scott G. *Revelation: A Book for the Rest of Us*. Berkeley, Calif.: Bibal Press, 1992.

Stuart, Moses. *A Commentary on the Apocalypse*. Volume 2. Andover: Allen, Morrill, and Wardwell, 1845.

Sweet, J. P. W. *Revelation*. Westminster Pelican Commentaries series. Philadelphia: Westminster Press, 1979.

Swete, Henry B. *The Apocalypse of St. John: The Greek Text with Introduction, Notes, and Indices*. Third edition. London: Macmillan and Co., 1909; reprint, 1911.

Tait, Andrew. *The Messages to the Seven Churches of Asia*. London: Hodder and Stoughton, 1884.

Thompson, Steven. *The Apocalypse and Semitic Syntax*. Cambridge: Cambridge University Press, 1985.

Tickle, John. *The Book of Revelation: A Catholic Interpretation of the Apocalypse*. Liguori, Mo.: Liguori Publications, 1983.

Tremmel, William C. *The Twenty-Seven Books that Changed the World: A Guide to Reading the New Testament*. New York: Holt, Rinehart and Winston, 1981.

Trench, Richard C. *Commentary on the Epistles to the Seven Churches in Asia*. New York: Charles Scribner & Co., 1872.

Van Hartingsveld, L. *Revelation: A Practical Commentary*. Translated from the Dutch by John Vriend. Grand Rapids, Mich.: William B. Eerdmans Publishing Co., 1985.

Walvoord, John F. *The Revelation of Jesus Christ*. Chicago: Moody Press, 1966.

Weiss, Bernhard. *A Commentary on the New Testament*. Volume 4: *Thessalonians-Revelation*, translated by George H. Schodde and Epiphanius Wilson. New York: Funk & Wagnalls Company, 1906.

Whiting, Charles C. *The Revelation of John*. Boston: Gorham Press, 1918.

Wilcock, Michael. *I Saw Heaven Opened: The Message of Revelation*. London: Inter-Varsity Press, 1975.

## Commentaries and Related Literature: Other Bible Books

Aune, David E. "Magic in Early Christianity." *Aufstieg und Niedergang der Romischen Welt*, II, 23.2, 1507–57. Berlin: Walter de Gruyter, 1980.

Avi-Yonah, Michael. *Views of the Biblical World*. Volume 5: *The New Testament*. Jerusalem [Israel]: International Publishing Company, 1961.

Bacon, Charles Foster. *The Work and Teachings of the Apostles*. Volume 6 of *The Historical Bible*. New York: Charles Scribner's Sons, 1916.

Baez-Camargo, Gonzalo. *Archaeological Commentary on the Bible*. Translated by Eugene A. Nida. Garden City, N.Y.: Doubleday & Company, 1984.

Barclay, William. *The Letters to the Philippians, Colossians, and Thessalonians*. Revised edition. Daily Study Bible series. Philadelphia: Westminster Press, 1975.

Bengel, John Albert. *Gnomon of the New Testament*. Volume 5. Translated by William Fletcher. Edinburgh [Scotland]: T. & T. Clark, 1859.

Beyer, Bryan. "Obadiah." In Bryan Beyer and John Walton, *Obadiah, Jonah: Bible Study Commentaries*. Grand Rapids, Mich.: Lamplight Books/Zondervan Publishing House, 1988.

Blaiklock, E. M. "The Acts of the Apostle as a Document of First Century History." In *Apostolic History and the Gospel*, edited by W. Ward Gasque and Ralph P. Martin, 41–54. [Great Britain]: Paternoster Press, 1970.

Bruce, F. F. *New International Commentary on the New Testament: The Epistles to the Colossians, to Philemon, and to the Ephesians*. Grand Rapids, Mich.: William B. Eerdmans Publishing Company, 1984.

Cadbury, Henry J. *The Book of Acts in History*. London: Adam and Charles Black, 1955.

Caird, G. B. *Paul's Letters from Prison: Ephesians, Philippians, Colossians, Philemon*. New Clarendon Bible Commentary series. Oxford: Oxford University Press, 1976.

Carson, Herbert M. *Colossians and Philemon*. Tyndale New Testament Commentary series. Grand Rapids, Mich.: William B. Eerdmans Publishing Company, 1960.

Cassidy, Richard J. *Society and Politics in the Acts of the Apostles*. Maryknoll, N.Y.: Orbis Books, 1987.

Daille, Jean. *An Exposition of the Epistle of Saint Paul to the Colossians*. 1648. Translated from the French by "F. S." Revised and corrected by James Sherman. Reprint English translation, Philadelphia: Presbyterian Board of Publication, 18– .

Dargen, Edwin C. "Colossians." In *An American Commentary on the New Testament: Corinthians to Thessalonians*. Philadelphia: American Baptist Publication Society, 1890.

Demarest, Gary. *Colossians: The Mystery of Christ*. Waco, Tx.: Word Books, 1979.

Duncan, George S. *St. Paul's Ephesian Ministry: A Reconstruction*. New York: Charles Scribner's Sons, 1930.

Earle, Ralph. "1 Timothy; 2 Timothy." In *Ephesians-Philemon*. Volume 11 in The Expositor's Bible Commentary. Grand Rapids, Mich.: Zondervan Publishing House, 1978.

Fairbairn, Patrick. *The Pastoral Epistles*. Edinburgh [Scotland]: T. & T. Clark, 1874.

Fee, Gordon D. *1 and 2 Timothy, Titus*. Good News Commentary series. San Francisco: Harper & Row, Publishing 1984.

Festugiere, Andre-Jean. *Personal Religion Among the Greeks*. Berkeley and Los Angeles: University of California Press, 1954.

Firminger Walter K. *Colossians and Philemon* ("Indian Church Commentaries"). Madras [India]: S.P.C.K., 1921.

Fornberg, Tord. *An Early Church in a Pluralistic Society: A Study of 2 Peter*. Translated by Jean Gray. [Sweden]: CWK Gleerup, 1977.

Goodspeed, Edgar J. *Introduction to the New Testament*. Chicago: University of Chicago Press, 1937.

Gritz, Sharon Hodgin. *Paul, Women Teachers, and the Mother Goddess at Ephesus: A Study of 1 Timothy 2:9–15 in Light of the Religious and Cultural Milieu of the First Century*. Lanham, N.Y.: University Press of America, 1991.

Guthrie, Donald. *The Apostles*. Grand Rapids, Mich.: Zondervan Publishing House, 1975.

———. *The Pastoral Epistles: An Introduction and Commentary*. Tyndale Commentary series. Grand Rapids, Mich.: William B. Eerdmans Publishing Company, 1957.

Hanson, A. T. *The Pastoral Epistles*. The New Century Bible Commentary series. Grand Rapids, Mich.: William B. Eerdmans

Publishing Company, [British edition: London: Marshall, Morgan & Scott, Publishers], 1982.

Harris, Murray J. *Colossians and Philemon*. Grand Rapids, Mich.: William B. Eerdmans Publishing Company, 1991.

Harvey, H. H. "First and Second Timothy." In *An American Commentary on the New Testament: Timothy to Peter*. Philadelphia: American Baptist Publication Society, 1890.

Hillard, A. E. *The Pastoral Epistles of St. Paul*. London: Rivingons, 1919.

Houlden, J. L. *Paul's Letters from Prison: Philippians, Colossians, Philemon, and Ephesians*. Westminster Pelican Commentaries series. Philadelphia: Westminster Press, 1977.

Hultgren, Arland J. "1 and 2 Timothy." In Arland J. Hultgren and Roger Aus, *I–II Timothy, Titus, II Thessalonians*. Augsburg Commentary on the New Testament series. Minneapolis, Minn.: Augsburg Publishing House, 1984.

Ironside, H. A. *Lectures on the Epistle to the Colossians*. New York: Bible Truth Press, 1929.

Jones, Maurice. *The Epistle of St. Paul to the Colossians*. London: Society for Promotion of Christian Knowledge, 1923.

Kelly, J. N. D. *A Commentary on the Pastoral Epistles*. Harper's New Testament Commentary series. New York: Harper & Row, 1963.

Kent, Homer A. *The Pastoral Epistles: Studies in I and II Timothy and Titus*. Chicago: Moody Press, 1958.

Lightfoot, J. B. *Saint Paul's Epistles to the Colossians and to Philemon*. Revised Edition. London: Macmillan and Company, 1879.

Lohse, Eduard. *Colossians and Philemon*. Edited by Helmut Koester. Translated from the German by William R. Poehlmann and Robert J. Harris. Philadelphia: Fortress Press, 1971.

Lyall, Francis. *Slaves, Citizens, Sons: Legal Metaphors in the Epistles*. Grand Rapids, Mich.: Academie Books: Zondervan Publishing House, 1984.

Martin, Ralph R. *Colossians and Philemon*. The New Century Bible Commentary series. Greenwood, S.C.: Attic Press, 1974.

———. *Ephesians, Colossians, and Philemon*. Atlanta, Ga.: John Knox Press, 1991.

Metzger, Bruce M. *Breaking the Code: Understanding the Book of Revelation*. Nashville, Tenn.: Abingdon Press, 1993.

Michaels, J. Ramsey. *Interpreting the Book of Revelation*. Grand Rapids, Mich.: Baker Book House, 1992.

Moellering, H. Armin. "1 and 2 Timothy." In *1 Timothy-Philemon*.

Concordia Commentary. Saint Louis, Mo.: Concordia Publishing House, 1970.

Nicholson, Roy S. "The Pastoral Epistles." In *Romans-Philemon*. Volume 50 in The Wesleyan Bible Commentaries. Grand Rapids, Mich.: William B. Eerdmans Publishing Company, 1965.

O'Brien, Peter T. *Word Biblical Commentary*. Volume 44: *Colossians, Philemon*. Waco, Tx.: Word Books, Publishers, 1982.

Oden, Thomas C. *First and Second Timothy and Titus*. The Interpretation Commentary series. Louisville, Ky.: John Knox Press, 1989.

Patzia, Arthur G. *Colossians, Philemon, Ephesians*. San Francisco: Harper & Row, Publishers, 1984.

Perowne, Stewart. *The Journeys of St. Paul*. London: Hamlyn, 1973.

Pfleiderer, Otto. *Primitive Christianity: Its Writings and Teachings in Their Historical Connections*. Volume 3. Translated from the German by W. Montgomery. London: Williams & Norgate, 1910.

Plummer, Alfred. *The Pastoral Epistles*. New York: A. C. Armstrong & Son, 1893.

Pokorny, Petr. *Colossians: A Commentary*. Translated from the German by Siegfried S. Schatzmann. Peabody, Mass.: Hendrickson Publishers, 1991.

Ralph, Margaret N. *Discovering the First Century Church: The Acts of the Apostles, Letters of Paul, and the Book of Revelation*. New York: Paulist Press, 1991.

Robertson, Archibald T. *Paul and the Intellectuals: The Epistle to the Colossians*. Garden City, N.Y.: Doubleday, Doran and Company, 1928.

Rutherford, John. *St. Paul's Epistles to Colossae and Laodicea*. Edinburgh [Scotland]: T. & T. Clark, 1908.

Schweizer, Eduard. *The Letter to the Colossians: A Commentary*. Translated from the German by Andrew Chester. Minneapolis, Minn.: Augsburg Publishing House, 1976.

Scott, E. F. *The Pastoral Epistles*. Moffatt New Testament Commentary series. London: Hodder and Stoughton, 1936; 1948 reprint.

Simpson, E. K. *The Pastoral Epistles*. London: Tyndale Press, 1954.

Stuart, Douglas. *Hosea-Jonah*. The Word Biblical Commentary series. Waco, Tx.: Word Books, 1987.

Thomas, W. H. Griffith. *Studies in Colossians and Ephesians*. Grand Rapids, Mich.: Kregel Publications, 1986.

Tolbert, Malcolm O. *Layman's Bible Book Commentary*. Volume 22:

*Colossians, Philippians, 1 and 2 Thessalonians, 1 and 2 Timothy, Titus, Philemon*. Nashville, Tenn.: Broadman Press, 1980.

Trevethan, Thomas L. *Our Joyful Confidence: The Lordship of Jesus in Colossians*. Downers Grove, Ill.: InterVarsity Press, 1981.

Turner, George A. "Colossians." In *Romans-Philemon*, edited by Charles W. Carter, et al. Volume 5 in The Wesleyan Bible Commentary. Grand Rapids, Mich.: William B. Eerdmans Publishing Company, 1965.

Unger, Merrill F. *The New Unger's Bible Handbook*. Revised by Gary N. Larson. Chicago: Moody Press, 1984.

Vaughn, Curtis. "Colossians." In *Ephesians-Philemon*, edited by Frank E. Gaebelein. Volume 11 in The Expositor's Bible Commentary. Grand Rapids, Mich.: Zondervan Publishing House, 1978.

Ward, Ronald A. *Commentary on 1 and 2 Timothy and Titus*. Waco, Tx.: Word Books, Publishers, 1974.

Watts, John D. W. *Books of Joel, Obadiah, Jonah, Nahum, Habakkuk, and Zephaniah*. In the *Cambridge Bible Commentary on the New English Bible*. Cambridge: Cambridge University Press, 1975.

White, E. R. O. "Colossians." In *2 Corinthians-Philemon*, edited by Clifton J. Allen. *The Broadman Bible Commentary*. Nashville, Tenn.: Broadman Press, 1971.

Williams, Charles B. *A Commentary on the Pauline Epistles*. Chicago: Moody Press, 1953.

## Histories and Related Works

Adams, J. Mckee. *Biblical Backgrounds*. Revised by Joseph A. Callaway. Nashville, Tenn.: Broadman Press, 1965.

Akurgal, Ekrem. *Ancient Civilizations and Ruins of Turkey: From Prehistoric Times Until the End of the Roman Empire*. Third edition. Ankara [Turkey]: Turkish Historical Society Press/Haset Kitabevi, 1973.

Applebaum, S. "The Legal Status of the Jewish Communities in the Diaspora." In *The Jewish People in the First Century: Historical Geography, Political History, Social, Cultural, and Religious Life and Institutions*, edited by S. Safari and M. Stern, 420–63. Volume 1. Assen [Netherlands]: Van Gorcum & Company, B.V., 1974.

———. "The Organization of the Jewish Communities in the Diaspora." In *The Jewish People in the First Century: Historical Geog-*

*raphy, Political History, Social, Cultural, and Religious Life and Institutions*, edited by S. Safari and M. Stern, 464–503. Volume 1. Assen [Netherlands]: Van Gorcum & Company, B. V., 1974.

Applebaum, Shimon. *Jews and Greeks in Ancient Cyrene*. Leiden: E. J. Brill, 1979.

Archibald, Zophia. *Discovering the World of the Ancient Greeks*. New York: Facts on File, 1991.

Arnold, W. T. *The Roman System of Provincial Administration*. Third edition. Revised by E. S. Bouchier. Oxford: Oxford University Press, 1914. Reprint, Chicago: Ares Publishers, 1974.

Aune, David E. "Magic in Early Christianity." In *Aufstieg und Niedergang der Romischen Welt*, II, 23.2, 1507–57. Berlin: Walter de Gruyter, 1980.

Aurenhammer, Maria. "Sculptures of Gods and Heroes from Ephesos." In *Ephesos: Metropolis of Asia–An Interdisciplinary Approach to Its Archaeology, Religion, and Culture*, edited by Helmut Koester, 251–80. Harvard Theological Studies 41. Valley Forge, Pa.: Trinity Press International, 1995.

Avery, Catherine B. *The New Century Classical Handbook*. New York: Appleton-Century, Crofts, 1962.

Badian, E. *Publicans and Sinners: Private Enterprise in the Service of the Roman Republic*. Oxford: Basil Blackwell, 1972.

Ballance, Michael H., and Olwen Brogan. "Roman Marble: A Link Between Asia Minor and Libya." In *Geology and History of Turkey*, edited by Angus S. Campbell, 33–38. Tripoli [Libya]: Petroleum Exploration Society of Libya, 1971.

Balsdon, J. P. V. D. *Romans and Aliens*. Chapel Hill, N.C.: University of North Carolina Press, 1979.

———. *Rome: The Story of an Empire*. New York: McGraw-Hill Book Company, 1970.

Bara, Musa. *Ephesus and Its Surroundings*. Translated by Hulya Terzioglu. Izmir [Turkey]: Molay Matbaacilik, 19– .

Baring, Anne and Jules Cashford. *The Myth of the Goddess: Evolution of an Image*. New York: Viking Arkana, 1991.

Barnes, Timothy. "Pagan Perceptions of Christianity." In *Early Christianity: Origins and Evolution to A.D. 600*, edited by Ian Hazlett, 231–43. Nashville, Tenn.: Abingdon Press, 1991.

Barr, David L. "Elephants and Holograms: From Metaphor to Methodology in the Study of John's Apocalypse." In *Society of Biblical Literature Seminar Papers Series: 1986*, edited by Kent H. Richards, 400–11. Atlanta, Ga.: Scholars Press, 1986.

Barton, George A. *Archaeology and the Bible*. Seventh edition. Revised. Philadelphia: American Sunday-School Union, 1937.

Bauer, Walter. *Orthodoxy and Heresy in Earliest Christianity*. Second German edition translated by Robert A. Kraft, David Hay, et al. Edited by Robert A. Kraft and Gerhard Krodel. Philadelphia: Fortress Press, 1971.

Baugh, S. M. "A Foreign World: Ephesus in the First Century." In *Women in the Church: A Fresh Analysis of 1 Timothy 2:9–15*, edited by Andreas J. Kostenberger, Thomas R. Schreiner, and H. Scott Baldwin, 13–52. Grand Rapids, Mich.: Baker Books, 1995.

Baus, Karl. *Handbook of Church History*. Volume 1: *From the Apostolic Community to Constantine*. Translated from the German. New York: Herder and Herder, 1965.

Beagley, Alan J. *The "Sitz Im Leben" of the Apocalypse with Particular Reference to the Role of the Church's Enemies*. Berlin: Walter de Gruyter, 1987.

Bean, George E. *Aegean Turkey: An Archaeological Guide*. New York: Frederick A. Praeger, Publishers, 1966.

————. *Turkey Beyond the Maeander*. Revised edition. London: Ernest Benn, 1980.

Becatti, Giovanni. *The Art of Ancient Greece and Rome–From the Rise of Greece to the Fall of Rome*. Translated by John Ross. Englewood Cliffs, N.J.: Prentice-Hall, 1967.

Bengston, Hermann. *History of Greece–From the Beginning to the Byzantine Era*. Translated from the German and updated by Edmund F. Bloedow. Ottawa [Canada]: University of Ottawa Press, 1988.

Benko, Stephen. "Pagan Criticism of Christianity During the First Two Centuries A.D." *Aufstieg und Niedergang der Romischen Welt*, II, 23.2, 1055–1118. Berlin: Walter de Gruyter, 1980.

————. *Pagan Rome and the Early Christians*. Bloomington [Ind.]: Indiana University Press, 1984.

————. *The Virgin Goddess: Studies in the Pagan and Christian Roots of Mariology*. New York: E. J. Brill, 1933.

Berrett, LaMar C. *Discovering the World of the Bible*. Provo, Utah: Young House, 1973.

Blaiklock, E. M. *The Archaeology of the New Testament*. Grand Rapids, Mich.: Zondervan Publishing House, 1970.

————. *The Christian in Pagan Society* ("The Tyndale New Testament Lecture for 1951"). London: The Tyndale Press, 19– .

————. *Cities of the New Testament.* London: Pickering & Inglis, 1965.

————. *Out of the Earth: The Witness of Archaeology to the New Testament.* Grand Rapids, Mich.: William B. Eerdmans Publishing Company, 1957.

Blue, Bradley. "Acts and the House Church." In *The Book of Acts in Its Graeco-Roman Setting,* edited by David W. J. Gill and Conrad Gempf, 119–222. Volume 2 of *The Book of Acts in Its First-Century Setting.* Grand Rapids, Mich.: William B. Eerdmans Publishing Company, 1994.

Boulton, W. H. *Archaeology Explains.* London: Epworth Press, 1952; 1953 reprint.

Bowersock, G. W. *Augustus and the Greek World.* Oxford: Clarendon Press, 1965.

————. *Hellenism in Late Antiquity.* Ann Arbor [Mich.]: University of Michigan Press, 1990.

————. "The Imperial Cult: Perceptions and Persistence." In *Jewish and Christian Self-Definition.* Volume 3: *Self-Definition in the Greco-Roman World,* edited by Ben F. Meyer and E. P. Sanders, 183–241. Philadelphia: Fortress Press, 1982.

Boyd, Robert T. *Tells, Tombs, and Treasure: A Pictorial Guide to Biblical Archaeology.* New York: Baker Books, 1969. Reprint, New York: Bonanza Books, 1975.

Brooten, Bernadette J. *Women Leaders in the Ancient Synagogue: Inscriptional Evidence and Background Issues.* Chico, Calif.: Scholars Press, 1982.

Broughton, T. Robert. "New Evidence on Temple-Estates in Asia Minor." In *Studies in Roman Economic and Social History–in Honor of Allan Chester Johnson,* edited by P. R. Coleman-Norton with the assistance of F. C. Bourne and J. V. A. Fine, 236–50. Princeton: Princeton University Press, 1951.

Broughton, T. R. S. "Roman Asia." In *An Economic Survey of Ancient Rome.* Volume 4. Edited by Tenney Frank, 499–918. Baltimore: Johns Hopkins Press, 1938.

Bruce, F. F. *The Spreading Flame: The Rise and Progress of Christianity from Its First Beginnings to the Conversion of the English.* Grand Rapids, Mich.: William B. Eerdmans Publishing Company, 1958.

Buchan, John. *Augustus.* Boston: Houghton Mifflin Company, 1937.

Buckler, W. H. "Labour Disputes in Asia Minor." In *Anatolian Studies–Presented to Sir William Mitchell Ramsay,* edited by W. H.

Buckler and W. M. Calder. Manchester [England]: Manchester University Press, 1923.

Budden, Charles W., and Edward Hastings. *The Local Colour of the Bible*. Volume 3: *Matthew-Revelation*. Edinburgh [Scotland]: T. & T. Clark, 1925.

Burford, Allison. *Craftsmen in Greek and Roman Society*. Ithaca, N.Y.: Cornell University Press, 1972.

Burkert, Walter. *Ancient Mystery Cults*. Cambridge, Mass.: Harvard University Press, 1972.

Cadoux, Cecil J. *Ancient Smyrna: A History from the Earliest Times to 324 A.D.* Oxford: Basil Blackwell, 1938.

Calder, W. M. "Smyrna as Described by the Orator Aelius Aristide." In *Studies in the History and Art of the Eastern Provinces of the Roman Empire*, edited by W. M. Ramsay, 95–116. Aberdeen, Scotland: Aberdeen University Press, 1906.

Calkin, John A. *Historical Geography of Bible Lands*. Philadelphia: Westminster Press, 1904.

Cannon, William R. *Journeys After Paul: An Excursion into History*. New York: Macmillan Company, 1963.

Carson, R. A. G. *Coins of the Roman Empire*. London: Routledge, 1990.

Cassidy, Richard J. *John's Gospel in New Perspective: Christology and the Realities of Roman Power*. Maryknoll, N.Y.: Orbis Books, 1992.

Cerfaux, Lucien. "The Church in the Book of Revelation." In *The Birth of the Church: A Biblical Study*, translated by Charles Underhill Quinn. Staten Island, N.Y.: Alba House, 1969.

Charlesworth, M. P. *Trade Routes and Commerce of the Roman Empire*. Second Edition. Revised. Chicago: Ares Publishers, 1926. Reprint, 197–.

Cole, Susan Guettel. "Demeter in the Ancient Greek City and Its Countryside." In *Placing the Gods: Sanctuaries and Sacred Space in Ancient Greece*, edited by Susan E. Alcock and Robin Osborne, 199–216. Oxford: Clarendon Press, 1994.

Coleman-Norton, P. R. "The Apostle Paul and the Roman Law of Slavery." In *Studies in Roman Economic and Social History–in Honor of Allan Chester Johnson*, edited by P. R. Coleman-Norton, with the assistance of F. C. Bourne and J. V. A. Fine, 155–77. Princeton: Princeton University Press, 1951.

Collins, Adela Y. "Numerical Symbolism in Jewish and Early Christian Apocalyptic Literature." In *Aufstieg und Niedergang der*

*Romischen Welt*, II, 21.2, 1221–87. Berlin: Walter de Gruyter, 1984.

―――. "Vilification and Self-Definition in the Book of Revelation." In *Christians Among Jews and Gentiles*, edited by George W. E. Nickelsburg and George W. MacRae, 308–20. Philadelphia: Fortress Press, 1986.

Cook, J. M. *The Greeks–In Ionia and the East*. New York: Frederick A. Praeger, Publisher, 1963.

Corley, Kathleen E. "Were the Women Around Jesus Really Prostitutes? Women in the Context of Greco-Roman Meals." In *Society of Biblical Literature 1989 Seminary Papers*, edited by David J. Lull, 1989, 487–521. Atlanta Ga.: Scholars Press, 1989.

Cornell, Tim, and John Matthews. *Atlas of the Roman World*. New York: Facts on File, 1982.

Countryman, L. William. "Welfare in the Churches of Asia Minor Under the Early Roman Empire." *Society of Biblical Literature 1979 Seminar Papers*. Volume 1. Edited by Paul J. Achtemeier, 131–46. Atlanta, Ga.: Scholars Press, 1979.

Crawford, Stephen J. *The Byzantine Shops at Sardis*. Cambridge, Mass.: Harvard University Press, 1990.

Cunliffe, Barry. *Rome and Her Empire*. New York: McGraw-Hill Book Company, 1978.

Davies, Roy W. "The Daily Life of the Roman Soldier Under the Principate." In *Aufstieg und Niedergang der Romischen Welt*, II, 1, 299–338. Berlin: Walter de Gruyter, 1974.

Davis, John J. *Biblical Numerology: A Basic Study of the Use of Numbers in the Bible*. Grand Rapids, Mich.: Baker Book House, 1968.

Delia, Diana. *Alexandrian Citizenship During the Roman Principate*. Atlanta, Ga.: Scholars Press, 1991. de Ste Croix, G. E. M. *The Class Struggle in the Ancient Greek World–from the Archaic Age to the Arab Conquests*. Ithaca, N.Y.: Cornell University Press, 1981.

de Polignac, Francois. *Cults, Territory, and the Origins of the Greek City-State*. Translated by Janet Lloyd. Chicago: University of Chicago Press, 1995.

―――. "Mediation, Competition, and Sovereignty: The Evolution of Rural Sanctuaries in Geometric Greece." In *Placing the Gods: Sanctuaries and Sacred Space in Ancient Greece*, edited by Susan E. Alcock and Robin Osborne, 5–18. Oxford: Clarendon Press, 1994.

Duff, A. M. *Freedmen in the Early Roman Empire*. Oxford University Press, 1928; reprint, Cambridge: W. Heffer & Sons, 1958.

Duncan-Jones, Richard. *The Economy of the Roman Empire: Quantita-*

*tive Studies*. Second Edition. Cambridge: Cambridge University Press, 1982.

Enslin, Morton S. "Rome in the East." In *Religions in Antiquity: Essays in Memory of Erwin Ramsdell Goodenough*, edited by Jacob Neusner. Leiden: E. J. Brill, 1968.

Farnell, Lewis R. *The Cults of the Greek States*. Volume 2. 1895. Reprint, Chicago: Aegean Press, 1971.

Ferguson, Everett. *Backgrounds of Early Christianity*. Second Edition. Grand Rapids, Mich.: William B. Eerdmans Publishing Company, 1993.

Ferguson, John. "China and Rome." In *Aufstieg und Niedergang der Romischen Welt*, II, 9.2, 581–603. Berlin: Walter de Gruyter, 1978.

———. "Divinities." In *Civilization of the Ancient Mediterranean*, edited by Michael Grand and Rachel Kitzinger, 2:847–60. New York: Charles Scribner's Sons, 1988.

———. *The Religions of the Roman Empire*. Ithaca, N.Y.: Cornell University Press, 1970.

Festugiere, Andre-Jean. *Personal Religion Among the Greeks*. Berkeley and Los Angeles: University of California Press, 1954.

Finegan, Jack. *The Archaeology of the New Testament: The Mediterranean World of the Early Christian Apostles*. Boulder, Colo.: Westview Press, 1981.

Finley, M. I. *The Ancient Economy*. Berkeley and Los Angeles: University of California Press, 1973.

———. *Atlas of Classical Archaeology*. New York: McGraw-Hill Book Company, 1977.

———. *Economy and Society in Ancient Greece*, edited by Brent D. Shaw and Richard P. Satler. London: Chatto & Winus, 1981.

Finn, T. M. "Social Mobility, Imperial Civil Service, and the Spread of Early Christianity." *Studia Patristica* 17, part 1, 31–37. Oxford: Pergamon Press, 1982.

Foss, Clive. *Ephesus After Antiquity: A Late Antique, Byzantine, and Turkish City*. Cambridge: Cambridge University Press, 1979.

Frank, Harry T. *An Archaeological Companion to the Bible*. London: SCM Press, 1972; Nashville, Tenn.: Abingdon Press, 1971.

———. *Bible Archaeology and Faith*. Nashville, Tenn.: Abingdon Press, 1971.

French, David. "Acts and the Roman Roads of Asia Minor." In *The Book of Acts in Its Graeco-Roman Setting*, edited by David W. J. Gill and Conrad Gempf, 49–58. Volume 2 of *The Book of Acts in*

*Its First-Century Setting*. Grand Rapids, Mich.: William B. Eerdmans Publishing Company, 1994.

Friend, W. C. *Martyrdom and Persecution in the Early Church: A Study of Conflict from the Maccabees to Donatus*. Oxford: Basil Blackwell, 1965.

Friesen, Steven. "The Cult of the Roman Emperors in Ephesos: Temple Wardens, City Titles, and the Interpretation of the Revelation of John." In *Ephesos: Metropolis of Asia–An Interdisciplinary Approach to Its Archaeology, Religion, and Culture*, edited by Helmut Koester, 229–50. Harvard Theological Studies 41. Valley Forge, Pa.: Trinity Press International, 1995.

Friesen, Steven J. *Twice Neokoros: Ephesus, Asia, and the Cult of the Flavian Imperial Family*. Leiden: E. J. Brill, 1993.

Gager, John G. *Kingdom and Community: The Social World of Early Christianity*. Englewood Cliffs, N.J.: Prentice-Hall, 1975.

———. "Religion and Social Class in the Early Roman Empire." In *The Catacombs and the Colosseum: The Roman Empire as the Setting of Primitive Christianity*, edited by Stephen Benko and John J. O'Rourke, 99–120. Valley Forge, Pa.: Judson Press, 1971.

Garlan, Yvon. *War in the Ancient World–A Social History*. Translated from the French by Janet Lloyd. New York: W. W. Norton & Co., 1975.

Garnsey, Peter. *Famine and Food Supply in the Graeco-Roman World: Responses to Risk and Crisis*. Cambridge: Cambridge University Press, 1988.

———. "Grain for Rome." In *Trade in the Ancient Economy*, edited by Peter Garnsey, Keith Hopkins, and C. R. Whittaker. Berkeley: University of California Press, 1983.

———. "Religious Toleration in Classical Antiquity." *Studies in Church History*. Volume 21: *Persecution and Toleration*, edited by W. J. Sheils, 1–28. [Great Britain]: Basil Blackwell, 1984.

———. *Social Status and Legal Privilege in the Roman Empire*. Oxford: Clarendon Press, 1970.

Garnsey, Peter, and Richard Saller. *The Roman Empire: Economy, Society, and Culture*. Berkeley and Los Angeles: University of California Press, 1987.

Garrison, Roman. *The Graeco-Roman Context of Early Christian Literature*. Journal for the Study of the New Testament, Supplement 137. Sheffield, England: Sheffield Academic Press, 1997.

Gill, David W. J. "Acts and Roman Religion: A. Religion in a Local Setting." In *The Book of Acts in Its Graeco-Roman Setting*, edited by David W. J. Gill and Conrad Gempf, 79–92. Volume 2 of *The*

*Book of Acts in Its First-Century Setting.* Grand Rapids, Mich.: William B. Eerdmans Publishing Company, 1994.

―――. "Acts and the Urban Elites." In *The Book of Acts in Its Graeco-Roman Setting,* edited by David W. J. Gill and Conrad Gempf, 93–103. Volume 2 of *The Book of Acts in Its First-Century Setting.* Grand Rapids, Mich.: William B. Eerdmans Publishing Company, 1994.

Godwin, Jocelyn. *Mystery Religions in the Ancient World.* San Francisco: Harper & Row, Publishers, 1981.

Goldenberg, Robert. "The Jewish Sabbath in the Roman World up to the Time of Constantine the Great." In *Aufstieg und Niedergang der Romischen Welt,* II, 19.1, 414–47. Berlin: Walter de Gruyter, 1979.

Gonen, Rivka. *Biblical Holy Places–An Illustrated Guide.* [Jerusalem], Israel: Palphot, 1987.

Goodspeed, Edgar J. *Introduction to New Testament.* Chicago: University of Chicago Press, 1937.

Grant, Michael. *Gladiators.* New York: Delacorte Press, 1967.

―――. *The Jews in the Roman World.* New York: Charles Scribner's Sons, 1973.

Grant, Robert M. *Augustus to Constantine: The Thrust of the Christian Movement into the Roman World.* New York: Harper & Row, Publishers, 1970.

―――. "The Social Setting of Second Century Christianity." In *Jewish and Christian Self-Definition.* Volume One: *The Shaping of Christianity in the Second and Third Centuries,* edited by E. P. Sanders, 16–29. Philadelphia: Fortress Press, 1980.

Greene, Kevin. *The Archaeology of the Roman Economy.* Berkeley and Los Angeles: University of California Press, 1986.

Gruen, Erich S. *The Hellenistic World and the Coming of Rome.* Volume 2. Berkeley: University of California Press, 1984.

Guthrie, Donald. *The Apostles.* Grand Rapids, Mich.: Zondervan Publishing House, 1975.

Halsberghe, Gaston H. *The Cult of Sol Invictus.* Leiden: E. J. Brill, 1972.

Hanfmann, George M. A. *From Croessus to Constantine: The Cities of Western Asia Minor and Their Arts in the Greek and Roman Times.* Jerome lectures, tenth series. Ann Arbor, Mich.: University of Michigan Press, 1975.

―――. "Historical Background." Chapter subsection in George M. A. Hanfmann, Louis Robert, and William E. Mierse, "The Hellenistic Period." In *Sardis: From Prehistoric to Roman Times–*

*Results of the Archaeological Exploration of Sardis, 1958–1975,* edited by George M. A. Hanfmann and William E. Mierse, 112–14. Cambridge, Mass.: Harvard University Press, 1983.

—————. "Introduction." Chapter subsection in George M. A. Hanfmann, Fikret K. Yegul, and John S. Crawford, "The Roman and Late Antique Period." In *Sardis: From Prehistoric to Roman Times–Results of the Archaeological Exploration of Sardis, 1958–1975,* edited by George M. A. Hanfmann and William E. Mierse, 139–48. Cambridge, Mass.: Harvard University Press, 1983.

—————. *Letters from Sardis.* Cambridge, Mass.: Harvard University Press, 1972.

—————. "Previous Research and the Harvard-Cornell Excavation." Chapter subsection in George M. A. Hanfmann, Louis Robert, and William E. Mierse, "The Hellenistic Period." In *Sardis: From Prehistoric to Roman Times–Results of the Archaeological Exploration of Sardis, 1958–1975,* edited by George M. A. Hanfmann and William E. Mierse, 109–11. Cambridge, Mass.: Harvard University Press, 1983.

—————. "Religious Life." Chapter subsection in George M. A. Hanfmann, Louis Robert, and William E. Mierse, "The Hellenistic Period." In *Sardis: From Prehistoric to Roman Times–Results of the Archaeological Exploration of Sardis, 1958–1975,* edited by George M. A. Hanfmann and William E. Mierse, 128–36 (text), 264–65 (footnotes).

Hanfmann, George M. A., and Jane C. Waldbaum. "New Excavations at Sardis and Some Problems of Western Anatolian Archaeology." In *Near Eastern Archaeology in the Twentieth Century: Essays in Honor of Nelson Glueck,* edited by James A. Sanders, 307–26. Garden City, N.Y.: Doubleday & Company, 1970.

—————. *A Survey of Sardis and the Major Monuments Outside the City Walls.* Cambridge, Mass.: Harvard University Press, 1975.

Hansen, Esther V. *The Attalids of Pergamon.* Second edition. Revised and expanded. Ithaca, N.Y.: Cornell University Press, 1971.

Hanson, John A. *Roman Theater-Temples.* Princeton, N.J.: Princeton University Press, 1959.

Harris, William V. *Ancient Literacy.* Cambridge, Mass.: Harvard University Press, 1989.

—————. "Towards a Study of the Roman Slave Trade." In *The Seaborne Commerce of Ancient Rome: Studies in Archaeology and History.* Memoirs of the American Academy in Rome, volume

36, edited by J. H. D'Arms and E. C. Kopff, 117–40. Rome: American Academy in Rome, 1980.

Harrison, Everett F. *The Apostolic Church*. Grand Rapids, Mich.: William B. Eerdmans Publishing Company, 1985.

Harrison, R. K. *Archaeology of the New Testament*. New York: Association Press, 1964.

Heichelheim, Fritz M. *An Ancient Economic History*. Volume Three. Translated by Mrs. Joyce Stevens. Leyden [Netherlands]: A. W. Sijthoff, 1970.

Helgeland, John. "Roman Army Religion." In *Aufstieg und Niedergang der Romischen Welt*, 16.2, 1470–1550. Berlin: Walter de Gruyter, 1978.

Hemer, C. J. "The Cities of the Revelation." In *New Documents Illustrating Early Christianity*, volume 3, edited by G. H. Horsley, 51–58. [Marrickville, Australia]: Macquarie University/Ancient History Documentary Research Centre, 1983.

———. "Seven Cities of Asia Minor." In *Major Cities of the Biblical World*, edited by R. K. Harrison, 234–48. Nashville, Tenn.: Thomas Nelson Publishers, 1985.

Hengel, Martin. *Jews, Greeks, and Barbarians: Aspects of the Hellenization of Judaism in the Pre-Christian Period*. Translated from the German by John Bowden. Philadelphia: Fortress Press, 1980.

———. *Judaism and Hellenism: Studies in Their Encounter in Palestine During the Early Hellenistic Period*. Translated from the German by John Bowden. Philadelphia: Fortress Press, 1974.

Henrichs, Albert. "Changing Dionysiac Identities." In *Jewish and Christian Self-Definition*. Volume Three: *Self-Definition in the Graeco-Roman World*, edited by Ben F. Meyer and E. P. Sanders, 137–60. Philadelphia: Fortress Press, 1982.

Heyob, Sharon K. *The Cult of Isis Among Women in the Graeco-Roman World*. Leiden: E. J. Brill, 1975.

Hopkins, Keith. *Conquerors and Slaves: Sociological Studies in Roman History*. Volume 1. Cambridge: Cambridge University Press, 1978.

Horbury, William. "The Jewish Dimension." In *Early Christianity: Origins and Evolution to A.D. 600*, edited by Ian Hazlett, 40–51. Nashville, Tenn.: Abingdon Press, 1991.

Horsley, G. H. "Doctors in the Graeco-Roman World." *New Documents Illustrating Early Christianity*, volume 2, edited by G. H. Horsley, 7–25. [Marrickville, Australia]: Macquarie University: Ancient History Documentary Research Centre, 1982.

———. "Expiation and the Cult of Men." In *New Documents Illustrat-*

*ing Early Christianity*, volume 3, edited by G. H. Horsley, 20–31. [Marrickville, Australia]: Macquarie University: Ancient History Documentary Research Centre, 1983.

———. "Inscriptions of Ephesus and the New Testament." In *New Documents Illustrating Early Christianity*, volume 3, edited by G. H. Horsley. [Marrickville, Australia]: Macquarie University: Ancient History Documentary Research Centre, 1983.

———. "Invitations to the *Kline* of Sarapis." In *New Documents Illustrating Early Christianity*, volume 1, edited by G. H. Horsley, 5–9. [Marrickville, Australia]: Macquarie University: Ancient History Documentary Research Centre, 1981.

———. "A Prefect's Circular Forbidding Magic." In *New Documents Illustrating Early Christianity*, volume 1, edited by G. H. Horsley, 47–51. [Marrickville, Australia]: Macquarie University: Ancient History Documentary Research Centre, 1982.

———. "The Purple Trade, and the Status of Lydia of Thyatira." In *New Documents Illustrating Early Christianity*, volume 2, edited by G. H. Horsley, 25–32. [Marrickville, Australia]: Macquarie University: Ancient History Documentary Research Centre, 1982.

Horsley, G. H. R. "Jews at Ephesos." In *New Documents Illustrating Early Christianity*, volume 4, edited by G. H. R. Horsley, 231–32. [Marrickville, Australia]: Macquarie University: Ancient History Documentary Research Centre, 1987.

———. "The Silversmiths at Ephesos." In *New Documents Illustrating Early Christianity*, volume 4, edited by G. H. R. Horsley, 7–10. [Marrickville, Australia]: Macquarie University: Ancient History Documentary Research Centre, 1987.

Humphrey, John H. *Roman Circuses: Arenas for Chariot Racing*. Berkeley and Los Angeles: University of California Press, 1986.

———. "Roman Games." In *Civilization of the Ancient Mediterranean* volume 2, edited by Michael Grant and Rachel Kitzinger, 1153–66. New York: Charles Scribner's, 1988.

Ilhan, Emil. "Earthquakes in Turkey." In *Geology and History of Turkey*, edited by Angus S. Campbell, 432–42. Tripoli [Libya]: Petroleum Exploration Society of Libya, 1971.

Inan, Jale, and Elisabeth Rosenbaum. *Roman and Early Byzantine Portrait Sculpture in Asia Minor*. London: British Academy by the Oxford University Press, 1966.

Jakobovits, Immanuel. *Jewish Medical Ethics: A Comparative and His-*

*torical Study of the Jewish Religious Attitude to Medicine and Its Practice.* New York: Bloch Publishing Company, 1959.

James, E. O. *The Cult of the Mother-Goddess: An Archaeological and Documentary Study.* London: Thames and Hudson, 1959.

Jayne, Walter A. *The Healing Gods of Ancient Civilizations.* 1925. Reprint, New Hyde Park, N.Y.: University Books, 1962.

Johnson, Allan C. *Egypt and the Roman Empire.* Jerome lectures, second series. Ann Arbor [Mich.]: University of Michigan Press, 1951.

Johnson, S. E. "The Present State of Sabazios Research." In *Aufsteig und Niedergang der Romischen Welt*, 17.3, 1583–1613. Berlin: Walter de Gruyter, 1984.

Johnson, Sherman E. "Asia Minor and Early Christianity." In *Christianity, Judaism, and Other Greco-Roman Cults: Studies for Morton Smith at Sixty*, volume 2, edited by Jacob Neusner, 77–145. Leiden: E. J. Brill, 1975.

————. "A Sabazios Inscription from Sardis." In *Religions in Antiquity: Essays in Memory of Erwin Ramsdell Goodenough*, edited by Jacob Neusner, 542–50. Leiden: E. J. Brill, 1968.

Johnston, Alan W., and Malcolm A. R. Colledge. "The Classical World." In *Atlas of Archaeology*, edited by K. Branigan, 50–91. New York: St. Martin's Press, 1982.

Jolowicz, H. F., and Barry Nicholas. *Historical Introduction to the Study of Roman Law.* Third edition. Cambridge: Cambridge University Press, 1972.

Jones, A. H. M. *The Cities of the Eastern Roman Provinces.* Second edition. Revised by Michael Avi-Yonah, et al. Oxford: Clarendon Press, 1971.

————. *The Decline of the Ancient World.* London: Longman, 1966.

————. *The Greek City: From Alexander to Justinian.* Oxford: Clarendon Press, 1940; 1971 reprint.

————. *A History of Rome Through the Fifth Century.* Volume 2: *The Empire.* London: Macmillan, 1970.

————. *The Roman Economy: Studies in Ancient Economic and Administrative History.* Edited by P. A. Brunt. Oxford: Basil Blackwell, 1974.

Jones, Allen H. *Essenes: The Elect of Israel.* Lanham, Md.: University Press of America, 1985.

Jones, Donald L. "Christianity and the Roman Imperial Cult." In *Aufstieg und Niedergang der Romischen Welt*, II, 23.2, 1023–54. Berlin: Walter de Gruyter, 1980.

Judge, E. A. *The Social Pattern of Christian Groups in the First Century.* London: Tyndale Press, 1960.

Kearsley, R. A. "The Asiarchs." In *The Book of Acts in Its Graeco-Roman Setting*, edited by David W. J. Gill and Conrad Gempf, 363–76. Volume 2 of *The Book of Acts in Its First-Century Setting.* Grand Rapids, Mich.: William B. Eerdmans Publishing Company, 1994.

————. "Ephesus: *Neokoros* of Artemis." In *New Documents Illustrating Early Christianity*, volume 6, edited by S. R. Llewelyn, 203–6. [Marrickville, Australia]: Macquarie University: Ancient History Documentary Research Centre, 1992.

————. "The Mysteries of Artemis at Ephesus." In *New Documents Illustrating Early Christianity*, volume 6, edited by S. R. Llewelyn, 196–202. [Marrickville, Australia]: Macquarie University: Ancient History Documentary Research Centre, 1992.

————. "Some Asiarchs of Ephesos." In *New Documents Illustrating Early Christianity*, volume 4, edited by G. H. R. Horsley, 46–55. [Marrickville, Australia]: Macquarie University: Ancient History Documentary Research Centre, 1987.

Kee, Howard, C. *Medicine, Miracle, and Magic in New Testament Times.* Cambridge: Cambridge University Press, 1986.

————. "Self-Definition in the Asclepius Cult." In *Jewish and Christian Self-Definition.* Volume 3: *Self-Definition in the Graeco-Roman World*, edited by Ben F. Meyer and E. P. Sanders, 118–36. Philadelphia: Fortress Press, 1982.

Kerenyi, C. *Asklepios: Archetypal Image of the Physician's Existence.* Translated from the German by Ralph Manheim. New York: Pantheon Books, 1959.

Keresytes, Paul. "The Imperial Government and the Christian Church. I. From Nero to the Severi." In *Aufstieg und Niedergang der Romischen Welt*, II, 23.1, 247–315. Berlin: Walter de Gruyter, 1979.

Keskin, Naci. *Ephesus.* Translated by Ertugrul Uckun. Ankara [Turkey]: Keskin Color Ltd. Co. Printing House, 19– .

Kidd, B. J. *A History of the Church to A.D. 461.* Volume 1. Oxford: Clarendon Press, 1922. Reprint, AMS, 1976 [n.p.].

Knibbe, Dieter. "*Via Sacra Ephesiaca:* New Aspects of the Cult of Artemis Ephesia." In *Ephesos: Metropolis of Asia–An Interdisciplinary Approach to Its Archaeology, Religion, and Culture*, edited by Helmut Koester, 141–155. Harvard Theological Studies 41. Valley Forge, Pa.: Trinity Press International, 1995.

Koester, Helmut. "Ephesos in Early Christian Literature." In *Ephesos: Metropolis of Asia–An Interdisciplinary Approach to Its Archaeology, Religion, and Culture*, edited by Helmut Koester, 119–40. Harvard Theological Studies 41. Valley Forge, Pa.: Trinity Press International, 1995.

―――. *History, Culture, and Religion of the Hellenistic Age*. Volume 1. Translated from the German. Philadelphia: Fortress Press, 1982.

―――. "The Red Hall in Pergamon." In *The Social World of the First Christians: Essays in Honor of Wayne A. Meeks*, edited by L. Michael White and O. Larry Yarbrough, 265–74. Minneapolis: Fortress Press, 1995.

Kotansky, Roy. "Incantations and Prayers for Salvation on Inscribed Greek Amulets." In *Magika Hiera: Ancient Greek Magic and Religion*, edited by Christopher A. Faraone and Dick Obbink, 107–37. New York: Oxford University Press, 1991.

Kottek, Samuel. "Medicinal Drugs in the Works of Flavius Josephus." In *The Healing Past: Pharmaceuticals in the Biblical and Rabbinic World*, edited by Irene and Walter Jacob, 95–105. Leiden: E. J. Brill, 1993.

Kraabel, A. Thomas. "The Diaspora Synagogue: Archaeological and Epigraphic Evidence Since Sukenik." In *Aufstieg und Niedergang der Romischen Welt*, II, 19.1, 477–510. Berlin: Walter de Gruyter, 1979.

―――. "Impact of the Discovery of the Sardis Synagogue." In *Diaspora Jews and Judaism: Essays in Honor of A. Thomas Kraabel*. South Florida Studies in the History of Judaism, number 41, edited by J. Andrew Overman and Robert S. MacLennan, 269–92. Atlanta, Ga.: Scholars Press, 1992.

―――. "Impact of the Discovery of the Sardis Synagogue." Chapter subsection in Andrew R. Seager and A. Thomas Kraabel, "The Synagogue and the Jewish Community." In *Sardis: From Prehistoric to Roman Times–Results of the Archaeological Exploration of Sardis, 1958-1975*, edited by George M. A. Hanfmann and William E. Mierse, 178–90. Cambridge, Mass.: Harvard University Press, 1983.

―――. "Paganism and Judaism: The Sardis Evidence." In *Diaspora Jews and Judaism: Essays in Honor of A. Thomas Kraabel*. South Florida Studies in the History of Judaism, number 41, edited by J. Andrew Overman and Robert S. MacLennan, 237–56. Atlanta, Ga.: Scholars Press, 1992.

―――. "Religious Propaganda and Missionary Competition in the

New Testament World." In *Immigrants, Exiles, Expatriates, and Missionary Competition in the New Testament World*, edited by Lukas Bormann, Kelly del Tredici, and Angela Standhartinger, 71–88. Leiden: E. J. Brill, 1994.

———. "The Synagogue at Sardis: Jews and Christians." In *Sardis: Twenty-seven Years of Discovery*, edited by Eleanor Gurainick, 62–73. Chicago: [n.p.], 1987.

Kraeling, Emil G. *Rand McNally Bible Atlas*. New York: Rand McNally & Company, 1956.

Kraemer, Ross S. "Hellenistic Jewish Women: The Epigraphical Evidence." In *Society of Biblical Literature Seminar Papers Series: 1986*, edited by Kent H. Richards, 183–200. Atlanta, Ga.: Scholars Press, 1986.

Kraft, Robert A. "Judaism on the World Scene." In *The Catacombs and the Colosseum: The Roman Empire as the Setting of Primitive Christianity*, edited by Stephen Benko and John J. O'Rourke, 81–98. Valley Forge, Pa.: Judson Press, 1971.

Krill, Richard M. "Roman Paganism Under the Antonies and Severans." In *Aufstieg und Niedergang der Romischen Welt*, 16.1, 27–44. Berlin: Walter de Gruyter, 1978.

Krodel, Gerhard. "Persecution and Toleration of Christianity Under Hadrian." In *The Catacombs and the Colosseum: The Roman Empire as the Setting of Primitive Christianity*, edited by Stephen Benko and John J. O'Rourke, 255–67. Valley Forge, Pa.: Judson Press, 1971.

Kunke, Wolfgang. *An Introduction to Roman Legal and Constitutional History*. Second edition (based on the sixth German edition). Translated by J. M. Kelly. Oxford: Clarendon Press, 1973.

Lambert, Royston. *Beloved and God: The Story of Hadrian and Antinous*. New York: Viking, 1984.

Lampe, Peter, and Ulrich Luz. "Post-Pauline Christianity and Pagan Society." Chapter translated by Annemarie S. Kidder. In *Christian Beginnings: Word and Community from Jesus to Post-Apostolic Times*, edited by Jergen Becker, 242–80. Louisville, Ky.: Westminster/John Knox Press, 1993.

Lane, Eugene N. "Men: A Neglected Cult of Roman Asia Minor." In *Aufstieg und Niedergang der Romischen Welt*, II, 18.3, 2161–74. Berlin: Walter de Gruyter, 1990.

Laney, J. Car. *Baker's Concise Bible Atlas: A Geographical Survey of Bible History*. Grand Rapids, Mich.: Baker Book House, 1988.

Leaney, A. R. C. *The Jewish and Christian World, 200 B.C. to A.D. 200*. Cambridge: Cambridge University Press, 1984.

Lease, Gary. "Mithraism and Christianity: Borrowings and Transformations." In *Aufstieg und Niedergang der Romischen Welt*, II, 23.2, 1306–32. Berlin: Walter de Gruyter, 1980.

Levick, Barbara. *Roman Colonies in Southern Asia Minor.* Oxford: Clarendon Press, 1967.

Levinskaya, Irina. *The Book of Acts in Its Diaspora Setting.* Volume 5 of *The Book of Acts in Its First-Century Setting.* Grand Rapids, Mich.: William B. Eerdmans Publishing Company, 1996.

LiDonnici, Lynn R. "Epidaurian Miracle Cures." In *Society of Biblical Literature 1988 Seminar Papers*, edited by David J. Lull, 272–76. Atlanta, Ga.: Scholars Press, 1988.

Liebeschuetz, J. H. W. G. *Continuity and Change in Roman Religion.* Oxford: Clarendon Press, 1979.

Lietzman, Hans. *A History of the Early Church.* Volume 1: *The Beginnings of the Christian Church.* Translated by Bertram L. Woolf. Second edition, 1949. Reprinted in one volume, London: Lutterworth Press, 1961.

Lloyd, Seton. "Anatolia and Soviet Armenia." In *Atlas of Ancient Archaeology*, edited by Jacquetta Hawkes, 131–45. New York: McGraw-Hill Book Company, 1974.

Ludwig, Charles. *Cities in New Testament Times.* Denver, Colo.: Accent Books, 1976.

McGiffert, Arthur C. *A History of Christianity in the Apostolic Age.* Edinburgh [Scotland]: T. & T. Clark, 1897.

MacKendrick, Paul. *The Greek Stones Speak: The Story of Archaeology in Greek Lands.* Second edition. New York: W. W. Norton & Company, 1981.

MacMullen, Ramsay. *Corruption and the Decline of Rome.* New Haven: Yale University Press, 1988.

———. *Paganism in the Roman Empire.* New Haven: Yale University Press, 1981.

———. "Peasants during the Principate." In *Aufstieg und Niedergang der Romischen Welt*, II, 1, 253–61. Berlin: Walter de Gruyter, 1974.

———. *Roman Social Relations: 508 B.C. to A.D. 284.* New Haven: Yale University Press, 1974.

Magie, David. *Roman Rule in Asia Minor to the End of the Third Century After Christ.* 2 volumes. Princeton, N.J.: Princeton University Press, 1950. Reprint, Salem, N.H.: Ayer Company, Publishers, 1988. (Volume 1 consists exclusively of text; volume 2 of notes and related materials. The page numbering is consecutive rather than beginning again in volume 2.)

Malina, Bruce J. *On the Genre and Message of Revelation: Star Visions and Sky Journeys*. Peabody, Mass.: Hendrickson Publishers, 1995.

Malkin, Irad. *Religion and Colonization in Ancient Greece*. Leiden: E. J. Brill, 1987.

Marco, Anthony D. "The Cities of Asia Minor Under the Roman Imperium." In *Aufstieg und Niedergang der Romischen Welt*, II, 7.2, 698–729. Berlin: Walter de Gruyter, 1980.

Marsh, Frank B. *The Reign of Tiberius*. [Oxford]: Oxford University Press, 1931.

Marti-Ibanez, Felix. *A Prelude to Medical History*. New York: MD Publications, 1961.

Martin, Luther H. *Hellenistic Religions: An Introduction*. New York: Oxford University Press, 1987.

———. "The Pagan Religious Background." In *Early Christianity: Origins and Evolution to A.D. 600*, edited by Ian Hazlett, 52–64. Nashville, Tenn.: Abingdon Press, 1991.

Maxnes, Halvor. "Patron-Client Relations and the New Community in Luke-Acts." In *The Social World of Luke-Acts: Models for Interpretation*, edited by Jerome H. Neyrey, 241–68. Peabody, Mass.: Hendrickson Publishers, 1991.

Mayerson, Philip. "What in the Roman World: An Addendum." *Classsical Quarterly* 34 (1984), 243–45. Reprinted in Philip Mayerson, *Monks, Martyrs, Soldiers, and Saracens: Papers on the Near East in Late Antiquity (1962–1993)*, 222–24. Jerusalem: Israel Exploration Society in Association with New York University, 1994.

Meeks, Wayne A. *The First Urban Christians: The Social World of the Apostle Paul*. New Haven: Yale University Press, 1983.

Meinardus, Otto F. A. "The Christian Remains of the Seven Churches of Asia." In *Biblical Archaeologist Reader, IV*, edited by Edward F. Campbell Jr. and David Noel Freedman, 345–58. Sheffield [England]: Almond Press, 1983.

Mellor, R. "The Goddess Roma." In *Aufstieg und Niedergang der Romischen Welt*, II, 17.2, 950–1030. Berlin: Walter de Gruyter, 1981.

Mierse, William E. "Artemis Sanctuary." Chapter subsection in George M. A. Hanfmann, Louis Robert, and William E. Mierse, "The Hellenistic Period." In *Sardis: From Prehistoric to Roman Times–Results of the Archaeological Exploration of Sardis, 1958–1975*, edited by George M. A. Hanfmann and William E. Mierse, 119–21.

Miles, M. F. "Ignatius and the Church." *Studia Patristica* 17, Part 2, 750–55. Oxford: Pergamon Press, 1982.

Miller, Helen H. *Bridge to Asia: The Greeks in the Eastern Mediterranean*. New York: Charles Scribner's Sons, 1967.

Miller, Ulrich B. "Apocalyptic Currents." Chapter translated by Annemarie S. Kidder. In *Christian Beginnings: Word and Community from Jesus to Post-Apostolic Times*, edited by Jurgen Becker, 281–329. Louisville, Ky.: Westminster/John Knox Press, 1993.

Mitchell, Stephen. *Anatolia: Land, Men, and Gods in Asia Minor*. Volume 1: *The Celts in Anatolia and the Impact of Roman Rule*. Oxford: Clarendon Press, 1993.

———. *Anatolia: Land, Men, and Gods in Asia Minor*. Volume 2: *The Rise of the Church*. Oxford: Clarendon Press, 1993.

———. "The Roman Empire in the East." In *The Cambridge Encyclopedia of Archaeology*, edited by Andrew Sherratt, 239–44. New York: Crown Publishers/Cambridge University Press, 1980.

Momigliano, Arnaldo. *On Pagans, Jews, and Christians*. Middletown, Conn.: Wesleyan University Press, 1987.

Mommsen, Theodor. *The Provinces of the Roman Empire*. Volume 1. Translated by William P. Dickson. London: 1909. Reprint, Chicago: Ares Publishers, 1974.

Mosse, Claude. "The Economist." In *The Greeks*, edited by Jean-Pierre Vernant, 23–52. Translated by Charles Lambert and Teresa Lavender Fagan. Chicago: University of Chicago Press, 1995.

Muckelroy, Keith, General Editor. *Archaeology Under Water: An Atlas of the World's Submerged Sites*. New York: McGraw-Hill Book Company, 1980.

Neils, Jenifer, editor. *Worshipping Athena: Panathenaia and Parthenon*. Madison, Wis.: University of Wisconsin Press, 1996.

Neusner, Jacob. *A History of the Jews in Babylonia*. Volume 1: *The Parthian Period*. Leiden [Netherlands]: E. J. Brill, 1965.

Newmyer, Stephen. "Aspah the Jew and Greco-Roman Pharmaceutics." In *The Healing Past: Pharmaceuticals in the Biblical and Rabbinic World*, edited by Irene and Walter Jacob, 107–20. Leiden: E. J. Brill, 1993.

Nielsen, Harald. *Ancient Opthamological Agents: A Pharmaco-historical Study of the Collyria and Seals for Collyria Used During Roman Antiquity, as Well as of the Most Frequent Components of the Collyria*. Translated from the Danish by Lars McBride. Odense, Denmark: Odense University Press, 1974.

Nilsson, Martin R. *Greek Popular Religion*. New York: Columbia University Press, 1940.

———. *Imperial Rome*. London: G. Bell & Sons, 1962. Reprint, New York: Schocken Books, 1967.

North, Robert. "Medical Discoveries of Biblical Times." In *Scripture and Other Artifacts: Essays on the Bible and Archaeology in Honor of Philip J. King*, edited by Michael D. Coogan, J. Cheryl Exum, and Lawrence E. Stager, 311–32. Louisville, Ky.: Westminster/ John Knox Press, 1994.

Oakman, Douglas E. "The Countryside in Luke-Acts." In *The Social World of Luke-Acts: Models for Interpretation*, edited by Jerome H. Neyrey, 151–79. Peabody, Mass.: Hendrickson Publishers, 1991.

Oliver, James H. *The Sacred Gerusia*. [Baltimore, Md.]: American School of Classical Studies at Athens, 1941.

Onen, U. *Ephesus: Ruins and Museum*. Translated by Nualla Yilmaz and Nanette T. Nelson. Izmir [Turkey]: Akademia, 1983.

Onen, Ulgur. *Ephesus: The Way It Was–The City Viewed in Reconstructions*. Translated by Nualla Yilmaz and Nanette T. Nelson. Izmir: Akademia, 1985.

O'Rouke, John J. "Roman Law and the Early Church." In *The Catacombs and the Colosseum: The Roman Empire as the Setting of Primitive Christianity*, edited by Stephen Benko and John J. O'Rourke, 165–86. Valley Forge, Pa.: Judson Press, 1971.

Oster, R. "Holy Days in Honour of Artemis." In *New Documents Illustrating Early Christianity*, volume 4, edited by G. H. R. Horsley, 74–82. [Marrickville, Australia]: Macquarie University: Ancient History Documentary Research Centre, 1987.

Oster, Richard E. "The Ephesian Artemis as an Opponent of Early Christianity." In *Jahrbuch fur Antike und Christentum*, volume 19 (1976) 24–44. Munster [Germany]: Aschendorffsche Verlagsbechhandlung, 1977.

———. "Ephesus as a Religious Center Under the Principate: I. Paganism Before Constantine." In *Aufstieg und Niedergang der Romischen Welt*, II, 18.3, 1661–1728. Berlin: Walter de Gruyter, 1990.

Palmer, Robert E. A. *Roman Religion and Roman Empire: Five Essays*. Philadelphia: University of Pennsylvania Press, 1974.

Parker, H.M.D. *The Roman Legions*, 1928. Reprint (with minor corrections of factual errors), Chicago, Ill.: Ares Publishers, 1954, 1980.

Parker, Robert. *Athenian Religion: A History.* Oxford: Clarendon Press, 1996.

Paul-Louis [no other name]. *Ancient Rome at Work: An Economic History of Rome from the Origins to the Empire.* Translated by E. B. F. Wareing, 1927. Reprint, New York: Barnes & Noble, 1965.

Pedley, John G. *Sardis in the Age of Croesus.* Norman [Oklahoma]: University of Oklahoma Press, 1968.

Pentreath, Guy. "Early Christianity in 'Asia.'" In *Geology and History of Turkey,* edited by Angus S. Campbell, 39–48. Tripoli [Libya]: Petroleum Exploration Society of Libya, 1971.

Perowne, Stewart. *Archaeology of Greece and the Aegean.* New York: A Studio Book/Viking Press, 1974.

Peters, F. E. *The Harvest of Hellenism: A History of the Near East from Alexander the Great to the Triumph of Christianity.* New York: Simon and Schuster, 1970.

Petit, Paul. *Pax Romana.* Translated by James Willis. London: B. T. Batsford, 1976.

Pfeiffer, Charles F., and Howard F. Vos. *The Wycliffe Historical Geography of Bible Lands.* Chicago: Moody Press, 1967.

Porter, Eliot. *The Greek World.* New York: E. P. Dutton, 1980.

Price, Martin J., and Bluma L. Trell. *Coins and Their Cities: Architecture on the Ancient Coins of Greece, Rome, and Palestine.* Detroit, Mich.: Wayne State University Press, 1977.

Price, S. R. F. *Rituals and Power: The Roman Imperial Cult in Asia Minor.* Cambridge: Cambridge University Press, 1984.

Ramage, Nancy H., and Andrew Ramage. *Roman Art–Romulus to Constantine.* New York: Harry N. Abrams, 1991.

Ramsay, W. M. *The Church in the Roman Empire Before A.D. 170.* London: Hodder and Stoughton, 1895.

———. *The Historical Geography of Asia Minor.* Volume 4 of Royal Geographical Society: Supplementary Papers. London: John Murray, 1890.

———. *Pauline and Other Studies in Early Christian History.* London: Hodder and Stoughton, 1916.

———. *St. Paul the Traveller and the Roman Citizen.* New York: G. P. Putnam's Sons, 1896; 1905 reprint.

Ramsay, William M. *Cities and Bishoprics of Phrygia.* Volume 1: *The Lycos Valley and South-Western Phrygia.* Oxford: Clarendon Press, 1895.

———. *The Social Basis of Roman Power in Asia Minor.* Aberdeen [Scotland]: Aberdeen University Press, 1941. Reprint, Amsterdam: Adolf M. Hakkert, Publisher, 1967.

Raschke, Manfred G. "New Studies in Roman Commerce with the East." In *Aufstieg und Niedergang der Romischen Welt*, II, 9.2, 604–1378. Berlin: Walter de Gruyter, 1978.

Rickmann, Geoffrey. *The Corn Supply of Ancient Rome*. Oxford: Clarendon Press, 1980.

Robertson, Martin. *A History of Greek Art*. Volume 1. Cambridge: Cambridge University Press, 1975.

Rogers, Robert S. *Studies in the Reign of Tiberius*. Baltimore: Johns Hopkins Press, 1943.

Rohrbaugh, Richard L. "The Pre-industrial City in Luke-Acts: Urban Social Relations." In *The Social World of Luke-Acts: Models for Intepretation*, edited by Jerome H. Neyrey, 125–49. Peabody, Mass.: Hendrickson Publishers, 1991.

Rose, H. J. *A Handbook of Greek Mythology–Including Its Extension to Rome*. Sixth edition. London: Methuen & Company, 1958; 1965 reprint.

Rostovtzeff, M. *The Social and Economic History of the Roman Empire*. Second edition. Revised by P. M. Fraser. (Two volumes with consecutive page numbering throughout.) Oxford: Clarendon Press, 1957.

Rowland, C. "Moses and Patmos: Reflections on the Jewish Background of Early Christianity." In *Words Remembered, Texts Renewed: Essays in Honour of John F. A. Sawyer*, edited by Jon Davies, Graham Harvey, and Wilfred G. E. Watson, 280–99. Journal for the Study of the Old Testament, Supplement 195. Sheffield, England: Sheffield Academic Press, 1995.

Russell, J. C. *Late Ancient and Medieval Population*. Philadelphia: American Philosophical Society, 1958.

Saffrey, H. D. "The Piety and Prayers of Ordinary Men and Women in Late Antiquity." In *Classical Mediterranean Spirituality: Egyptian, Greek, Roman*, edited by A. H. Armstrong. New York: Crossroad, 1986.

Scarborough, John. "Roman Medicine to Galen." In *Aufstieg und Niedergang der Romischen Welt*, II, 27.1, 3–48. Berlin: Walter de Gruyter, 1993.

Scherrer, Peter. "The City of Ephesos from the Roman Period to Late Antiquity." In *Ephesos: Metroplis of Asia–An Interdisciplinary Approach to Its Archaeology, Religion, and Culture*, edited by Helmut Koester, 1–25. Harvard Theological Studies 41. Valley Forge, Pa.: Trinity Press International, 1995.

Schlatter, Adolph. *The Church in the New Testament Period.* Translated from the German by Paul P. Levertoff. London: S.P.C.K., 1961.

Schmidt, Evamaria. *The Great Altar of Pergamon.* Boston: Boston Book and Art Shop, 1965.

Schoedel, William R. "Theological Norms and Social Perspectives in Ignatius of Antioch." In *Jewish and Christian Self-Definition.* Volume 1: *The Shaping of Christianity in the Second and Third Centuries,* edited by E. P. Sanders, 30–56. Philadelphia: Fortress Press, 1980.

Schonfield, Hugh J. *The Bible Was Right: New Light on the New Testament.* London: Frederick Muller, 1958.

Scott, Kenneth. *The Imperial Cult Under the Flavians.* Stuttgart [Germany]: W. Kohlhammer, 1936. Reprint, New York: Arno Press, 1975.

Seager, Andrew. "The Architecture of the Dura and Sardis Synagogues." In *The Dura-Europos Synagogue: A Re-evaluation (1932–1992),* edited by Joseph Gutmann, 79–116. Atlanta, Ga.: Scholars Press, 1992.

―――. "The Building." Chapter subsection in Andrew R. Seager and A. Thomas Kraabel, "The Synagogue and the Jewish Community." In *Sardis: From Prehistoric to Roman Times–Results of the Archaeological Exploration of Sardis, 1958–1975,* edited by George M. A. Hanfmann and William E. Mierse, 168–78. Cambridge, Mass.: Harvard University Press, 1983.

Segal, Charles. "Spectator and Listener." In *The Greeks,* edited by Jean-Pierre Revnant, 184–217. Translated by Charles Lambert and Teresa Lavender Fagan. Chicago: University of Chicago Press, 1995.

Seltman, Charles. *Riot in Ephesus: Writings on the Heritage of Greece.* London: Max Parrish, 1958.

Shanks, Hershel. *Judaism in Stone: The Archaeology of Ancient Synagogues.* New York: Harper & Row, Publishers/Washington, D. C.: Biblical Archaeological Society, 1979.

Sherwin-White, A. N. "The Roman Citizenship: A Survey of Its Development into a World Franchise." In *Aufstieg und Niedergang der Romischen Welt,* I, 2, 23–58. Berlin: Walter de Gruyter, 1972.

―――. *Roman Society and Roman Law in the New Testament.* The Sarum Lectures, 1960–61. Oxford: Clarendon Press, 1963.

Sherwin-White, Susan, and Amelie Kuhrt. *From Samarkhand to*

*Sardis: A New Approach to the Seleucid Empire.* London: Duckworth, 1993.

Signe, Isager. "Kings and Gods in the Seleucid Empire: A Question of Landed Property." In *Religion and Religious Practice in the Seleucid Kingdom,* edited by Per Bilde, Troels Engberg-Pedersen, Lise Hannestad, and Jan Zahle. [Denmark]: Aarhus University Press, 1990.

Simon, Marcel. *Verus Israel: A Study of the Relations Between Christians and Jews in the Roman Empire (135-425).* Translated from the French by H. McKeating. Oxford: Oxford University Press, 1986.

Sitwell, M. H. H. *Roman Roads of Europe.* New York: St. Martin's Press, 1981.

Smallwood, H. Mary. *The Jews Under Roman Rule: From Pompey to Diocletian.* Volume 20 of *Studies in Judaism in Late Antiquity,* edited by Jacob Neusner. Leiden: E. J. Brill, 1978.

Smith, Charles E. *Tiberius and the Roman Empire.* Baton Rouge, La.: Louisiana State University Press, 1942.

Smith, Jonathan Z. *Map Is Not Territory: Studies in the History of Religions.* Leiden: E. J. Brill, 1978.

Speidel, Michael P. "Legionaries from Asia Minor." In *Aufstieg und Niedergang der Romischen Welt,* II, 7.2, 730–46. Berlin: Walter de Gruyter, 1980.

Stambaugh, John D., and David L. Balsh. *The New Testament in Its Social Environment.* Philadelphia: Westminster Press, 1986.

Stark, Freys. *Rome on the Euphrates: The Story of a Frontier.* London: John Murray, 1966.

Stephens, William H. *The New Testament World in Pictures.* Nashville, Tenn.: Broadman Press, 1987.

Stoneman, Richard. *Land of Lost Gods: The Search for Classical Greece.* Norman [Oklahoma]: University of Oklahoma Press, 1987.

Strong, Donald. *Roman Art.* Prepared for press by J. M. C. Toynbee. Revised and annotated by Roger Ling. Middlesex [England]: Penguin Books, 1988.

Strubbe, J. H. M. "Cursed Be He That Moves My Bones." In *Magika Hiera: Ancient Greek Magic and Religion,* edited by Christopher A. Faraone and Dirk Obbink, 33–59. New York: Oxford University Press, 1991.

Sutherland, C. H. V. *Roman History and Coinage, 44 B.C.-A.D. 69: Fifty Points of Relation from Julius Caesar to Vespasian.* Oxford: Clarendon Press, 1987.

Tam Tinh, Tran. "Sarapis and Isis." In *Jewish and Christian Self-Definition*. Volume Three: *Self-Definition in the Greco-Roman World*, edited by Ben F. Meyer and E. P. Sanders, 101–17. Philadelphia: Fortress Press, 1982.

Tarn, W. W. *Hellenistic Civilization*. Third edition. Revised by W. W. Tarn and G. T. Griffith. London: Edward Arnold & Co., 1952.

Taylor, Lily R. "Artemis of Ephesus." In *The Beginnings of Christianity, Part 1: The Acts of the Apostles* (Volume 5), edited by Kirsopp Lake and Henry J. Cadbury, 251–55. London: Macmillan and Company, 1933.

———. "Asiarchs." In *The Beginnings of Christianity, Part 1: The Acts of the Apostles* (Volume 5), edited by Kirsopp Lake and Henry J. Cadbury, 256–61. London: Macmillan and Company, 1933.

Taylor, Lily Ross. *The Divinity of the Roman Emperor*. Middletown: American Philological Association, 1931. Reprint, Philadelphia, Pa.: Porcupine Press, 1975.

Tenney, Merrill C. *New Testament Times*. Grand Rapids, Mich.: William B. Eerdmans Publishing Company, 1965; 1984 reprint.

Thelen, Mary F. *Historical Introduction to the Christian Religion*; Part 1: *The Old Testament and the Hellenistic Background*. [n.p.], 1956.

Thomas, Christine. "At Home in the City of Artemis: Religion in Ephesos in the Literary Imagination of the Roman Period." In *Ephesos: Metropolis of Asia–An Interdisciplinary Approach to Its Archaeology, Religion, and Culture*, edited by Helmut Koester, 81–117. Harvard Theological Studies 41. Valley Forge, Pa.: Trinity Press International, 1995.

Thomas, Garth. "Magna Mater and Attis." In *Aufstieg und Niedergang der Romischen Welt*, II, 17.3, 1500–1535. Berlin: Walter de Gruyter, 1984.

Thompson, J. A. *The Bible and Archaeology*. Grand Rapids, Mich.: William B. Eerdmans Publishing Company, 1972.

Thompson, Wesley E. "Insurance and Banking." In *Civilization of the Ancient Mediterranean* (Volume 2), edited by Michael Grant and Rachel Kitzinger, 829–36. New York: Charles Scribner's Sons, 1988.

Throckmorton, Peter. "Romans on the Sea." In *A History of Seafaring–Based on Underwater Archaeology*, edited by George F. Bass, 65–86. New York: Walker and Company, 1972.

Throckmorton, Peter, and A. J. Parker. "A Million Tons of Marble."

In *The Sea Remembers: Shipwrecks and Archaeology*, edited by Peter Throckmorton, 72–77. New York: Weidenfeld & Nicolson, 1987.

Toksoz, Cemil. *Ephesus: Legends and Facts*. Translated by Ahmet E. Uysal. Ankara [Turkey]: Ayvildiz Matbaasi, 1969.

———. *Pergamum: Its History and Archaeology*. Translated by Ahmet E. Uysal. Ankara [Turkey]: Ayvildiz Matbaasi, 1969.

———. *A Travel Guide to the Historic Treasures of Turkey*. Istanbul [Turkey]: Mobil Oil Turk A.S., 1977.

Tomlinson, R. A. *Greek Sanctuaries*. New York: St. Martin's Press, 1976.

Toutain, Jules. *The Economic Life of the Ancient World*. Translated by M. R. Dobie. London: Kegan Paul, Trench, Trubner & Co., 1930.

Townsend, John T. "Ancient Education in the Time of the Early Roman Empire." In *The Catacombs and the Colosseum: The Roman Empire as the Setting of Primitive Christianity*, edited by Stephen Benko and John J. O'Rourke, 139–64. Valley Forge, Pa.: Judson Press, 1971.

Trachtenberg, Joshua. *Jewish Magic and Superstition: A Study in Folk Religion*. New York: Behrman's Jewish Book House, 1939.

Trebilco, Paul. "Asia." In *The Book of Acts in Its Graeco-Roman Setting*, edited by David W. J. Gill and Conrad Gempf, 291–362. Volume 2 of *The Book of Acts in Its First-Century Setting*. Grand Rapids, Mich.: William B. Eerdmans Publishing Company, 1994.

Trebilco, Paul R. *Jewish Communities in Asia Minor*. Cambridge: Cambridge University Press, 1991.

Trell, Bluma L. *The Temple of Artemis at Ephesos*. New York: American Numismatic Society, 1945.

Trevett, Christine. *The Study of Ignatius of Antioch in Syria and Asia*. Lewiston [New York]: Edwin Mellen Press, 1992.

Turner, Cuthbert H. *Studies in Early Church History*. Oxford: Clarendon Press, 1912.

Van Der Heyden, A. A. M. and H. H. Scullard. *Atlas of the Classical World*. London: Thomas Nelson & Sons, 1959.

Van Der Horst, Peter W. *Essays on the Jewish World of Early Christianity*. Gottingen [Germany]: Vandenhoech & Ruprecht, 1990.

van Tilborg, Sjef. *Reading John in Ephesus*. Leiden: E. J. Brill, 1996.

Vegetti, Mario. "The Greeks and Their Gods." In *The Greeks*, edited by Jean-Pierre Vernant, 254–84. Translated by Charles Lambert and Teresa Lavender Fagan. Chicago: University of Chicago Press, 1995.

Vermaseren, Maaten J. *Cybele and Attis–The Myth and the Cult.* London: Thames and Hudson, 1977.

Vermeule, Cornelius C. *Roman Imperial Art in Greece and Asia Minor.* Cambridge, Mass.: Belknap Press of Harvard University Press, 1968.

Vernant, Jean-Pierre. "Introduction." In *The Greeks*, edited by Jean-Pierre Vernant, 1–22. Translated by Charles Lambert and Teresa Lavender Fagan. Chicago: University of Chicago Press, 1995.

Versnel, H. S. *Inconsistencies in Greek and Roman Religion 1: Ter Unus–Isis, Dionyson, Hermes; Three Studies in Henotheism.* Leiden: E. J. Brill, 1990.

Vickers, Michael. *The Roman World.* Second edition. New York: Peter Bedrick Books, 1989.

Vos, Howard F. *Archaeology in Bible Lands.* Chicago: Moody Press, 1977.

Waldbaum, Jane C. "Metalwork and Metalworking in Sardis." In *Sardis: Twenty-Seven Years of Discovery*, edited by Eleanor Guralnick, 36–45. Chicago: [n.p.], 1987.

Walden, John W. H. *The Universities of Ancient Greece.* New York: Charles Scribner's Sons, 1909; 1910 printing.

Walters, James. "Egyptian Religions in Ephesos." In *Ephesos: Metropolis of Asia–An Interdisciplinary Approach to Its Archaeology, Religion, and Culture*, edited by Helmut Koester, 281–310. Harvard Theological Studies 41. Valley Forge, Pa.: Trinity Press International, 1995.

Ward-Perkins, J. B. *Roman Imperial Architecture.* London: Penguin Books, 1981.

Watterson, Barbara. *The Gods of Ancient Egypt.* London: B. T. Batsford, 1984.

Webber, Randal C. "Group Solidarity in the Revelation of John." In *Society of Biblical Literature 1988 Seminar Papers*, edited by David I. Lull, 132–40. Atlanta, Ga.: Scholars Press, 1988.

Webster, Graham. *The Roman Imperial Army of the First and Second Centuries A.D.* Third edition. Totowa, N.J.: Barnes & Noble Books, 1985.

Wengst, Klaus. *Pax Romana and the Peace of Jesus Christ.* Translated from the German by John Bowden. Philadelphia: Fortress Press, 1987.

Westermann, William L. *The Slave Systems of Greek and Roman Antiquity*. Philadelphia: American Philosophical Society, 1955.

White, K. D. *Greek and Roman Technology*. Ithaca, N.Y.: Cornell University Press, 1984.

White, L. Michael. "Urban Development and Social Change in Imperial Ephesos." In *Ephesos: Metropolis of Asia–An Interdisciplinary Approach to Its Archaeology, Religion, and Culture*, edited by Helmut Koester, 27–79. Harvard Theological Studies 41. Valley Forge, Pa.: Trinity Press International, 1995.

Wiedermann, Thomas. *Emperors and Gladiators*. London: Routledge, 1992.

———. *Greek and Roman Slavery*. London: Routledge, 1981.

Wight, Fred H. *Highlights of Archaeology in Bible Lands*. Chicago: Moody Press, 1955.

Wild, Robert A. "The Known Isis-Sarapis Sanctuaries from the Roman Period." In *Aufstieg und Niedergang der Romischen Welt*, II, 17.4, 1739–1851. Berlin: Walter de Gruyter, 1984.

Winter, Bruce W. "Acts and Food Shortages." In *The Book of Acts in Its Graeco-Roman Setting*, edited by David W. J. Gill and Conrad Gempf, 59–78. Volume 2 of *The Book of Acts in Its First-Century Setting*. Grand Rapids, Mich.: William B. Eerdmans Publishing Company, 1994.

———. "Acts and Roman Religion: . . . B. The Imperial Cult." In *The Book of Acts in Its Graeco-Roman Setting*, edited by David W. J. Gill and Conrad Gempf, 93–103. Volume 2 of *The Book of Acts in Its First-Century Setting*. Grand Rapids, Mich.: William B. Eerdmans Publishing Company, 1994.

Witt, R. E. "The Importance of Isis for the Fathers." *Studia Patristica* 8, part 2, 135–45. Berlin: Akademie-Verlag, 1966.

Wright, G. Ernest. *Biblical Archaeology*. Philadelphia: Westminster Press, 1957.

Yamauchi, Edwin. "Archaeology and the New Testament." In *Archaeology and the Bible: An Introductory Study*, edited by Donald J. Wiseman and Edwin Yamauchi, 63–109. Grand Rapids, Mich.: Zondervan, 1979.

———. *The Archaeology of New Testament Cities in Western Asia Minor*. Grand Rapids, Mich.: Baker Book House, 1980.

———. *Harper's World of the New Testament*. San Francisco: Harper & Row, 1981.

Zabehlicky, Heinrich. "Preliminary Views of the Ephesian Harbor." In *Ephesos: Metropolis of Asia–An Interdisciplinary Approach to Its Archaeology, Religion, and Culture*, edited by Helmut Koester,

201–15. Harvard Theological Studies 41. Valley Forge, Pa.: Trinity Press International, 1995.

## Articles

Amitai, Pinchas. "Scorpion Ash Saves Woman's Eyesight." *Bible Review* 11 (April 1995): 36–37.

Anderson, C. P. "Hebrews Among the Letters of Paul." *Studies in Religion/Sciences Religieuses* 5 (1975–76): 258–66.

Anderson, Charles P. "Who Wrote 'the Epistle from Laodicea'?" *Journal of Biblical Literature* 85 (1966): 436–40.

Arnold, Irene R. "Festivals of Ephesus." *American Journal of Archaeology* 76 (1972): 17–22.

Atkinson, K. M. T. "The Governors of the Province of Asia in the Reign of Augustus." *Historia* 7 (1958): 300–30.

Aune, David E. "The Influence of the Roman Imperial Court Ceremonial on the Apocalypse of John." *Biblical Research* 28 (1983): 5–26.

———. "The Social Matrix of the Apocalypse of John." *Biblical Research* 26 (1981): 16–32.

Bammer, Anton. "Recent Excavations at the Altar of Artemis in Ephesus." *Archaeology* 27 (1974): 202–5.

Barnett, Paul W. "Revelation in Its Roman Setting." *Reformed Theological Review* 50 (May-August 1991): 59–68.

Bell, Albert A., Jr. "The Date of John's Apocalypse: Evidence of Some Roman Historians Reconsidered." *New Testament Studies* 25 (1978–79): 93–102.

Bent, J. Theodore. "What St. John Saw on Patmos." *Nineteenth Century* 24 (1888): 813–21.

Blasi, Anthony J. "Office Charisma in Early Christian Ephesus." *Sociology of Religion* 56 (Fall 1995): 245–55.

Bonz, Marianne P. "Differing Approaches to Religious Benefaction: The Late Third-Century Acquisition of the Sardis Synagogue." *Harvard Theological Review* 86 (April 1993): 139–50.

Borgen, Peder. "Moses, Jesus, and the Roman Emperor: Observations in Philo's Writings and the Revelation of John." *Novum Testamentum: An International Quarterly for New Testament and Related Studies* 38 (April 1996): 145–59.

Boring, M. Eugene. "The Voice of Jesus in the Apocalypse of John." *Novum Testamentum: An International Quarterly for New Testament and Related Studies* 34 (October 1992): 334–59.

Botha, P. J. J. "God, Emperor Worship, and Society: Contemporary Experiences and the Book of Revelation." *Neotestamentica: Journal of the New Testament Society of South Africa* 22 (1988): 87–102.

————. "The Historical Domitian—Illustrating Some Problems of Historiography." *Neotestamentica: Journal of the New Testament Society of South Africa* 23 (1989): 45–59.

Brettler, Marc Z., and Michael B. Poliakoff. "Rabbi Simeon ben Lakish at the Gladiator's Banquet: Rabbinic Observations on the Roman Arena." *Harvard Theological Review* 83 (January 1990): 93–98.

Bruce, F. F. "Colossian Problems, Part I: Jews and Christians in the Lycus Valley." *Bibliotheca Sacra* 141 (January-March 1984): 3–15.

Burton, G. P. "Proconsuls, Assizes, and the Administration of Justice Under the Empire." *Journal of Roman Studies* 65 (1975): 92–106.

Charles, J. Daryl. "Imperial Pretensions and the Throne-Vision of the Lamb: Observations on the Function of Revelation 5." *Criswell Theological Review* 7 (Fall 1993): 85–97.

Cole, Dan P. "Corinth and Ephesus: Why Did Paul Spend Half His Journeys in These Cities?" *Bible Review* 4 (December 1988): 20–30.

Cotter, Wendy. "Women's Authority Roles in Paul's Churches: Countercultural or Conventional?" *Novum Testamentum: An International Quarterly for New Testament and Related Studies* 36 (October 1994): 350–72.

Crawford, John S. "Multiculturalism at Sardis: Jews and Christians Live, Work, and Worship Side by Side." *Biblical Archaeology Review* 22 (September-October 1996): 38–47, 70.

D'Angelo, Mary Rose. "'Abba' and 'Father': Imperial Theology and the Jesus Traditions." *Journal of Biblical Literature* 111 (Winter 1992): 611–30.

Daniel, Jerry L. "Anti-Semitism in the Hellenistic-Roman Period." *Journal of Biblical Literature* 98 (1979): 46–65.

deSilva, David A. "Exchanging Favor for Wrath." *Journal of Biblical Literature* 115 (Spring 1996): 91–116.

————. "The 'Image of the Beast' and the Christians in Asia Minor: Escalation of Sectarian Tension in Revelation 13." *Trinity Journal* 12 (Fall 1991): 185–208.

Elderkin, George W. "The Bee of Artemis." *American Journal of Philology* 60 (1939): 202–13.

Filson, Floyd. "Ephesus and the New Testament." *Biblical Archaeologist* 8 (1945): 73–80.

Fitzgerald, Michael. "The Ship of Saint Paul, Part 2: Comparative Archaeology." *Biblical Archaeologist: Perspectives on the Ancient World from Mesopotamia to the Mediterranean* 53 (March 1990): 31–39.

Ford, J. Massynberde. "Bookshelf on Prostitution." *Biblical Theology Bulletin* (Fall 1993): 128–34.

Foss, Clive. "A Neighbor of Sardis: The City of Tmolus and Its Successors." *Studies in Classical Antiquity* 1. (*California Studies in Classical Antiquity*, 13), 178–201.

Friesen, Steven. "Ephesus: Key to a Vision in Revelation." *Biblical Archaeology Review* 19 (May-June 1993): 24–37.

———. "Revelation, Reality, and Religion: Archaeology in the Interpretation of the Apocalypse." *Harvard Theological Review* 88 (July 1996): 291–314.

Ginsburg, Michael J. "Fiscus Judaicus." *Jewish Quarterly Review* 21 (1930–31): 281–91.

Goldsmith, Raymond W. "An Estimate of the Size and Structure of the National Product in the Early Roman Empire." *Review of Income and Wealth* 30 (1984): 263–88.

Gordon, Mary. "The Freedman's Son in Municipal Life." *Journal of Roman Studies* 21 (1931): 65–77.

Goulder, Michael D. "The Visionaries of Laodicea." *Journal for the Study of the New Testament* 43 (September 1991): 15–39.

Habicht, Christian. "New Evidence on the Province of Asia." *Journal of Roman Studies* 65 (1975): 64–91.

Hanfmann, George M. A., and Jane C. Waldbaum. "Kybele and Artemis: Two Anatolian Goddesses at Sardis." *Archaeology* 22 (1969): 264–69.

Hardy, E. R. "The Priestess in the Greco-Roman World." *Churchman: A Quarterly Journal of Anglican Theology* 84 (1970): 264–70.

Hill, Andrew E. "Ancient Art and Artemis: Toward Explaining the Polymastic Nature of the Figurine." *Journal of the Ancient Near Eastern Society* 21 (1992): 91–94.

Hirschfeld, Nicolle. "The Ship of Saint Paul, Part 1: Historical Background." *Biblical Archaeologist: Perspectives on the Ancient World from Mesopotamia to the Mediterranean* 53 (March 1990): 25–30.

Hopkins, Keith. "Taxes and Trade in the Roman Empire (200 B.C.-A.D. 400)." *Journal of Roman Studies* 70 (1980): 102–25.

Horsley, S. H. R. "The Inscriptions of Ephesus and the New Testament." *Novum Testamentum* 34 (April 1992): 105–68.

Jewell, James Stewart. "Topography of Ephesus." *Methodist Review* 53 (April 1871): 279–96.

Johnson, David R. "The Library of Celsus, an Ephesian Phoenix." *Wilson Library Bulletin* 54, 1980: 651–53.

Johnson, Richard R. "Ancient and Medieval Accounts of the 'Invention' of Parchment." *California Studies in Classical Antiquity*, 3: 115–22.

Johnson, Sherman E. "The Apostle Paul and the Riot in Ephesus." *Lexington Theological Quarterly* 14 (October 1979): 79–88.

———. "Early Christianity in Asia Minor." *Journal of Biblical Literature* 77 (1958): 1–17.

———. "Laodicea and Its Neighbors." *Biblical Archaeologist* 13 (February 1950): 1–18.

Kee, Alistair. "The Imperial Cult: The Unmasking of an Ideology." *Scottish Journal of Religious Studies* 8 (Autumn, 1985): 112–28.

Kerkaslager, Alan. "Apollo, Greco-Roman Prophecy, and the Rider on the White Horse in Revelation 6:2." *Journal of Biblical Literature* 112 (Spring 1993): 116–21.

Koester, Helmut. "A Political Christmas Story." *Bible Review* 10 (October 1994): 23, 58.

Kraemer, Rose S. "On the Meaning of the Term 'Jew' in Greco-Roman Inscriptions." *Harvard Theological Review* 82 (January 1989): 36–53.

Kramer, Ross S. "Ecstasy and Possession: The Attraction of Women to the Cult of Dionysos." *Harvard Theological Review* 72 (January 1979): 55–80.

Kreitzer, Larry. "Apotheosis of the Roman Emperor." *Biblical Archaeologist: Perspectives on the Ancient World from Mesopotamia to the Mediterranean* 53 (December 1990): 210–17.

Kreitzer, Larry J. "A Numismatic Clue to Acts 19:23–41: The Ephesian Cistophori of Claudius and Agrippina." *Journal for the Study of the New Testament* 30 (1987): 59–70.

Laeuchli, Samuel. "Urban Mithraism." *Biblical Archaeologist* 31 (1968): 73–99.

Levick, Barbara. "Domitian and the Provinces." *Latomus* 41 (1982): 50–73.

Lewis, Kevin. "John on Patmos and the Painters." *ARTS: The Arts in Religious and Theological Studies* 5 (Summer 1993): 18–23.

Lynn R. LiDonnici, "The Images of Artemis Ephesia and Greco-Roman Worship: A Reconsideration," *Harvard Theological Review* 85 (October 1992): 389–415.

McMinn, Joe B. "Fusion of the Gods: A Religio-astrological Study of the Interpenetration of the East and the West in Asia Minor." *Journal of Near Eastern Studies* 15 (1956): 201–13.

MacMullen, Ramsay. "Imperial Bureaucrats in the Roman Provinces." *Harvard Studies in Classical Philology* 68 (1964): 305–16.

———. "Late Roman Slavery." *Historia* 36 (1987): 359–82.

———. "Women in Public in the Roman Empire." *Historia* 29 (1980): 208–18.

Malherle, Abraham H. "The Beasts at Ephesus." *Journal of Biblical Literature* 87 (1968): 71–80.

Malina, Bruce J. "Mediterranean Sacrifice: Dimensions of Domestic and Political Religion." *Biblical Theology Bulletin* 26 (Spring 1996): 26–44.

Marshall, A. J. "Flaccus and the Jews of Asia (Cicero Pro Flacco 28. 67–69)." *Phoenix* 29 (1975): 139–54.

Mellink, Machteld J. "Archaeology in Asia Minor." *American Journal of Archaeology* 81 (1977): 289–321.

Mitchell, Stephen. "The Plancii in Asia Minor." *Journal of Roman Studies* 64 (1974): 27–39.

Mitten, David Gordon. "A New Look at Ancient Sardis." *Biblical Archaeologist* 29 (1966): 38–68.

Moore, Stephen D. "The Beatific Vision as a Posing Exhibition: Revelation's Hypomasculine Deity," *Journal for the Study of the New Testament* 60 (December 1995): 27–55.

Osborne, Robert E. "Paul and the Wild Beasts." *Journal of Biblical Literature* 85 (1966): 225–30.

Oster, Richard E. "Numismatic Windows in the World of Early Christianity: A Methodological Inquiry." *Journal of Biblical Literature* 101 (1982): 195–223.

Parvis, Merrill M. "Archaeology and St. Paul's Journey in Greek Lands—Part IV: Ephesus." *Biblical Archaeologist* 8 (1945): 62–73.

Pilch, John J. "Lying and Deceit in the Letters to the Seven Churches: Perspectives from Cultural Anthropology." *Biblical Theology Bulletin* 22 (Fall 1992): 126–35.

Price, S. R. F. "Between Man and God: Sacrifice in the Roman Imperial Cult." *Journal of Roman Studies* 70 (1980): 28–43.

Provan, Iaian. "Foul Spirits, Fornication, and Finance: Revelation

18 from an Old Testament Perspective." *Journal for the Study of the New Testament* 64 (December 1996): 81–100.

Ramsay, William. "Ephesus." *Biblical World* 17 (1901): 167–77.

———. "A Sketch of the History of Asia Minor." *National Geographic* 42 (November 1922): 553–70.

Roscoe, Will. "Priests of the Goddess: Gender Transgression in Ancient Religion." *History of Religions* 35 (February 1996).

Rudwick, M. J. S., and E. M. Green, "The Laodicean Lukewarmness." *Expository Times* 69 (1957–58): 176–78.

Scherer, Steven J. "Signs and Wonders in the Imperial Cult—Revelation 13:13–15." *Journal of Biblical Literature* 103 (1984): 599–610.

Scobie, Charles H. H. "Local References in the Letters to the Seven Churches." *New Testament Studies* 39 (October 1993): 606–24.

Sellew, Philip. "Laodiceans and the Philippians Fragments Hypothesis." *Harvard Theological Review* 87 (January 1994): 17–28.

Sherwin-White, A. N. "The Early Persecutions and Roman Law Again." *Journal of Theological Studies* 3 (1952): 199–213.

Silberschlag, E. "The Earliest Record of Jews in Asia Minor." *Journal of Biblical Literature* 52 (1933): 66–77.

Smith, Philip K. "The Apocalypse of St. John and the Early Church." *Journal of Bible and Religion* 25 (1957): 187–96.

Sokolowski, F. "A New Testimony to the Cult of Artemis of Ephesus." *Harvard Theological Review* 58 (1965): 427–31.

Stanley, Christopher D. "'Neither Jew Nor Greek': Ethnic Conflict in Graeco-Roman Society." *Journal for the Study of the New Testament* 64 (December 1996): 101–24.

Stoops, Robert F., Jr. "Riot and Assembly: The Social Context of Acts 19:23–41." *Journal of Biblical Literature* 108 (Spring 1989): 73–91.

Thompson, A. "Domitian and the Jewish Tax." *Historia* 31 (1982): 329–42.

Thompson, Leonard. "A Sociological Analysis of Tribulation in the Apocalypse of John." *Semeia* 36 (1986): 147–74.

Trudinger, Paul. "The Ephesus Milieu." *Downside Review* 105 (October 1988): 286–98.

Tyree, E. Loeta, and Evangelia Stefanoudaki. "The Olive Pit and Roman Oil Making." *Biblical Archaeologist: Perspectives on the Ancient World from Mesopotamia to the Mediterranean* 59 (September 1996): 171–78.

Ulansey, David. "Solving the Mithraic Mysteries." *Biblical Archaeology Review* 20 (September/October 1994): 41–53.

Vinson, Steve. "Ships in the Ancient Mediterranean." *Biblical Archaeologist: Perspectives on the Ancient World from Mesopotamia to the Mediterranean* 53 (March 1990): 13–18.

Ward, Roy B. "Women in Roman Baths." *Harvard Theological Review* 85 (April 1992): 125–47.

Wendel, Clarence A. "Land-tilting or Silting? Which Ruined Ancient Harbors?" *Archaeology* 22 (1969): 322–24.

Wilson, J. Christian. "The Problem of the Domitianic Date of Revelation." *New Testament Studies: An International Journal* 39 (October 1993): 587–605.

Wood, Peter. "Local Knowledge in the Letters of the Apocalypse." *Expository Times* 73 (1961–62): 263–64.

Wotschitzky, Alfons. "Ephesus: Past, Present, Future of an Ancient Metropolis." *Archaeology* 14 (1961): 205–12.

Yamauchi, Edwin M. "Magic Bowls: Cyrus H. Gordon and the Ubiquity of Magic in the Pre-Modern World." *Biblical Archaeologist: Perspectives on the Ancient World from Mesopotamia to the Mediterranean* 59 (March 1996): 51–55.

Zinderman, J. Irving. "Seashells and Ancient Purple Dyeing." *Biblical Archaeologist: Perspectives on the Ancient World from Mesopotamia to the Mediterranean* 53 (June 1990): 98–101.

## Dissertations and Theses

*Italicized titles are of published dissertations; titles in quotation marks are unpublished ones.*

Bartchy, S. Scott. *First-Century Slavery and the Interpretation of I Corinth 7:21.* Dissertation Series, 11. Missoula, Mont.: Society of Biblical Literature, 1973.

Baugh, Steven M. "Paul and Ephesus: The Apostle Among His Contemporaries." Ph.D. dissertation, University of California (Irvine), 1990.

Birge, Darice E. "Sacred Groves in the Ancient Greek World." Ph.D. dissertation, University of California–Berkeley, 1982.

Foss, Clive. "Byzantine Cities of Western Asia Minor." Ph.D. dissertation, Harvard University, 1972.

Hemer, Colin J. *The Letters to the Seven Churches of Asia in Their Local Setting.* Sheffield, England: University of Sheffield, 1986. Journal for the Study of the New Testament, Supplement Series 11.

Hollinshead, Mary B. B. "Legend, Cult, and Architecture at Three

Sanctuaries of Artemis," Ph.D. dissertation, Bryn Mawr College, 1979.

Kraabel, A. Thomas. "Judaism in Western Asia Minor Under the Roman Empire, with a Preliminary Study of the Jewish Community of Sardis, Lydia." Ph.D. dissertation, Harvard University, 1968.

Kraybill, J. Nelson. "Cult and Commerce in Revelation 18." Ph.D. dissertation, Union Theological Seminary (Richmond, Va.), 1992.

Saltman, Ellen S. "The Jews of Asia Minor in the Greco-Roman Period: A Religious and Social Study." M.A. thesis, Smith College, 1971.

Saunders, Fuller B. "The Seven Churches of the Apocalypse." Ph.D. dissertation, Southern Baptist Theological Seminary, 1949.

Showerman, Grant. "The Great Mother of the Gods." Ph.D. dissertation, University of Wisconsin, 1900. Reprinted in *Bulletin of the University of Wisconsin, Philology and Literature Series*. Volume 1, number 3, Madison, Wis. (May 1901): 221–329.

# Index

Aegean Sea, 54

Angdistis (god): 65

Anti-semitism (*see also* Jews): efforts to prevent payment of temple tax by Asian Jews to Jerusalem, 75–76; in Egypt, 174 n. 161; reasons for intense Roman pressure on Asian cities to grant religious rights to local Jewish communities, 74–75; seizure of temple tax from Jews in Egypt, 77–78; tensions versus violent outbursts the norm in Asia by first century A.D., 72–73

Apocalyptic literature, similarities and differences with John's "Revelation," 85–86

Apollo, 94

Armenia, 47

Army: *see* Legions (Roman)

Artemius (goddess): 62, 94

Asclepius (god): 30

Asia (*see also* Anti-semitism, Christianity and Christians, Jews): agricultural crops, 55; architecture, 57–58; bestowal to Rome of area by Attalus III, 43–44; burial customs, 58–59; changing of calendar to honor Augustus, 52; cost of living, 16; Christianity in, 81–84; debt bondage in, 42; dialects, 8; dispute over when capital officially shifted from Pergamon to Ephesus, 47–50; earthquakes, 55–57; economic strength of under Byzantine Empire, 68–69; excessive government expenditures by local cities, 63–64; exporters of, 70–71; farmers in, 14; imperial cult pervasive within, 120; Jews in, 71–81; judicial districts within, 51, 107; labor unrest, 69–70; legion dispositions in, 20; life span of residents, 7–8; lifestyle and practices in non-urban areas, 64–65; literacy, 8;

249

123–126; early recognition its members were distinct from traditional Judaism, 82–83; ethical/moral roots of pagan opposition, 125–126; even when members became increasingly numerous, the movement generally ignored by educated society, 83; lack of general heavy persecution in Asia, 125; number of churches in Asia, 100–101; social composition of movement, 84

Cicero, 16, 39, 77; defends seizure of Jewish temple tax in Asia, 76; on economic impact of loss of Asia to Mithridates, 45; on wealth of Asia, 68

Cities: and public education, 63; employee salaries, 62; firefighting in, 63; formal religious activities sponsored by, 62; games sponsored by, 62; gymnasiums built and maintained by, 62; Jewish leadership participation within, 75; limitations of relying on voluntary civic donations by the rich as substitute for formal taxation, 61–62; price control efforts, 69; property regulations, 60; right of Romaus to force solvency of local governments, 63–64; sizable personal economic cost of holding government office, 60–61; varied taxes of, 59–60

Claudius, 9, 13, 19; downgraded worship of individual emperors, 116, 117; on value of traditional herbal remedies, 32

Colossae, 55, 100

Cybele (goddess): 24

Cyprus, 73

Cyrenaica, 73

Decurions (Roman): requirements to be, 9

Dio Chrysostom, 16

Diocletian (emperor): 119

Dionysius of Alexandria, 88, 89, 90

Domitian, 11, 17, 79, 121, 128; attempt to limit grape growth in Asia to create a more self-sufficient agriculture, 67; avid believer in personal godhood of individual emperors, 117

Egypt, 42; abandoned farms in, 16; Alexandria, 20; exporter of food to province of Asia, 66;